Soviet Foreign Trade

Soviet Foreign Trade

Purpose and Performance

William Nelson Turpin
Appalachian State University

Lexington Books

D.C. Heath and Company
Lexington, Massachusetts
Toronto

Library of Congress Cataloging in Publication Data

Turpin, William Nelson.
    Soviet foreign trade.

    Includes index.
    1. Russia—Commerce. I. Title.
HF3626.5.T87   382'.0947   76-47337
ISBN 0-669-01143-6

Published simultaneously in Canada

Printed in the United States of America

International Standard Book Number: 0-669-01143-6

Library of Congress Catalog Card Number: 76-47337

To my mother, and to the memory of my father
and my late wife.

Contents

List of Tables

Preface

This book began as a doctoral dissertation at The George Washington University; its subject and much of its form originated with my director, John P. Hardt, Professorial Lecturer in Economics and Senior Specialist in Soviet Economics at the Congressional Research Service. He is, of course, in no way responsible for my interpretations or for the correctness of my conclusions; but the inspiration for the book and much of its final shape are due to him.

My debt to my colleagues in the American Foreign Service, in other agencies of the U.S. government, and in the services of other governments will be obvious to the reader. It would be invidious to name any without mentioning a very large number. I have also benefitted from the comments of an anonymous referee. Needless to say, none of them is responsible for my errors whether of fact or of judgment.

My friend and colleague at Appalachian, Dr. Charles J. Haulk, was of inestimable assistance in the statistical work which underlies Chapter 4. I am deeply grateful to him, and not less so to his wife, June, who painstakingly and voluntarily prepared the index. All translations are the author's, except for the quotation from the Solzhenitsyn letter.

I am grateful to *The New York Times* for permission to quote from its issue of September 18, 1955, its account of Khrushchev's interview with a group of American Senators; to *The Economist Newspaper,* Ltd., for permission to quote two of its reports, one of July 12, 1958, and the other of January 6, 1973; and to the Index on Censorship in association with Writers and Scholars International, Ltd., London, for permission to quote Alexander Solzhenitsyn's "Letter to the Soviet Leaders."

Finally, to the librarians, typists, and secretaries in the Department of State and at Appalachian, who have put up with so much bother from me, I want to express particular appreciation.

William Nelson Turpin

Soviet Foreign Trade

1   Introduction

Critics examine a role in a drama from two distinct but intimately related points
of view: They treat the various aspects of the personality portrayed, their consistency, and contradictions by studying the totality of the character as an entity
in itself; and they deal with the role as it relates to other characters in the drama
and to the unfolding of the whole play. We shall attempt in this study to deal
similarly with the functioning, and the function, of the trading relations of the
Soviet Union with developed capitalist countries. This aspect of Soviet economic
relations is organizationally separate from the economic dealings of the USSR
with other socialist countries and with the developing world and is categorized
separately by Soviet officials and scholars (being placed, incidentally, after the
others in the listing and treatment of the subdivisions of the subject). But it is
not normally singled out for separate theoretical treatment when the benefits
and purposes of trade are being discussed.

Accordingly, we shall be interested in both the organization and the operation of the Soviet foreign trading system in themselves and as they relate to the
use by the Soviet government and party of trade with developed capitalist countries to further Soviet purposes, domestic and international.

We shall commence our examination with an attempt to test the hypothesis
that the conventional Western view of the purpose and nature of Soviet trading
relations with the developed economies is correct. As we shall see presently,
Western scholars frequently assert the hypothesis, but have offered little evidence
that it is true.

The consensus among American, British, German, and other scholars is indeed strong, both with respect to the nature of the Soviet system of foreign
trade and with respect to the policy purposes it has been made to serve. But this
consensus, as we shall see by examining what is, at least, a representative sampling
of Western statements on the subject and, at most, a nearly exhaustive compilation of the most important ones, while showing differences in emphasis, is really
based on subjective judgments that are largely undocumented and almost entirely
untested statistically. Our evidence will be seen to suggest that the conventional
wisdom is generally accurate, and it will put for the first time a systematic ana-
lytical and statistical foundation under it.

We shall, then, first show what we have called the conventional wisdom that
is, indeed, the accepted view. We then present the evidence that is available from
Soviet sources and show that it correctly describes Soviet policy and practice,

1

even though Soviet authorities do not formulate it in the same way. Finally, we examine the statistical evidence that the system has, in fact, operated in a manner consistent with the hypothesis.

The next stage of our examination will present the central features of the Soviet foreign trading system as they have existed up to the present time, from both an organizational and an operational point of view. In so doing, we lay the groundwork for an examination of the proposition that Soviet export and import decisions have not been and cannot possibly be made primarily on the basis of relative prices, whether external (world market) or internal (ruble) prices are considered.

We shall then inquire into the reasons that have led the Soviet Union to adopt this pattern of governing its external economic relations. We shall consider the question of whether the system as it has been (and is) was a logical consequence of the economic structure and policies of the Soviet Union and see how it fits into the economic machinery devised to carry out those policies.

We shall then turn to the question of whether, as many Western and Soviet experts argue and as some Soviet party and government actions and pronouncements imply, this system is no longer suitable for the Soviet Union in today's world. We shall examine the hypothesis that interdependence, rather than isolation, is more appropriate to the world's second largest industrial power in the last quarter of this century. We shall look at the reasons being urged by Soviet authorities for change, at some of the implications of making changes, and at the evidence that a radical shift is not only being suggested, but is actually being put into place. We shall comment on some of the significant features of the possible, as well as the actual, changes.

Finally, we attempt an evaluation of the likelihood of major changes in the pattern and in the purposes of foreign trade in the general Soviet economic and foreign policy game plan. We shall note the domestic political costs entailed in making major changes, and we shall see that whatever the possible economic benefits of more "normal" behavior, there is evidence that the present system suits Soviet purposes at least well enough to make the pressures for fundamental change tolerable. Indeed, our study of the nature of the changes necessary to make the Soviet foreign trading system more efficient (from a Western point of view) will indicate that those changes would entail unacceptable political costs for the Communist Party and more specifically for its leaders. Hence, it would seem, there is no reason for Western policymakers to reckon on liberalizing effects on the Soviet system in the foreseeable future. In conclusion, we attempt to deduce some policy implications from our analysis, for the United States and its industrialized allies, and to suggest some ways in which these implications might effectively be dealt with.

2

The "Received" Western View of Soviet Foreign Trade

In this chapter we shall present the Western "conventional wisdom" on the nature of Soviet foreign trade and on the role of prices within it. But first, we had best define the time periods within which our remarks apply.

The economic history of the Soviet Union is customarily divided, by Soviet and Western students alike, into (1) the period of War Communism; (2) the years of the New Economic Policy; (3) the (Stalinist) Plan Era; and, (4) the post-Stalin period. These conventional demarcations will serve our purposes, if we remember that certain features of Soviet foreign trading organization and practice have been constant through the whole period, and that, indeed, some predate the October Revolution. We should also bear in mind that the application of Soviet policies has varied from time to time within these periods. For example, machinery imports and agricultural exports were at a much higher level during the first than during later five-year plans; the second World War period was not surprisingly an exception to many generalizations; experience since Stalin's death has reflected a degree of uncertainty, or of vacillation, that Stalin at least never allowed to become visible.

It also seems fair to say that whereas the changes from War Communism to NEP and from the latter to the Plan Era were sharp, open, and dramatic, the transition to the post-Stalin era has been a less clear-cut break with the past. It could be argued that Khrushchev's Secret Speech to the XX Party Congress was a repudiation of Stalin without a repudiation of Stalinism; in any case, it is clear that many, if not most, of the central characteristics of the Stalinist system of operating the Soviet economy continue twenty years after his death.

These propositions, which could be debated but with which most students would probably agree, are germane to our purposes, primarily because the task of analyzing the organization as well as the functioning of the Soviet foreign trading system, which entails analysis of the broader economic system of which it is part, is made difficult by reason of the Soviet habit of abstracting from particular temporal circumstances and discussing as timeless general principles things that may well be only temporary phenomena. (It would scarcely be denied that Western economists do the same thing, of course.) Moreover, as Soviet economic writing is naturally intended for a Soviet, and often for an expert Soviet, audience, the readers are assumed to have knowledge that a foreigner cannot have gained at first hand and may well not have at all. Hence, Soviet economic writers do not necessarily, or usually, explain changes in policies or circumstances. One has, therefore, always to consider whether and how conditions formerly prevailing have changed—and if so, how much.

That said, however, we may take it as our intitial assumption that the general outlines of Soviet foreign trading organization and operational methods, like those of the planned economy of which they are a part, have remained essentially the same since 1928. Later, when we come to examine the question of possible change, we shall be concerned with the question of whether a new era has begun since the death of Stalin, or perhaps more precisely, how different that era is. In the penultimate chapter we shall look at the question of whether yet another, newer era is necessary, likely, or possible.

There appears to be no readily accessible and explicit statement of the received view with respect to the importance of foreign trade to the Soviet Union; the neglect of the subject in the standard works, and especially of this aspect, suggests that Soviet and Western commentators alike have taken for granted that the proportion of trade turnover to national output would be small. While the purposes of trade, and its role in a planned economy, are discussed more amply, as we shall see, the question of its size seems to have attracted little explicit attention.

The best short statement of the conventional wisdom on the role of foreign trade in the Soviet economic system is that of Alan A. Brown and Egon Neuberger:

The traditional view is that CPE's regard trade as a means of obtaining necessary imports, and that the level of trade is based primarily on the planners' evaluation of imports necessary to fulfill the plans, while exports are adjusted to finance these imports.[1]

One of the contributors to that symposium spells the matter out somewhat:

Imports were used primarily to fill temporary gaps in the capital stock, and temporary and not-so-temporary gaps in the supply of inputs required in the domestic economy. Traditional exports and goods in temporary surplus supply were then exported in amounts "necessary to pay for the imported goods, to form foreign exchange reserves, and to meet obligations for mutual deliveries and deliveries on credit."[2]

That this is the generally accepted view is indicated by other remarks by Western students: "Foreign trade does not have the same function in the economy of the Soviet Union as it does in market-economy countries."[3] A more recent comment is

In the Soviet Union's planned economy model, foreign trade was assigned essentially solely the task of closing gaps in the supplying of its own country. Exports had in the main to secure the foreign exchange which was necessary for paying for vitally needed imports.[4]

As the earliest Western study on Soviet foreign trade puts it:

In the Soviet economic system export trade is solely a means of paying for *indispensable* imports.[5]

Again:

. . . the main motives for the planners to engage in foreign trade under the Stalinist model were to relieve bottlenecks in the balancing process, to import technology embodied in capital goods, or to shortcircuit the transformation of surplus into investment goods, rather than to increase GNP through the benefits of specialization and comparative advantage.[6]

We may note, as well, Alexander Gerschenkron's remark:

In general, however, Russia exports solely in order to obtain the wherewithal for payments for imports. In this sense she is likely to live up to the classical doctrine of foreign trade and to reject the tenets of mercantilism . . . . From the Russian point of view, exports are a loss and not a gain.[7]

A post-Stalin study of East-West trade expresses a similar view:

Whereas in the developed market economies the emphasis appears to be on exports, in the centrally planned economies it is imports that occupy the focus of attention. Imports are the starting side in the planning process, since they are considered as indispensable to meet developmental targets. Exports are essentially looked upon as a sacrifice to secure the required imports.[8]

A more pragmatic study takes the same line in attempting to predict the future course of Soviet foreign trade strategy:

The Soviets seem to be indicating that in the future they will be most interested in American production equipment and in American technology. They have always been interested, of course, in acquiring the machinery and equipment that produces products rather than the products themselves.[9]

The author continues, with respect to imports:

There are, of course, certain limiting factors—such as Soviet purchasing power—or, at least, there are the limits the Soviet Government believes it necessary to impose on the expenditures of foreign exchange for the importation of foreign products and technology.[10]

In like vein, perhaps the most prolific American writer on Soviet foreign trade remarks:

First, among the eastern nations, foreign trade is conducted primarily to obtain essential imports. Exports are considered not as an end in themselves, but as a means to finance the necessary imports.[11]

The same student said some years earlier:

First, Soviet trade has been heavily oriented to the needs of the State in its industrialization drive . . . . Second, the U.S.S.R. has attempted to minimize trade. It has followed a policy of autarky or self-sufficiency . . . . The policy of autarky stems from the prior objective of securing and maintaining military and economic independence from the capitalist world. Third, the Soviet planners are primarily interested in imports rather than exports. Foreign trade is conducted to obtain essential goods, which are either temporarily or permanently unavailable. Exports are viewed as a necessary evil—necessary to pay for imports—and are limited to the value required for desired imports.[12]

An official of the Department of Commerce told the Joint Economic Committee:

Foreign trade remains a small part of overall Soviet economic activity and its basic economic function in the Soviet scheme of things has remained essentially unchanged. That is, the procurement from abroad of goods needed for plan fulfillment, when they are not available domestically, with exports thus primarily serving the purpose of financing necessary imports.[13]

Holzman's introduction of the term *autarky* opens up a range of inquiry related to, but different from, our present subject, to which we shall return. It is closely related to another peripheral element in the received doctrine of Soviet foreign trade policy, namely, the assertion that the USSR limits its trade to the minimum necessary. Both elements appear in the analysis of Soviet trade policy of Abram Bergson:

Thus a cardinal aim of the U.S.S.R. has been to limit trade relations with non-Communist countries. In some degree this has been felt in order because of a concern to limit foreign trade generally, for such trade is not easily integrated with the system of central planning by which the U.S.S.R. administers its economy. More basically, political and military considerations have also argued for economic independence of the capitalist West. I refer to the famous policy of self-sufficiency that was pursued over a very long period by Stalin. It is still pursued by Khrushchev, although not as relentlessly as by Stalin.

While seeking to limit trade with non-Communist countries, the Soviet Government has not by any means wished to have it extinguished. Thus, from its standpoint trade still has the merit that it permits the economic acquisition of supplies which because of resource limitations would be especially costly to produce domestically. It is also a device for alleviation of short-run bottlenecks in the domestic economy for achieving rapid expansion of stocks of specialized machinery without investing more in plant to produce it than is required to meet replacement needs, and for the profitable disposition of shortrun surpluses. Then too through imports of machinery exploitation of western technological innovations is much facilitated.[14]

The Legislative Reference Service of the Library of Congress in a 1965 study of East-West trade for the Senate Foreign Relations Committee[15] treated the policy problem in analagous fashion; we shall look at this material when we consider the autarky problem. A later (1970) study similarly assumed the conventional wisdom when it said:

The U.S.S.R. attaches special importance to this trade (*scilicet* with the industrial West) because of its need for Western equipment and technology and other materials which are in short supply in the U.S.S.R. Until recently the failure of the U.S.S.R. to generate sufficient hard currency earnings through exports led to disequilibrium in Soviet hard currency trade, characterized by substantial annual deficits and sizeable sales of gold to finance these deficits.[16]

Glen Alden Smith makes the same assertion:

The import and export policies of the Soviet Union limit imports to those goods that contribute to socialist development and exports to those necessary to pay for the needed imports.[17]

We shall consider the views of Andrea Boltho[18] in more detail below, when we take up the question of autarky, but his general discussion is consistent with the received view, even though he does not summarize quotably with respect to the Soviet Union.

Despite the recent rapid expansion in Soviet imports from developed capitalist countries, which Foreign Trade Minister Nikolai Patolichev has described as signifying a "qualitatively new stage,"[19] the most recent authoritative American study of Soviet foreign trade continues to assume the same purpose and practices as fundamental to Soviet trading policy. The volume of trade may be larger, as we shall see, but the fundamental lines remain unchanged.[20]

The authorities we have consulted, who are not merely a representative, but a somewhat exhaustive, collection of Western commentators on Soviet foreign trade, seem to be in close agreement on the basic nature of Soviet policies in that area. It is perhaps worth noting, however, that with the exception of Holzman's remarks in the Bergson and Kuznets volume quoted above,[21] no evidence is presented in support of this widely held opinion. And Holzman quotes only a single prewar Soviet author, whose position we shall consider in the following chapter. For the rest, received opinion is, precisely, undocumented opinion.

Some confusion has been introduced into the question of Soviet intentions with respect to foreign trade as a result of a common usage of the term *autarky* in what may appear to be a somewhat imprecise sense. And, as that characterization is not infrequently used as a one-word summation of the situation, and as some discussion has arisen in recent years as to whether the USSR has abandoned its alleged policy of maintaining or striving for autarky, we may usefully conclude this chapter by examining the hypothesis that autarky is an accurate, if not necessarily a useful, word to apply to Soviet foreign trade policy.

It might well be considered that it would be best to avoid the term altogether in view of the wide varieties of meaning attached to it. The dictionary definition, which refers to the desirability of maintaining a "self-sufficient and independent" national economy, does not help very much, as both terms can be and are used in a relative as well as an absolute sense. "Autarky," at least among economists, carries a pejorative tinge; its dictionary synonyms do not. What follows is an attempt to clarify the question, which may be justified precisely because of the frequency of the application of the term, with somewhat imprecise and undefined connotations, to the Soviet economy.

Examples of this usage are frequent, not to say customary, in Western discussions of Soviet (and East European) foreign trade policies. We may take the following remarks as typical:

It can only be assumed, therefore, that the new world that the Bolshevik leaders were planning to build was conceived of as a world without normal external economic relations, a world in which such legal and moral refinements as the inviolability of the economic rights of former owners would no longer have to be respected.[22]

If the autarkic policy which has characterized Soviet trade in the past is maintained, and I believe it will be . . . .[23]

Self-sufficiency in virtually all respects has been and is a continuing goal of Communist planners.[24]

The Soviet Union is committed to a policy of ultimate economic self-sufficiency for Eastern Europe.[25]

The export and import policies of the Soviet Union were based on the principle of autarky . . . .[26]

The latter author then cites Under Secretary of State C. Douglas Dillon's 1959 description of Soviet trade policy as autarkic. A leading British student of Soviet economics remarks, almost in passing, that "The U.S.S.R. . . . is largely self-sufficient and was anxious for most of its history to make itself so."[27]

A German scholar gives his version of the reasons for autarky in saying the Soviets practice it:

Because of the historical development, the geographic circumstances, and the central planning of the socialist economy, the Soviet economy tends on the whole towards autarky.[28]

Bergson remarks: "Given the policy of autarky . . . "[29] while Boltho says:

The beginning of the Five Year Plans period for the Soviet Union and of the "Cold War" for the smaller Eastern European countries led to an increasing degree of autarky . . . . While the drive to autarky was subsequently abandoned . . . .[30]

And others might be cited.

As we shall see in a later chapter, the Soviet Union has certainly not achieved autarky; its external trade has not disappeared, nor has it shown a consistent tendency to decline. It may well be, although it is difficult to demonstrate conclusively, that, as Pryor says, Eastern Europe in general trades "below its potential."[31]

The very concept of autarky may be, as Professor Brown asserts, "vague and ambiguous,"[32] in that, as he argues, it includes both the notion of "the greatest possible economic self-sufficiency" and that of reducing trade "as much as possible." And, hence, it might be as well to avoid the use of the term. But there can be no doubt that for reasons and in ways we shall examine in detail, Soviet foreign trade is run on different principles from those prevailing in commerce among market economies, and it is perhaps worth pausing a moment to look for a description of the phenomenon that the widespread use of the term *autarky* in reference to it denotes.

"Reducing trade to a minimum" obviously does not imply its complete abolition. Achieving the "greatest possible self-sufficiency" is an aspect of Soviet policy to which these phrases correctly call attention. It signifies the desire to have under one's control all the essentials for achieving one's purposes. We need not here examine Leninist ideas about controlling rather than being controlled, or their implications for the whole notion of mutual trust among members of a society; but it is perhaps legitimate to refer to the well-known tendency of Soviet enterprise directors to prefer their own to any sort of external sources of supply. Complaints about the unwillingness of directors to rely on specialized shops for castings, gears, and other components are legion in the Soviet press and familiar to all students of Soviet economics. Official disapproval, however, does not prevent the directors from making every effort (legal or illegal)[33] to procure necessary additional supplies, or to hoard materials that might come in handy. The parallel to foreign trade policy is obvious.

It seems important for clarifying this aspect of Soviet behavior to bear in

mind "two basic characteristics in the men of the 'Stalin epoch'—a sense of irre-
ducible bipolarity in the world coupled with a supreme readiness to eradicate
everything that cannot be effectively controlled."[34] Foreign trade was and is a
drug, to be used when helpful, but to which the patient must not become
addicted. For American, and for other non-Soviet polities, the expansion of
world trade is believed desirable as very nearly an end in itself; for the USSR it
is a tool and a weapon, to be judged on pragmatic standards.

We shall be concerned later with the ways in which this tool is and has
been used; for the moment, we need only be clear as to the sense in which the
term *autarky* can properly be used with reference to the USSR. With a change
of one word, as suggested by the preceding discussion, we may adopt the following definition of autarky, and hope that its use will further, rather than
obscure, understanding:

Autarky is to be understood as the expression of an *intention* to be self-
sufficient (*lege* not dependent on the outside world). This implies that all
that needs to be considered is imports, since an autarkic nation, so defined,
is free to export *at its discretion.*[35]

This definition, rightly understood, implies correctly that the USSR is determined
to avoid dependence on foreign and particularly Western sources of supply so far
as possible, while remaining free to use the Western market for tactical and strategic advantage, but without accepting any obligation to participate responsibly in
the operations, the improvement, or the maintenance of that market. The Soviet
Union is, as we shall see in detail, seeking so much economic isolation or independence as will insure that it is not forced to subordinate any significant interest
to the needs of its commercial interconnections with the world outside, while
retaining the liberty to take such advantage of the existence of that world as
seems beneficial to it. In the case of the Soviet Union, it seems clear that the
primary constraint on trade is the determination not to give hostages to fortune,
even to the extent of providing information about its possible actions, let alone
making its internal policies dependent on outside markets, in either direction.

The purpose of the whole discussion is to draw attention to the fact that
the Soviet Union does not and does not want to participate in world trade in
the same way as free world companies and governments do, but rather wants to
use the existence of the outside world to further its ends. Moreover, as Chapter
5 shows, its administrative system is consciously designed to promote autarky
in this, but not in the pure, sense of the word.

Notes

1. Alan A. Brown and Egon Neuberger, *International Trade and Central*

Planning: An Analysis of Economic Interactions (Berkeley and Los Angeles: University of California Press, 1968), p. 12. CPE stands for Centrally Planned Economy (ibid., p. 3).

2. Herbert S. Levine, "The Effects of Foreign Trade on Soviet Planning Practice," in ibid., pp. 274-75. The inner quotation is from P. Cherviakov, *Organizatsiya i Tekhnika Vneshnei Torgovlyi SSSR,* 1st ed. (Moscow: Vneshtorgizdat, 1958), p. 66.

3. Oliver von Gajzago, *Der Sowjetische Aussenhandel mit den Indus-trielaendern* (Berlin: Duncker & Humboldt, 1960), p. 5.

4. Adam Zwass, *Die Waehrung im Aussenhandel der RGW Laendern* (Vienna: Wiener Institut fuer Wirtschaftsvergleiche, 1973), p. 2.

5. Alexander Baykov, *Soviet Foreign Trade* (Princeton, N.J.: Princeton University Press, 1946), p. 50.

6. Robert W. Campbell, *The Soviet-Type Economies,* 3rd ed. (Boston: Houghton Mifflin, 1974), p. 127.

7. Alexander Gerschenkron, *Economic Relations with the U.S.S.R.* (New York: The Committee on International Economic Policy, 1945), p. 47. Cited by Franklyn P. Holzman, "Foreign Trade Behavior of Centrally Planned Econo-mies," in Henry Rosovsky, ed., *Industrialization in Two Systems: Essays in Honor of Alexander Gerschenkron* (New York: John Wiley & Sons, 1966), p. 240.

8. Jozef Wilczynski, *The Economics and Politics of East-West Trade* (New York: Frederick A. Praeger, 1969), p. 60.

9. James Henry Giffen, *The Legal and Practical Aspects of Trade with the Soviet Union* (New York: Frederick A. Praeger, 1969), p. 6.

10. Ibid.

11. Holzman, "Foreign Trade Behavior," p. 246.

12. Franklyn D. Holzman, "Foreign Trade," in Abram Bergson and Simon Kuznets, eds., *Economic Trends in the Soviet Union* (Cambridge, Mass.: Harvard University Press, 1963), pp. 301-02.

13. Hertha W. Heiss, "The Soviet Union in the World Market," in U.S. Congress, Joint Economic Committee, *New Directions in the Soviet Economy* (Washington, D.C.: U.S. Government Printing Office, 1966), p. 919.

14. Abram Bergson in U.S. Congress, Joint Economic Committee, *Hearings on East-West Trade* (Washington, D.C.: U.S. Government Printing Office, 1964), p. 22.

15. Legislative Reference Service, *A Background Study of East-West Trade* (Washington, D.C.: U.S. Government Printing Office, 1965), passim.

16. Robert S. Kovach and John T. Farrell, "Foreign Trade of the U.S.S.R.," in U.S. Congress, Joint Economic Committee, *Economic Performance and the*

Military Burden in the U.S.S.R. (Washington, D.C.: U.S. Government Printing Office, 1970), p. 105.

17. Glen Alden Smith, *Soviet Foreign Trade Organization, Operations, and Policy, 1918-1971* (New York: Praeger Publishers, 1973), p. 45.

18. Andrea Boltho, *Foreign Trade Criteria in Socialist Economies* (Cambridge: The University Press, 1971), pp. 53-54.

19. Cf. U.S. Congress, Joint Economic Committee, *Soviet Economy in a New Perspective* (Washington, D.C.: U.S. Government Printing Office, 1976), p. 678.

20. Jack Brougher, "U.S.S.R. Foreign Trade: Greater Role for Trade with the West," in ibid., pp. 678-94.

21. Holzman, "Foreign Trade," pp. 301-02.

22. Leon G. Herman, "The Promise of Economic Self-Sufficiency under Soviet Socialism," in Vladimir G. Treml, ed., *The Development of Soviet Economy* (New York: Frederick A. Praeger, 1968), p. 314.

23. Holzman, "Foreign Trade," p. 310.

24. Legislative Reference Service, *A Background Study,* p. 16.

25. Ibid., p. 2.

26. Smith, *Soviet Foreign Trade Organization,* p. 24.

27. Alec Nove, *The Soviet Economy* (New York: Frederick A. Praeger, 1961). p. 193.

28. Theodor D. Zotschew, *Die Aussenwirtschaftlichen Verbindungen der Sowjetunion,* Kieler Studien No. 97 (Tuebinging: J.C.B. Mohr [Paul Siebeck], 1969), p. 1.

29. Bergson, Hearings, p. 318.

30. Boltho, *Foreign Trade Criteria,* p. 3.

31. Frederick L. Pryor, *The Communist Foreign Trade System* (Cambridge, Mass.: MIT Press, 1963), p. 27.

32. Alan A. Brown, "Towards a Theory of Centrally Planned Foreign Trade," in Brown and Neuberger, eds., *International Trade and Central Planning,* p. 58.

33. Joseph Berliner, " 'Blat' Is Higher than Stalin," *Problems of Communism,* vol. III, no. 1 (January-February 1954), p. 22; and Berliner, "The Informal Organization of the Soviet Firm," *Quarterly Journal of Economics,* August 1952, p. 342.

34. Alexander Erlich, *The Soviet Industrialization Debate, 1924-1928,* Cambridge, Mass.: Harvard University Press, 1960), p. 180.

35. Andre Marchal, "The Problems of the Common Market," in Paul A. Samuelson, ed., *International Economic Relations: Proceedings of the Third*

Congress of the International Economic Association (London: Macmillan; New York: St. Martin's Press, 1969), p. 178. Emphasis added.

3 Soviet Theories of Foreign Trade

In this chapter, we investigate Soviet statements concerning the purposes for carrying on foreign trade in order to seek evidence that will support or confute the Western "received opinion" on the subject we have just examined. In doing so, we need to bear in mind certain problems peculiar to the Soviet literature. For one thing, Soviet publications addressed to and intended to influence foreign audiences are to be looked at in the light of their intended purpose. For another, there is a tendency in much Soviet scholarly economic writing to confuse what actually is with what the authors believe should be the case. In other words, much Soviet scholarly output in the economic field is intended to persuade Soviet decisionmakers of the desirability of certain changes and hence is not exclusively concerned with the elucidation of the present, actual operation of Soviet economic processes. Finally, much Soviet economic literature is designed for instructional purposes, either as textbooks or as *agitprop* literature (a term that is not to be interpreted as pejorative) and accordingly is not intended as scientific scholarship in the conventional Western sense. In drawing conclusions about the inaccessible world of Soviet economic decision making, all these sources of information are valuable, but must be used with due attention to the intentions of their authors.

Soviet official and academic treatment of the subject of foreign trade is in comparison with the literature in other fields both scanty in quantity and superficial, often propagandistic, in content. Serious analysis of the economics, as distinguished from the mechanics, of foreign trade is, indeed, a phenomenon of quite recent years. Western commentators and Soviet writers alike have noted this fact, together with the noticeable lack of professional economic sophistication displayed. It is not too much to say that Soviet economists have treated foreign trade as a stepchild. There are signs, as we shall see, that this attitude is changing and that a decidedly more technical and professional approach to questions of foreign trade is becoming acceptable, even though, thus far, its impact on actual Soviet policies and practices is hard to discern.

The amount of material on foreign trade published in the Soviet Union and the western European countries before 1956 is very limited. Apart from a few statistics and some descriptions of the organization of the foreign trade ministry, there is an almost total lack of discussion of the more important problems of planning foreign trade and deciding on the structures of imports and exports.[1]

The most recent American work on the subject notes a number of Soviet works published before 1935, but only five nonstatistical works on foreign trade since that year.[2] A Soviet writer deplores the lack of serious treatment of foreign trade, and lists two dissertations and two monographs as the only serious recent Soviet works in the field.[3] There are works that deal primarily with trade among and with capitalist states;[4] the Nauchno-issledovatelskii Institut compendium mentioned below, for example, and a number dealing with trade among the socialist countries. There are also straight propaganda works; for example, Minister of Foreign Trade Patolichev's *Foreign Trade*,[5] and Alexander Bykov's *Untapped Reserves of World Trade*.[6]

From the opposite point of view, standard Soviet textbooks on planning[7] have no detailed treatment of the planning of foreign trade, nor do they incorporate references to the use of foreign trade in the planning process. Standard works on the all-important supply-sales planning process[8] are similarly silent. The standard textbook on political economy[9] devotes two pages to the subject, most of which is a discussion of the state monopoly.

Since the late sixties, the professional journals (*Vneshnaya Torgovlya, Voprosy Ekonomiki, Planovoye Khozyaistvo*) have printed a number of articles on the effectiveness of foreign trade, which we shall examine later. But the sparseness of the general literature is on the whole unrelieved.

Students of Soviet affairs are familiar with two contrasting, though not mutually exclusive, themes running through Soviet declarations on foreign relations in general and on foreign economic relations in particular. On the one hand, Soviet statements show signs of fear of what the surrounding, and by definition hostile, capitalist world might do to the Soviet Union. On the other, they demonstrate an eager desire to be accepted as equal and well-intentioned members of the world community.

The nationalization of foreign trade by the decree of April 22, 1918[10] was, in the words of the leading Soviet economic historian of the period:

> . . . very important from an economic and political point of view. It put into the hands of the Soviet state all foreign economic relations of the country with the capitalist world. From then on, the monopoly of foreign trade has been the unshakeable basis for the economic relations of the Soviet republic with the capitalist world.[11]

Lenin's motivation was primarily the protection of Russian industry from foreign competition. He rejected Bukharin's argument that tariff protection would be sufficient by saying that the "unbelievably rich" capitalist countries could easily overcome Soviet tariff barriers by means of subsidies.[12] This fear of "assaults" (*nastupleniya*) continued to dominate Soviet thinking on the subject throughout the NEP period.[13]

At the same time, however, the other side of the Soviet attitude toward foreign trade comes through in another *Lenin-Zitat*, the source of which, Foreign

Trade Minister N. S. Patolichev, simultaneously illustrates the continuation of this point of view into present times:

Lenin pointed out that the Soviet Union, despite the differences that existed between its socio-political system and the socio-political system of the capitalist countries, would willingly use the equipment and other goods manufactured in those countries, which, in their turn, were interested in Russian raw materials.[14]

Soviet authorities are not, of course, unaware of the political importance of international economic relations. Former Premier Khrushchev may have overstated the case somewhat in his famous remark:

"We value trade least for economic reasons and most for political reasons as a means for promoting better relations between our countries," Mr. Khrushchev told the senators who saw him last week.[15]

A more balanced and approximately contemporary statement of the same thing is contained in a collection of essays on foreign trade with a series of capitalist countries:

Cooperation in the economic field through foreign trade provides the prerequisites for strengthening political relations among states. Therefore foreign political relations are inseparable from foreign economic relations.[16]

Or again:

Trade and other forms of economic scientific cooperation in relations between socialist and capitalist countries is a specific form of the struggle of the two world systems in conditions of peaceful coexistence.[17]

While one would not wish to lay undue emphasis on this aspect of Soviet motivation, clearly the Soviet authorities have been and are well aware of the desire of the "capitalists" to do business with them, and they have been suspected of using this desire to promote such political aims as detente, or, in earlier days, peaceful coexistence.

On a more purely economic basis, the fear of external interference in the Soviet economy is undoubtedly one of the principal reasons for the existence of a state monopoly of foreign trade, as Soviet writers have often asserted:

At the same time, the monopoly of foreign trade protects the countries of the democratic camp from the aggressive attempts of the imperialists to subordinate their markets and sources of raw materials to their control.[18]

The basic principle, however, as Soviet writers constantly reiterate, is the subordination of foreign trade to the development of the Soviet economy, and specifically, to the demands of the plan.

Foreign trade must cooperate in the best use of the advantages of the international division of labor for speeding up the tempo of construction of communism in our country, winning time in the competition with the most developed capitalist countries.[19]

This is a scarcely noticeable change from the view expressed a decade earlier in an official textbook:

Foreign trade in the period of building a socialist society is subordinated to the task of liquidating economic backwardness, the one-sided economic development of a country, and facilitates industrialization, the liquidation of economic dependency on imperialist states and securing its economic independence.
    The foreign trade of the socialist state speeds up the development of productive forces of the country and the increase of the material well-being of the people and is based on the uninterruptedly and rapidly growing internal market of the country.[20]

More specific pronouncements, coinciding closely with the Western "received view," appear in the relatively sparse Soviet literature on foreign trade.
    A recent, detailed, and authoritative statement on Soviet policy and objectives was published in 1967 in *Vneshnaya Torgovlya* by the then (and now) Minister, N. S. Patolichev:

Foreign trade plays an important role in increasing the tempos of broadening socialist reproduction. With the help of foreign trade the structure of social production is improved, technical progress speeded up, the productivity of socially necessary labor is increased. Foreign trade facilitates the elevation of the material well-being and cultural level of the toilers of our country. Through the channels of foreign trade the import into the Soviet Union of capital equipment and other production of the machine-building of foreign countries is secured. This speeds up technical progress in domestic industry, and increases the effectiveness of domestic production. Significant resources in the course of a number of years are spent for the purchase of machines and equipment for branches producing consumers' goods. The import of such equipment facilitates an accelerated establishment of more rational proportions in the economy.
    By supplementing internal resources foreign trade secures the supply of the national economy with those sorts of equipment, raw materials and consumers' goods the domestic production of which at the given point of time does not yet meet the needs of the economy, and also with those goods which could be obtained from other countries with smaller outlays of means or in shorter time periods than would be needed for producing them at home.[21]

The almost-buried reference to comparative advantage tucked away in the last sentence of the passages quoted does not, of course, distinguish between imports from socialist and from capitalist countries. Nor does it hint at the fundamental question of *how* the Soviet decisionmakers can tell what can be imported "with smaller outlays of means" than if it were produced at home. These questions of reliability of supply and of comparative advantage (in real terms), as well as the matter of Soviet use of foreign sources to meet unplanned shortages, will concern us later. Here we are merely examining official public statements of Soviet purposes and trade policies.

On the purposes of export, Patolichev is less explicit, and less definitive, than other authorities we shall look at in a moment. He evidently takes for granted the necessity of paying for imports and the desirability of accumulating foreign exchange reserves and stresses that "exporting in its turn exercises a beneficent effect on the improvement of the branch structure of social production, on speeding up technical progress, and on the economy of social labor," thus emphasizing the potential dynamic effects of trade on the domestic productive apparatus.[22] His principal thrust appears to be that of assuring Soviet readers that the USSR is not content to remain a provider of raw materials in a perhaps unconscious expression of the "technological snobbery" that "remains dominant among Communists" and "operates with particular strength in foreign trade."[23] But he is also concerned with assuring socialist countries, in particular, that they need not fear the drying-up of Soviet raw material sources.

The strengthening of the export of finished products does not mean that the export of raw materials will be cut off. On the contrary, under suitable conditions that export can develop in economically rational degree.[24]

The most explicit statements on the subject date from the principal prewar work on foreign trade: "The basic task of Soviet importation is to use foreign goods, and first of all machinery, for the most rapid accomplishment of the plans of socialist construction, for industrialization and the technical reconstruction of the economy, for the technical-economic independence of the U.S.S.R."[25] On the other side, "the basic task of Soviet exportation is to receive foreign exchange for paying costs of imports and to help accumulate foreign exchange reserves in the country."[26] In summary, "since exporting secures payment for imports, and imports have played in fulfilling the tasks of socialist construction an exceptional role, the gigantic economic-political importance of our export work is comprehensible."[27]

The same spirit is expressed in a postwar Stalinist-epoch work on foreign trade, which is primarily concerned with bilateral relations with individual countries, but notes among its few general remarks:

The export of commodities serves first of all as a source of means for paying for the import of goods necessary for speeding up the tempo of socialist construction, and also the process of economic cooperation with brotherly [i.e., socialist] peoples.[28]

As is evident from the statistics on Soviet trade presented in Chapter 4, since the death of Stalin, Soviet interest in foreign trade, especially with capitalist countries, has expanded enormously and become politically respectable. Soviet statements since 1953 reflect this change, but show a rationale for importing and exporting that is not fundamentally different in kind.

Thus one writer in 1964 remarks that "Soviet foreign trade *in accordance with the plan of the development of the economy of the U.S.S.R.* helps solve problems of the further elevation of the socialist economy and the establishment of the material-technical basis of communism in the U.S.S.R."[29] He is thus in the direct line of descent from Lenin's pronouncement in a resolution of the IV Party Congress that "Foreign trade must be completely subordinated to the needs of the economic plan."[30] But now the emphasis, while still on the utility of importing, includes expansion of trade: "It is clear that the Soviet Union will in the future steadily develop commerce on mutually advantageous terms with all countries of the world. That means that it will increase its purchases of goods needed for the development of the economy of the country and satisfying the growing needs of the Soviet people."[31]

Writing for foreign consumption at some period in the mid-sixties, Patolichev picked up the Leninist theme and expanded on it with reference to contemporary policy in a way which further illustrates the Soviet attitude to exporting and importing, as we have seen.[32]

More concretely he adds:

In planning imports (on the basis of input-output tables) the main consideration is to secure for the country additional supplies of those producer and consumer goods (over and above the amount produced in the country) which would at the given period most effectively promote the development of the productive forces of the country and improve living standards . . . . The total amount of imports is linked to export possibilities.

In planning exports the chief consideration is to cover import payments and build currency reserves. Other factors in determining the composition and volume of exports are the availability of the given goods so that their export would not be detrimental to the planned development of the national economy, the estimated currency receipts in comparison to the costs and the demand for the commodity on the foreign market.[33]

In addition to the note of what we might call creeping comparative advantage, Soviet statements in the sixties increasingly included among the objectives of foreign trade two new considerations. On the import side, the desirability of importing consumers' goods (in sharp contrast to the Stalinist doctrine and practice) appears as a major though not primary purpose; and on the export side, the technical and public relations gains from exporting capital goods receives attention along with, though by no means displacing, the more traditional objectives we have already noticed.

Thus:

. . . the export of means of production including complex equipment for entire factories is economically profitable, expressing a high level of the technique of production in the enterprises of socialist industry and a rapid and uninterrupted growth in the productivity of labor.

On the other hand, it is necessary to remark in the import field a broadened import of contemporary, technically excellent equipment and at the same time the purchase in significant quantities of food and industrial consumption goods.[34]

More recently, a writer in the journal *Vneshnaya Torgovlya* (Foreign Trade) made a bow in the direction of the concept of comparative advantage while still showing signs of the older view of the purpose of Soviet trade:

Using foreign trade, the country gains the possibility of exchanging a part of its output for other goods with greater social utility (when domestic production does not match home needs exactly).[35]

In what may be the most comprehensive concise statement of post-Khrushchevian doctrine on the matter, G. Smirnov, writing in the authoritative academic economic journal *Voprosy Ekonomiki* (Questions of Economics) characterized Soviet foreign trade objectives in this way:

In the final analysis (if one excludes the necessity for obtaining foreign exchange from exports for its subsequent use for purposes not connected with the import of goods or services), the purpose of foreign trade is the procurement of certain imported goods: (a) which are not produced within the country at all, (b) are produced, as a result of whatever temporary reasons, in insufficient quantity, (c) whose production within the country is more expensive than their purchase on the foreign market.[36]

All this is not very different from the view expressed in the first post-Stalin handbook on trade with capitalist countries:

As for the foreign trade of the U.S.S.R., it fulfills great economic roles. Through trade with other countries the Soviet economy receives a part of the goods necessary for its development: certain sorts of equipment for outfitting industrial enterprises, some types of raw materials for processing industry, a series of other goods for satisfying the ever-increasing demand of industry and the population.[37]

Another post-Stalin authority expresses Soviet intentions in this way:

Foreign trade also participates in the accomplishments of internal social-economic tasks of which may be noted the diminution of heavy physical labor, improving the conditions of work and of domestic life, the development of safety techniques, the establishment of conditions for the coming together of the two forms of property, for overcoming the differences between city and country, between mental and physical work. The development of the economy of the national republics, oblasts, and economic regions of the U.S.S.R. has great importance.[38]

This formulation perhaps deserves a bit of interpretation, on the basis of the observations on the purposes of Soviet scholarly writing above. The book in which it appeared seems to have as its major, though unstated, purpose persuading its readers of the virtues of expanded and rationalized foreign trade. The author is therefore not unnaturally concerned first to demonstrate that doing as he advocates will advance the specific Soviet goals of the moment, which were those he mentioned, and further to suggest to his readers that many if not most of the goals would be more rapidly and completely attained if foreign sources of technology, in particular, were tapped.

The post-Khrushchev expressions of doctrine, finally, show some diminution of the concern we noted earlier regarding possible damage from increased external intercourse and stress more clearly the advantages its advocates see for the attainment of Soviet economic ends. The 1957 study quoted above contains one sentence that portrays the ambiguity of Soviet feelings in the post-Stalin period quite clearly:

With the help of the monopoly of foreign trade the U.S.S.R. makes possible in the best way the development of the productive forces of the country; on the other hand, it protects the Soviet economy from the corrupting (*tletvornogo*) influence of the capitalist economy.[39]

By 1967, the journal *Vneshnaya Torgovlya* was able to put a more positive face on the same dichotomy, in an article on the juridical aspects of the monopoly of foreign trade, and thus to lead its readers to see the advantages of such trade when carefully controlled by the state:

More concretely, the foundations of the socialist monopoly of foreign trade, expressing its essence, include the securing (a) of the independent development of the planned economy of the given socialist country and (b) of the planned character of the economic relations of the given country with the surrounding world.[40]

And finally:

The job of foreign exchange policy and of the legislation of the U.S.S.R. expressing it is the planned organization of the international accounts of the U.S.S.R. in order to secure the concentration of foreign exchange resources coming into the country in the hands of the State and the most rational (*tselesoobrazno*) use of them in accordance with the tasks of the economic plans, directed toward strengthening the socialist economy and of building communism.

At the same time, the foreign exchange policy and foreign exchange legislation of the U.S.S.R. subserves the goal of protecting the independence of the socialist economy, barring it off from the chaos of the capitalist market, from foreign exchange speculation and all sorts of efforts by capitalist countries to damage Soviet foreign trade.[41]

The same authority continues:

For this purpose, together with a significant expansion of exports, we were the main source of securing the foreign exchange necessary for paying for imports, measures were taken to increase gold production and for gathering into the State offices the foreign exchange valuables in the hands of the population and for increasing the income of transfers through non-commercial channels from abroad to the U.S.S.R.[42]

This treatment of foreign exchange—that is, of the balance of payments as distinguished from the balance of trade—shows at the same time the dependence of exchange policy on the purposes of trade and the acceptance in separate though related instances of government of the basic Soviet strategy of protection and import coverage.

We noted above the strain in Soviet pronouncements on foreign trade policy that shows the fear of interference from abroad with Soviet economic development; as we saw in Chapter 1, this has been interpreted by foreign analysis as implying a policy of autarky. While that topic is seldom explicitly touched on by Soviet authorities, at least one categorical denial of such a policy is quoted in an English work on Soviet foreign trade from the mid-thirties:

What are the prospects of Soviet foreign trade? In his speech at the World Economic Conference, Litvinov answered the question in the following way: "Thanks to the successful accomplishment of the first Five-Year Plan, we have ample opportunity of developing new construction, independently of foreign imports; nevertheless, my Government has no intention of cutting itself off from the outer world by economic barriers and retiring into its own economic shell. In distinction from other countries, we with a great increase of our own output, do not aspire to autarchy [*sic*] and do not resist an advantageous import of foreign goods."[43]

On the other hand, the prewar treatise quoted earlier, which was, at least, not written under the pressure of a public performance by the Foreign Affairs Commissar, states frankly that "the importation of the U.S.S.R. is so constructed as to accomplish its liberation from importing as soon as possible."[44] And in 1939, Trade Commissar Mikoyan told the 29th Party Congress that the goal had been achieved:

In the period when we were still backward and poor, when we did not have our own developed machine-building industry and we had to build industry at any cost, we were forced to export abroad a great deal of raw materials and foodstuffs which we needed ourselves, and we exported these in order to obtain foreign exchange, and to use those earnings to buy machine tools for industry, equipment for tractor and automobile plants.[45]

The theme was echoed after the war by N. A. Voznesensky, the chief wartime economic planner:

The U.S.S.R. will continue in the future to maintain economic ties with foreign countries in accordance with the tested line of the Soviet Government, which is directed towards the attainment of the technical and economic independence of the Soviet Union.[46]

But the goal continues to elude the Soviet leaders; the rainbow's end is still beyond the horizon:

I want to add that our plans are by no means plans calculated on autarky. We are not bearing a course toward the isolation of our country from the outside world. On the contrary, we start from the position that it [the country] will develop under conditions of growing, universal cooperation with the outside world, and therewith not only with socialist countries, but also in significant degree with states of an opposing social system.[47]

Thus said Leonid Brezhnev in his 1973 television address to the German people.

From what has been said, it would seem permissible to conclude that while as a rule Soviet statements on the subject do not formulate the "received Western view" in entirely Western terms, they are by no means inconsistent with it and taken in their entirety and their context, furnish substantial support for it. They provide ample confirmation, if that were needed, that the USSR operates a monopoly of foreign trade for two primary purposes: to isolate the USSR from "interference" with its development by external economic forces, and to subordinate all foreign trade to the economic purposes of the country's rulers. The possibilities of using trade and the opportunity to trade for political purposes in dealings with capitalist countries is frankly admitted:

It would be useless to enumerate here all the pronouncements on foreign trade made by the Soviet rulers. All embroider the same theme: the USSR wants to broaden its commercial relations with foreign countries, and if they don't make rapid enough progress, the fault must be attributed to a discriminatory policy practiced by the westerners with respect to the USSR. However, this official position does not yet demonstrate that the USSR really wants to carry on a developed foreign trade.[48]

If one reads behind the phrases about "socialist cooperation," one sees the possibility, if nothing more, of Soviet concern to maintain control through foreign trade over the development patterns of the other European CEMA members. Finally, one sees no Soviet admission that it proposes complete withdrawal from foreign economic relations into strict autarky, nor even a clear determination that CEMA should become entirely self-sufficient itself. One does, however, notice a continuing fear of becoming *dependent* on sources of supply not under direct Soviet control and a determination not to let that happen.

Notes

1. Andrea Boltho, *Foreign Trade Criteria in Socialist Economies* (Cambridge: The University Press, 1971), p. 49.

2. Glen Alden Smith, *Soviet Foreign Trade Organization, Operations, and Policy, 1918-1971* (New York: Praeger Publishers, 1973), pp. 350-80.

3. V. S. Pozdnyakov, *Gosudarstvennya Monopoliya Vneshnei Torgovlyi v SSSR* (Moscow: Mezhdunarodnye Otnosheniya, 1969), p. 34.

4. I. S. Potapov, G. S. Roginskii, Yu. N. Kapelinski, and M. G. Shereshevskii, *Organizatsionnye Formy i Tekhnika Vneshnetorgovykh Operatsii* (Moscow: Vneshtorgizdat, 1957).

5. Nikolai Patolichev, *Foreign Trade* (n.p. [New Delhi?]: Novosti Press Publishers House, n.d.).

6. Alexander Bykov, *Untapped Reserves of World Trade* (n.p.: Novosti Publishing House, n.d.; presumably New Delhi, about 1972).

7. M. V. Breev, ed., *Planirovaniya Narodnogo Khozyaistva SSSR* (Moscow: Izdatelstvo Politicheskoi Literatury, 1963); more recently M. G. Kolodny and A. P. Stepanov, *Planirovaniye Narodnogo Khozyaistva SSSR* (Kiev: Vishcha Shkola, 1975).

8. P. A. Shein, *Materialno-tekhnicheskoe Snabzheniye Sotsialistecheskogo Promyshelennogo Predpriyatiya* (Moscow: Gospolitizdat, 1959); the textbook edited by E. Yu. Lokshin, *Ekonomika materialno-tekhnicheskogo Snabzheniya* (Moscow: Gosudarstvennoe Izdatelstvo Politicheskoi Literatury, 1960).

9. Collective of Authors, *Politicheskaya Ekonomika: Uchebnik* (Moscow: Gosudarstvennoe Izdatelstvo Politicheskoi Literatury, 1954), pp. 515-17.

10. *Sbornik Uzakonenii i Rasporyazhenii Rabochekrestyanskogo Pravitel stva*, no. 33 (1918), p. 432; cited by P. I. Lyashchenko, *Istoriya Narodnogo Khozyaistva SSSR, Tom III, Sotsializm* (Moscow: Gosudarstvennoe Izdatelstvo Politicheskoi Literatury, 1956), p. 612.

11. Lyashchenko, *Istoriya Narodnogo Khozyaistva*, pp. 26-27.

12. Pozdnyakov, *Gosudarstvennya Monopoliya*, p. 34.

13. Ibid., p. 54.

14. N. Patolichev, "Stroitelstvo materialnotekhnicheskogo Bazy kommuniz-ma v SSSR," in *Vneshnaya Torgovlya*, no. 11 (1967), p. 3.

15. *The New York Times*, September 18, 1955, p. 4-B. The authenticity, and even more the accuracy, of this report is open to some doubt.

16. Nauchno-Isseledovatelskii Konyunkturny Institut MVT SSSR, *Vneshnaya Torgovlya SSSR s Kapitalisticheskimi Stranami* (Moscow: Vneshtorgizdat, 1957), p. 5.

17. G. M. Prokhorov, *Vneshe-ekonomicheskii Svyazi i Ekonomicheskii Rost Sotsialistisheskikh Stran* (Moscow: Mezhdunarodnye Otnosheniya, 1972), p. 195.

18. Potapov et al., *Organizatsionnye*.

19. D. F. Fokin, *Vneshnaya Torgovlya SSSR [1946-1963 gg.]*, (Moscow: Mezhdunarodnye Otnosheniya, 1964), pp. 186-87.

20. Potapov et al., *Organizatsionnye*, p. 417.

21. Patolichev, *Stroitelstvo,* pp. 10-11.

22. Ibid., p. 12.

23. P. J. D. Wiles, *Communist International Economics* (Oxford: Basil Blackwell, 1968), p. 179. In this respect, Wiles points out, and as is well known, the Soviets do not differ except perhaps in degree from other technologically retarded countries. Soviet fascination with the biggest plants and the most advanced techniques has been exemplified from the days of the Magnitogorsk-Kuzbas Shuttle to the Kama River Truck Plant. It is not without affinities with the familiar penchant of Western scientists, doctors, and engineers for the latest and most advanced equipment and techniques, regardless of cost-effectiveness. Given the fact that most Soviet economic administrators and executives are engineers by training, their proclivities in this regard are understandably given freer rein then they would be in more profit-oriented societies.

24. Patolichev, *Stroitelstvo,* p. 12.

25. D. D. Mishustin, *Vneshnaya Torgovlya SSSR* (Moscow: V/O Mezhdunarodnaya Kniga, 1941), p. 6.

26. Ibid., p. 7.

27. Ibid.

28. Potapov et al., *Organizatsionnye*, p. 417.

29. Fokin, *Vneshnaya Torgovlya*, p. 3. Emphasis added.

30. Cited by Louis Kawan, *La Nouvelle Orientation du Commerce Extérieur Soviètique* (Brussels: Centre National pour l'Etude des Pays à Régime Communiste, 1958), p. 124.

31. Fokin, *Vneshnaya Torgovlya*, p. 188. Emphasis added.

32. Ibid., p. 27.

33. Patolichev, *Foreign Trade*, p. 8.

34. Fokin, *Vneshnaya Torgovlya*, p. 11.

35. A. Borisenko, "Formirovaniye Struktury Eksporta i Importa (Postanovleniye voprosa)," *Vneshnaya Torgovlya*, no. 2 (1967), p. 17.

36. G. Smirnov, "K Voprosu Ob Otsenki Ekonomicheskoi Effektivnosti Vneshnei Torgovlyi SSSR" *Voprosy Ekonomiki*, no. 12, (1965), p. 94.

37. N. I. Konyunkturnyi Institut, *Vneshnaya Torgovlya*, p. 5.

38. G. M. Tuchkin, *Ekonomicheskaya Effektivnost Vneshnei Torgovlyi* (Moscow: Mezhdunarodnye Otnosheniya, 1969), p. 43.

39. N. I. Konyunkturnyi Institut, *Vneshnaya Torgovlya*, p. 6.

40. E. Usenko, "Sushchnost i Formy Sotsialisticheskoi Monopolii Vneshnei Torgovlyi," *Vneshnaya Torgovlya*, no. 6 (1967), p. 39.

41. A. M. Smirnov, *Mezhdunarodnye Valyutnye i Kreditnye Otnosheniya SSSR* (Moscow: Vneshtorgizdat, 1969), p. 25.

42. Ibid., p. 42.

43. J. D. Yanson, *Foreign Trade in the U.S.S.R.* (London: Victor Gollancz, Ltd., 1934), p. 3.

44. Mishustin, *Vneshnaya Torgovlya*, p. 6.

45. Quoted by Leon G. Herman, "The Promise of Economic Self-Sufficiency under Soviet Socialism," in Vladimir G. Treml, ed., *The Development of Soviet Economy* (New York: Frederick A. Praeger, 1968), p. 227.

46. N. A. Voznesensky, in *Planovoye Khozyaistvo*, no. 2 (1946), p. 67; quoted by Herman, ibid., p. 228.

47. Text in *Pravda*, May 22, 1973, p. 1.

48. Kawan, *La Nouvelle Orientation*, p. 23.

Statistical Evidence on the
"Received" View

This chapter sets out to test the hypothesis that the Soviet Union exports in order to pay for needed imports. As the hypothesis deals with *ex ante* intentions, the *ex post* evidence recorded in the trade statistics cannot provide direct confirmation or refutation. The most that can be expected is that the evidence of Soviet actions in the trade field, as reflected in the trade statistics, be consistent with the hypothesis, and with its implications. It is clearly impossible to prove intent from results, but we may, for example, hypothesize that if a significant sequence of deficits and surpluses in the foreign trade balance appears, then either deficits in one year are being covered in the following year or surpluses earned are being spent later.

The "received view" of Soviet foreign trade policy includes, as we have seen, an interpretation, or misinterpretation, of "autarky" that is susceptible of statistical examination. It may be summarized as holding that the Soviets, perhaps because their imports are limited by their ability to export, minimize imports. It is also held, as we have seen above, that there has been a change, either since the death of Stalin, or since the reform period began in 1965, so that complete independence of imports is no longer a Soviet objective. Both these views are supported by Soviet statements we have already examined. The former is confirmed by the Soviet record during the first and second five-year plans, as summarized by Baykov[1] and Smith.[2] Imports in 1936, according to the latter, had dropped to $120 million from a 1931 high of $569 million as a result of Soviet ability to produce its own industrial inputs, although the validity of this contention is somewhat vitiated by Smith's misdating of the low point (it was, in fact, in 1934 that Soviet imports reached their nadir, according to Smith's table[3] and official Soviet data.[4] Nevertheless, the foreign trading record before 1940 is clearly consistent with a policy of importation of capital goods in large quantities followed by increasing reliance on domestic production and hence leads to the interpretation that Soviet policy was indeed directed toward minimizing dependence on foreign sources.

Data from a prewar foreign trade statistical handbook shows the declining dependence on imports, as a proportion of total consumption, during the first five-year plan in selected major industrial branches: machines, 19.0% (1930), 13.0% (1931), 7.3% (1932); tractors (horsepower), 81.2% (1930), 59.3% (1931), 0.0% (1932); automobiles, 66.4% (1930), 43.1% (1931), 3.9% (1932); cotton, 19.3% (1930), 13.6 (1931), 5.2% (1932); rolled ferrous metals, 0.0% (1930), 23.0% (1931), 17.0% (1932); and copper, 3.16% (1930), 35.5% (1931), 17.3% (1932).[5]

These data are illustrative only of a declared Soviet intention and of the degree to which, within a remarkably short period of time, it was carried out. They are, of course, selective. Data available in the West do not permit the extension of the investigation into other areas or over other periods, to the best of the author's knowledge. Similarly, we have no consumption figures; the statistical handbooks available show only total production, not consumption of goods in these categories—if they show them at all. It is, of course, possible that the difficulties of exporting during the Depression reduced Soviet imports below what they might have been; but the remarks of Mikoyan, quoted earlier, indicate that Soviet reaction to marketing difficulties was cutting prices to the extent necessary to fulfill the export plan in value terms.

For a country with the resource endowment and the sheer size of the Soviet Union, foreign trade is naturally less important than for smaller, less self-sufficient countries; so much is commonplace. Nevertheless, it may be illuminating to look at Soviet foreign trade in the postwar period as a proportion both of Soviet Gross National Product, as calculated by Western experts, and of Net Material Product (NMP), as presented in Soviet statistics. These data are presented in Tables 4-1 and 4-2.

The data are, it should be noted, illustrative only. The figures for foreign trade turnover are subject to the usual reservations regarding foreign trade statistics summarized by Morgenstern.[6] Soviet foreign trade statistics are f.o.b. in both directions and include re-exports;[7] the Western import data re c.i.f.[8] and exclude them. Soviet trade data are given in foreign trade (valuta) rubles; the valuta ruble has no known determinate connection with the domestic ruble in which "net material product" is expressed.[9]

Moreover, due to the special nature of the political and economic relationship established between the Soviet Union and the other CEMA countries after World War II, the preponderance of the total Soviet trade carried on with them (56 percent in 1971, for example)[10] should be considered in a different light from the more nearly normal commercial relations with the developed capitalist countries; hence, we also show the trade with those latter countries as an *even smaller* fraction of GNP or NMP.

Further reservations with respect to the numbers apply to the GNP figures. The expression of Soviet GNP in dollars is liable to distortions going beyond those familiar from the work of Gilbert and Kravis;[11] see especially Abraham Becker, *Comparisons of United States and U.S.S.R. National Output: Some Rules of the Game*[12] and Peter Wiles, "The Theory of International Comparisons of Economic Volume."[13] Even with respect to the Soviet national output figures in rubles, for reasons set out in Chapter 6 and the Appendix,[14] there is good reason to go beyond the reservations that led Bergson to "adjust" the ruble to take account of turnover taxes and subsidies. We doubt that *any* ruble total involving the aggregation of Soviet price data is comparable to a total based on prices in a market economy.

Table 4-1
Soviet Foreign Trade and GNP

Year	(1) Soviet GNP in Current U.S. $ billion, Western Estimates (a)	(b)	(c)	(d)	(2) Soviet Foreign Trade Turnover, U.S. $ million (d)	(3) (2) as % of (1) (a)	(b)	(c)	(d)	(4) Soviet Trade with Free World Countries, $ million	(5) (4) as % of (1)	(6) Soviet Trade with COCOM Countries, $ million	(7) (6) as % of (1)
1975	803			786	70.5	8.7			10.0	9,688	1.6		
1974	719			704	52,156	5.9			6.0	8,313	1.5		
1973	632			622	42,317	6.7			6.8	7,791	1.5		
1972	598			546	31,774	5.3			5.8	7,044	1.6	5,925	0.99
1971	570			500	26,259	4.6			5.3	6,231	1.5	4,457	0.78
1970	526	497	638	475	24,508	4.7	4.9	5.9	5.2	5,669	1.5 1.6	4,217	0.80 0.85 0.66
1969	444			417	21,982	5.0			5.3	5,445	1.5	3,801	0.85
1968	429	532	414	388	20,044	4.7	3.8	4.8	5.2	4,901	1.5 1.2	3,386	0.80 0.64 0.82
1967	377			350	18,189	4.8			5.2	4,512	1.5	3,024	0.80
1966	357			325	16,754	4.7			5.2	3,915	1.4	2,958	0.83
1965	317			294	16,233	5.1			5.5	3,580	1.3	2,376	0.75
1964	293			272	15,420	5.3			5.7	3,121	1.3	2,350	0.80
1963	268			249	14,331	5.3			5.8	2,896	1.1	2,046	0.76
1962	258			240	13,486	5.2			5.6	2,380	1.0	1,736	0.67
1961	250	255		227	11,826	4.7	4.6		5.2	2,072	1.2	1,774	0.71 0.70
1960	229			213	11,192	4.9			5.3	2,059		1,561	0.68
1959	214			201	10,513	4.9			5.3	1,632		1,132	0.513
1958	202			189	8,640	4.3			5.2			992	0.49
1957	NA			168	8,311				4.6			969	
1956	NA			160	7,221				5.0			815	
1955	212.4	148	184	141	6,481	3.1	4.4	3.5	4.6	1,267	0.6 0.9 0.7	620	0.29 0.42 0.34
1950	98			92	3,248	3.3			3.5	NA		NA	

Sources: Column 1, (a)

1975, 1974, 1973: Indexes from Rush V. Greenslade, "The Real Gross National Product of the USSR, 1950-1975," in Joint Economic Committee, Soviet Economy in a New Perspective. (Washington, D.C.: U.S. Government Printing Office, 1976), p. 271, applied to 1970 figure from Joint Economic Committee, Soviet Economic Prospects for the Seventies, (Washington, D.C.: U.S. Government Printing Office, 1973), p. xvi.

1972, 1971, 1970: Joint Economic Committee, Prospects, p. xvi.

1969, 1968, 1967: Stanley H. Cohn, "General Growth Performance of the Soviet Economy", in Joint Economic Committee, Economic Performance and the Military Burden in the USSR. (Washington, D.C.: US Government Printing Office, 1970), p. 14.

1966, 1965: Joint Economic Committee, Soviet Economic Performance: 1966-67. (Washington, D.C.: US Government Printing Office, 1968), p. 16.

1964, 1963, 1962: Stanley H. Cohn, "Soviet Growth Retardation: Trends in Resource Availability and Efficiency," in Joint Economic Committee, New Directions in the Soviet Economy, (Washington, D.C.: U.S. Government Printing Office, 1966), p. 109.

1961: Soviet Economic Performance, p. 16.

Table 4-1 – *(Continued)*

1960: Cohn, "General Growth Performance", p. 14.
1959: Cohn, ibid., gives 1958 figure, and on page 9 gives the growth, 1958 to 1959, as 4.5 percent.
1958: Ibid.
1955: M. Bornstein, "A Comparison of Soviet and United States National Product," in Joint Economic Committee, Comparisons of the United States and Soviet Economies (Washington, D.C.: U.S. Government Printing Office, 1966), p. 175.

Column 1, b.
1970: U.S. Arms Control Disarmament Agency, *World Military Expenditures, 1971,* (Washington, D.C.: U.S. Government Printing Office, 1972), pp. 10-11, cited in Joint Economic Committee, *Prospects,* p. 124.
1968: F.W. Dresch, W.T. Lee, M.M. Earle, et. al., "A Comparison of US/USSR Gross National Product, National Security Expenditures, and Expenditures for RDT&E," SSC-TN-2010-1, SRI, Strategic Studies Center, Menlo Park, Calif., pp. V-5, VI-5. (December, 1972), cited in Joint Economic Committee, *Prospects,* p. 124.
1961: Joint Economic Committee, *Performance 1966-67,* p. 16.
1955: Dresch, etc., *Comparison,* p. 124.

Column 1, c.
1970: Dresch, etc., *Comparison,* p. 124.
1968: Cohn, "General Growth Performance," p. 14.
1955: Ibid.

Column 1, d.
Herbert Block, "Soviet Economic Power Growth–Achievements Under Handicaps," in Joint Economic Committee, *Soviet Economy in a New Perspective* (Washington, D.C., 1976), p. 246, deflated.
Column 2: Ministry of Foreign Trade of the USSR, *Vneshnaya Torgovlya SSSR za 19 god* (Moscow: Mezhdunarodnye Otnosheniya), appropriate years. (Cited hereafter as *Vneshnaya Torgovlya*). Converted to dollars at official exchange rates.
Columns 4 and 6: U.S. Department of State, *Battle Act Reports,* (Washington, D.C.: U.S. Department of State, appropriate years.

Note: All Soviet GNP figures have been converted from a price base of the year in which they were calculated to a current-year price basis by applying U.S. GNP deflators from *Survey of Current Business.*

Table 4-2
Soviet Foreign Trade as Proportion of National Income (Soviet Figures)

Year	(1) National Income Produced (Bil. rubles, current prices)	(2) Total Trade Turnover (Mil. 1961 valuta rubles, current prices)	(3) % of NMP	(4) Trade with Non-socialist Countries (Mil. 1961 valuta rubles, current prices)	(5) % of NMP	(6) Trade with Developed Industrial Countries (Mil. 1961 valuta rubles, current prices)	(7) % of NMP
1974	353.7	39,572	11.2	21,396	6.1	12,404	3.5
1973	337.8	31,346	9.34	18,332	5.4	8,339	2.5
1972	313.6	26,037	8.3	9,240	3.0	5,882	1.9
1971	305.0	23,657	7.7	8,181	2.3	5,085	1.7
1970	289.9	22,079	7.6	7,676	2.7	4,694	1.6
1969	261.9	19,784	7.5	6,844	2.6	4,331	1.7
1968	244.1	18,040	7.4	5,889	2.4	3,852	1.6
1967	225.5	16,370	7.3	5,280	1.4	3,374	1.5
1966	207.4	15,079	7.3	5,056	2.4	3,181	1.5
1965	193.5	14,610	7.6	4,560	2.4	2,816	1.5
1964	181.3	13,878	7.7	4,200	2.3	2,768	1.4
1963	168.8	12,898	7.6	3,821	2.1	2,416	1.3
1962	164.6	12,137	7.4	3,614	2.2	2,198	1.3
1961	159.2	10,645	6.7	3,022	1.9	1,990	1.3
1960	146.6	10,073	6.9	2,702	1.8	1,917	1.3
1959	137.5	9,471	6.9	2,335	1.7	1,508	1.1
1958	127.7	7,784	6.1	2,044	1.6	1,224	0.9
1957	113.3	7,487	6.6	1,970	1.7	1,271	1.1
1956	106.1	6,505	6.1	1,583	1.5	1,093	1.0
1955	93.7	5,839	6.2	1,208	1.3	904	1.0

Sources: Column 1
1965-1974: Tsentralnoye Statisticheskoye Upravleniye pri Sovete Ministrov SSSR, *Narodnoye Khozyaistvo SSSR, v 1974 g.* (Moscow: Statistika, 1975), p. 578. (Cited hereafter as *Narkhoz 74*).
1960-1965: Narodnoye Khozyaistvo SSSR v 1972 g. p. 531.

Table 4-2 – *(Continued)*

1955-1959: Computed from index in *Narodnoye Khozyaistvo SSSR v 1959 godu*, p. 62, applied to 1958 figure from F.W. Dresch, W.T. Lee, M.M. Earle, et. al., "A Comparison of US/USSR Gross National Product, National Security Expenditures, and Expenditures for RDT&E," SSC-TN-2010-1, Strategic Studies Center, Menlo Park, Calif., pp. V-5, VI-6 (December 1972), cited in Joint Economic Committee, *Soviet Economic Prospects for the Seventies* (Washington, D.C.: U.S. Government Printing Office, 1973, p. 124.)

Columns 2, 4, and 6.
Ministerstvo Vneshei Torgovlyi SSSR, *Vneshnaya Torgovlya SSSR za 19-god.* (Moscow: Mezhdunarodnye Otnosheniya, year following year in title.), and ibid., *Vneshnaya Torgovlya SSSR, Statisticheskii Sbornik, 1918-1966.* (Moscow: Mezhdunarodnye Otnosheniya, 1967) 1975 data from Joint Economic Committee, *Soviet Economy in a New Perspective.* (Washington, D.C.: U.S. Government Printing Office, 1976), p. 693, citing *Vneshnaya Torgovlya SSSR za 1975 god*, which was not available to the author.

Finally, in Table 4-3, we attempt an even more dubious translation of *valuta* into domestic rubles. This calculation, it may be suggested, may give a better notion of the real importance of foreign trade, and of foreign trade with Western countries, to the USSR than the other two calculations.

The Soviet statistical yearbooks, beginning in 1960, give two figures for national income: one "produced," the other "used."

In the yearbook together with data on the rate of growth of National Income produced, in the interest of comparability with the plan data are also given on the rate of growth of National Income used for consumption and accumulation. For each individual year the overall sum of consumption and accumulation (i.e., National Income used for consumption and accumulation) in actual prices differs from National Income as the total of the pure production of the branches of material production (national income produced) by the amount of replacement of losses and the foreign trade balance. But when national income used for production and consumption is calculated for a series of years in comparable prices, in this case national income used will differ from national income produced mainly not because of the replacement of losses and the foreign trade balance, but most of all on account of the structure of its material composition, which

Table 4-3

The Implicit Valuta Ruble Domestic Ruble Exchange Rate (Billion Rubles)

Year	National Income Generated[a]	National Income Used[a]	(1) - (2)	"Losses"	Foreign Trade Balance (billion domestic rubles)	Foreign Trade Balance, (million valuta rubles)	Implied Exchange Rate (5) (6)
1960	145.0[b]	142.8	1.3	1.3		−58.3	
1961	152.9[b]	151.2	1.7	1.7		153.7	
1962	164.6[b]	162.9	1.6	1.6		517.6	
1963	168.8	166.6	2.2	2.2		292.3	
1964	181.3	180.0	1.3	1.3		−47.9	
1965	193.5	190.4	3.0	1.7	−1.3	104.7	12.5
1966	207.4	202.2[b]	5.2	1.8	−3.4	835.4	4.1
1967	225.5	221.0	4.5	2.0	−2.5	1004.1	2.5
1968	244.1	238.7	5.4	2.1	−3.3	1101.9	3.0
1969	261.9	256.6	5.3	2.3	−3.0	1195.6	2.5
1970	289.9	285.2	4.4	2.5	−1.9	961.6	1.9
1971	305.0	299.3	4.9	2.6	−2.3	1194.7	
1972	313.6	310.7	2.9	2.7		−574.8	0.35
1973	337.2	334.1	3.1	2.9	−0.2	261.0	0.77
1974	353.7	348.2	5.5	3.0	−2.5	1903.4	1.32

[a]Tsentralnoye Statisticheskoye Upravleniye pri Sovete Ministrov SSSR, *Narodnoye Khozyaistvo SSSR v 19-- g.* (Moscow, Statistika, year following year in title).

[b]Narodnoye Khozyaistvo 1969, p. 42. National Income used given as 107 percent of 1965.

under dynamic conditions changes in different ways. In this connection the revaluation into comparable prices produces a somewhat different dynamic of used and produced national income.[15]

Now the foreign trade balance (*sal'do*) is calculated, as we shall see in more detail in a moment, as the balance in external prices multiplied by a coefficient to translate this balance into domestic prices.[16] It is this coefficient that we seek.

The formula for calculating it was discovered in the Ivanov article just cited apparently by Vladimir Treml and was first referred to in print by Abraham Becker.[17] Becker and following him, Holzman,[18] use in addition a United Nations source that is not available to the writer and treat the problem as one in national income accounting and input-output analysis. Ivanov, however, appears quite unequivocal as to the way in which the foreign trade balance figure is calculated in fact. Because of the obscurity of Holzman's treatment of the problem, it may be worth quoting Ivanov's account in full.

The entries on Lines and Columns 2-4 characterize the resources of the gross social product (i.e., production plus imports) and their final use for consumption (productive and non-productive), accumulation, losses, and exports. This relationship is widely known and does not need special explanation. In our view, the entries characterizing foreign trade operations deserve more detailed explanation. In the balance of the national economy, and correspondingly in the matrix, are entered the differences between the following indicators relating to foreign trade: 1) exports and imports (I and E) at internal prices, 2) the foreign trade balance (Z), 3) the gross product of foreign trade (X).

The indicators of exports and imports express the value of goods crossing the customs borders. The corresponding entries I and E can be found on line 45 and column 45. Further, the difference between exports and imports at internal prices is divided into two items (points 2 and 3): into the export-import balance (Z) and the gross product of foreign trade (X). Accordingly, $I - E = Z + X$. To explain how this division is carried out, we provide certain symbols.

Let I_0 and E_0 be imports and exports in world prices, re-evaluated into domestic currency at the official rate. Then $K = I:I_0$ and $m = E:E_0$ are coefficients showing the relationship between world and internal prices.

In this case the balance (*sal'do*) of exports and imports is determined on the basis of the following equations: $Z = (I_0 - E_0)K$, if $I_0 > E_0$, or $Z = (I - E):m_0$, if $I_0 < E_0$. The gross product of trade (X) in this case is easily calculated as the difference $X = (I - E) - Z$.

Obviously, for the purpose of analysis it would be convenient to have in the material balance [this appears to be a misprint for "matrix of the balance"] all three indicators. But in order to make them correspond, it is necessary to introduce a correction, equal to the negative quantity of the gross product of foreign trade (-X). And so, in one case the gross product of foreign trade is added to the production of other branches in order to get the amount of gross social product (see line 9 of the matrix), and in the other case it is excluded from the total or resources of the social product (line 46) so as to balance them with the indicators of final use. (Obviously, the necessity of such a procedure disappears, if we replace the absolute indicators of imports and exports in the scheme with the indicator of the balance of exports and imports (Z) which is in fact what is done for practice.)[19]

For our purposes, however, all that is necessary is the two ratios K and m. If we knew the amount of *"poteri,"* we could calculate m_O at least for 1972, in which the trade balance was in deficit in valuta rubles, since we know I_O - E_O). The same reasoning would hold, and we could calculate m_O for the other years since 1965, when the balance of trade in valuta rubles was positive, if the subscript o in Ivanov's second equation should have been attached, not to m as it is, but to the I and E within his parenthesis. Is this possible? The wish may well be fathering the thought, but it seems not impossible. The equations would then at least be consistent; there is no immediately obvious reason why both should not be doing the same thing, namely, transforming the balance in valuta rubles into domestic rubles, in order to adjust social product for the effects on domestic availabilities of imports and exports. Moreover, Ivanov gives no hint of any reason why he should have changed his symbols and attached the subscript where it appears. Finally, we have noted what appears to be another misprint in the use of "material" instead of "matrix" in the preceding paragraph.

Given the fact that we do not know the amount of "losses" and that that circumstance vitiates the analysis in any case, the whole exercise may be too fanciful to be significant. But we have some basis for attempting to estimate "losses," or at least to suggest limits within which they may fall.

Admittedly, the Soviet statistical annuals for 1972 and subsequent years contain a revised series for national income generated that differs slightly for some years from the numbers given in the annual volumes. Comparison of the two series does not suggest that the revision includes putting the foreign trade balance in retrospectively; the discrepancies are too small for that.

The volumes for 1960 and 1961 say that the difference between NI produced and NI consumed is attributable to "losses." From 1962 to 1964, inclusive, the expression is "after deducting undistributed expenditures and losses," which we may perhaps be justified in considering as an increase in precision rather than a change of definition. From 1965 on, the phrase is, "after deducting the replacement of losses and the foreign trade balance." But here, in contrast to the earlier situation, there is a marked rise in the difference between the two national income figures; it may not be too much to hope that it reflects a real change in procedure.

There is a further minor problem with the series. For the year 1966, the annual volume was replaced by a multi-year work;[20] the figure of national income used is not given. However, in *Narodnoye Khozyaistvo SSSR v 1969g.*[21] it is said to be 107 percent of 1965, which enables us to calculate the missing number; but the percentage is "in comparable prices," and rough calculations based on the current and the "comparable price" percentage figures for national income produced for various years in *Narodynoye Khozyaistvo SSSR v 1972 g*[22] show substantial discrepancies. From the statement in the 1972 annual that the comparable price base since 1966 has been the prices of 1965, one might expect that the discrepancy would be small; however, a calculation of the percentage increase in NI produced in current prices from 1965 to 1966 yields an increase of 7.2 percent; the increase in comparable prices is 8.1. Applying this proportion to the 7 percent comparable price increase in national income used gives a figure of 6.2 percent, which works out to a national income used (1966) of 202.2, which is that shown in the table.

Our next problem is to find some reasonable estimate of "losses." The average for the years 1960 to 1964 is 1.6 billion rubles; the annual variations do not show a steady growth or, indeed, any consistent pattern. It is curious that the occasional 1972 and later revisions of both "produced" and "used" figures leave the differences unaltered. It is, therefore, clearly improper merely to assume that losses have increased in proportion to the growth of national income. Moreover, the produced-used difference does not vary in proportion to the foreign trade balance in valuta rubles, as presumably it should if K is constant over time, and m is approximately equal to K, as Holzman believes.[23] And they should be, unless the composition of Soviet foreign trade and the internal pricing of the goods entering into it have changed significantly. (Admittedly, it is interesting to observe that the differences between constant and current price series and indices suggest that the USSR has kept prices roughly constant over the 1960-1972 period [1972 output in current prices was 216 percent of 1960, in constant prices 218.6 percent] despite considerable year-on-year swings.)

This circumstance may perhaps justify the expectation that even though "losses" do not grow consistently in proportion to the growth of national income, increasing the 1960-1964 average "losses," taken as a base, by the annual growth in national income may give a reasonably accurate estimate of the general movement in losses. The figures we present in column 4 of Table 4-3 are so calculated.

Unfortunately, the "losses" figure for 1972 does not exceed the "discrepancy," as it would have to if the import surplus of that year were to have its predicted effect. This may suggest that K and m are really quite different; certainly, the exchange rate for 1972 on our assumptions works out to 0.35 domestic rubles to one valuta ruble, whereas in the previous years the average ratio is 4.4; even if 1973 is included, the ratio is still 3.0. In 1974, the ratio rises again to 1.32 and while except for a bobble in 1968, the ratio falls steadily; the drop to 0.35 and 0.77 for 1972 and 1973 raises doubts. On the other hand, the exchange rates are not all that far from Paul Marer's implied rate when he says the overvaluation of East European exchange rates in comparison with purchasing power parities is "often two-to-three hundred percent or more."[24]

In short, the attempt to estimate an exchange rate indicating the relative values of the domestic and of the valuta ruble seems to yield reasonably satisfactory results as an indication of order-of-magnitude until 1972. Considering the heroic assumptions necessary to make any estimates at all, in particular the clearly contrary-to-fact assumption that "losses" increase in proportion to national income, this result is perhaps as good as could be expected. To the extent that it is valid, it indicates that the real importance of foreign trade to the USSR is substantially greater than would appear from figures based on official exchange rates.

We next examine the question of the degree to which the statistical evidence available supports the hypothesis that the Soviet Union imports to compensate for shortfalls in domestic production.

If the conventional explanation of Soviet foreign trade policy is correct, the statistics should show some correlation between shortfalls (or overages) in production of specific commodities and imports in the following year, since that explanation includes the suggestion that imports are an emergency source of resources for the USSR. In market economies, the problem of periodization would be severe and perhaps insuperable, since there is no reason why shortages should be apparent in one year and met in the year immediately following. But given the Soviet planning period of a year, it is not impossible that the lags should be of that dimension.

Ideally, our procedure should be the establishment of the occurrences of unanticipated shortfalls for specific commodities and the examination of the changes in the planned imports for the year following the occurrence. Unhappily, we have (except for the 1970-1975 five-year plan) no *ex ante* data on the output of the relevant commodities, and we have none on planned imports. These *lacunae* in our information make it difficult to be very precise.

There is also a problem in the selection of commodities for examination. We are interested primarily in imports from the noncommunist world, since these are the only ones subject to commercial purchase rather than Bloc barter agreements. Most finished manufactured goods are too broadly classified in both the production and the import statistics to permit precise matching. Nonferrous metals and synthetic rubber are not isolated in the production statistics. Paper and cardboard are traded in insignificant quantities. We are left, then, with steel pipe, wheat, cotton, wool, and sugar as possible subjects for investigation. Cotton and sugar are unfortunate necessities, since the relations of the USSR with Egypt and Cuba have caused imports (and exports) of these commodities to vary for reasons having nothing to do with economics, narrowly construed.

In Tables 4-4 and 4-5 we set out the data on the basis of annual targets laid down in the ninth five-year plan, and the available import statistics.

Of the commodities selected, steel pipe (Table 4-4) and cotton (Table 4-5) were produced over-plan. Grain imports (Table 4-7) during the three years on

Table 4-4

Steel Pipe: Planned and Actual Production and Trade, Ninth Five-Year Plan (Million Metric Tons)

Year	Plan	Actual	Overplan Production	Imports	Exports	Balance
1971	13.2	13.4	0.2	1.4	0.5	0.9
1972	13.7	13.8	0.1	1.5	0.4	1.1
1973	14.6	14.4	−0.2	2.0	0.3	1.7
1974	16	15.0	−1.0	2.2	0.3	1.9

Sources: Plan: N. Baibakov, ed., *Gosudarstvenyi Plan Razvitiya Narodnogo Khozyaistva SSSR na 1971-1975 gg.* (Moscow: Izdatelstvo Politicheskoi Literatury, 1972), p. 111. (Cited hereafter as *Ninth Plan*)

Actual: *Narkhoz 1974*, p. 227.

Exports and Imports: *Vneshnaya Torgovlya*, appropriate years.

which we have figures show a correlation of sorts between shortfalls of state purchases in one year and imports in the next. There was a shortfall of 11 million tons of state procurements in 1971, and the following year imports (net) were 10.9 million. In 1972 a shortfall of 18 million tons led to imports of 19 million tons in 1973.

Wool (Table 4-6) presents special problems. While all the statistics, on production and trade alike, are noted as being converted to washed weight, the state purchase figure (which, to judge from a footnote on page 296 of *Narodnoye Khozyaistvo SSSR v 1972 g,* is virtually the whole output) is recalculated by multiplying "the physical weight by the established zonal norm of yield of pure fiber from washed wool." But the note goes on, somewhat confusingly: "For example, a kolkhoz sells the State 800 kg. of wool with a yield of pure fiber of 38 percent, while the established norm is 35 percent; in this case the calculated weight is 860 kg. (800.38%/35%)." There is, of course, no indication of the relationship between these numbers and the tonnages of wool imported. However, the annual foreign trade volumes give "production" in their Table XVI ("Production, exports, and imports of most important products"), and the numbers for wool bear no visible relationship to those from the official statistical volumes. (They are much smaller—that is, for 1972, the foreign trade volume puts production of wool at 275,000 tons, while the "straight" output number from *Narodnoe Khozyaistvo SSSR v 1972 g.* [25] [pp. 294 and 370] is 420,000 and the "recalculated" figure [p. 299] is 452,000. For cotton fiber, the foreign trade and the statistical annuals give identical numbers.)

Nevertheless, it appears from Table 4-6 that 12,000 tons of over-plan production in 1971 was followed by a slight decrease in net imports in 1972,

Table 4-5
Cotton: Planned and Actual Production and Trade Ninth Five-Year Plan (Thousand Metric Tons)

| | Production | | | | | | Trade | | |
| | Raw Cotton | | Cotton Fiber | | | | Cotton Fiber | | |
Year	(1) Plan	(2) Actual	(3) Plan	(4) Actual	(5) Extraction Rate	(6) Apparent Surplus	(7) Imports	(8) Exports	(9) Balance
1971	6,200	7,100	[2,046]	2,361	0.38	[315]	243	547	304
1972	6,638	7,300	[2,134]	2,360	0.32	[236]	167	652	485
1973	6,800	7,660	[2,176]	2,471	0.32	[295]	131	728	597
1974	7,000	8,410	[2,030]	2,476	0.29	[446]	140	730	598

Sources: Raw Cotton: Plan: *Ninth Plan*, p. 360. Actual: *Narkhoz* 1974, p. 319.

Cotton Fiber: Plan: Calculated on the assumption that the actual rate of extraction of fiber from raw cotton was the planned rate. Actual: *Narkhoz* 1974, p. 269.

Exports and Imports: *Vneshnaya Torgovlya*, appropriate years.

Table 4-6

Wool: Planned and Actual Production and Imports, Ninth Five-Year Plan (Thousand Metric Tons)

| | Production | | | | | | Trade | | | |
| | Plan | % Increase | Actual | % Increase | Shortfall (−) or Surplus (+) | % | Imports | Exports | Imports % Increase | Total Availabilities |
Year										
1970	NA		441				82.7	17.7		65.0
1971	445.0		457	3.6	+12	2.7	86.1	14.1	10.7	72.0
1972	465.2	4.5	452	−1.1	−13	−2.8	83.0	12.1	−1.5	70.9
1973	479.0	2.9	470	4.0	−9	−1.9	96.0	7.5	24.8	88.5
1974	496.8	3.7	507	7.9	−10	−2.0	100.3	5.9	6.9	74.4

Sources: Plan: *Ninth Plan*, p. 169. Actual: *Narkhoz 1974*, p. 319. Exports and Imports: *Vneshnaya Torgovlya*, appropriate years.

Table 4-7
State Purchases of Grain, Planned and Actual, and Imports, Ninth Five-Year Plan
(Million Metric Tons)

Year	Plan	Actual	Shortfall	Imports	Exports	Balance
1970	NA	73.3		2.2	5.7	−3.5
1971	75	64.1	17	3.5	8.6	−5.1
1972	78	60.0	18	15.5	4.6	+10.9
1973	81	79.7	1	23.9	4.9	+19.0
1974	84	73.3	11	7.1	7.0	+0.1

Sources: Plan: *Ninth Plan,* p. 180. Actual: *Narkhoz* 1974, p. 319.

Exports and Imports: *Vneshnaya Torgovlya,* appropriate years.

while a 13,000 ton shortfall in that year led to an increase in net imports of 17,690 tons in 1973. And 5,000 tons of this change in the balance resulted from the termination or suspension of exports of wool to the GDR, which may have been unexpected. In any case, the increase in imports from the free world was 13,000 tons, whereas in the previous year, after the over-plan production of 1971, there had been a 3,000 ton drop in imports from the free world, to which should be added a decline in exports to the Bloc of 2,200 tons. In 1973, production was 9,000 tons short of plan; and net imports in 1974 responded by increasing 5.9 thousand tons.

Thus, with respect to wool, the figures move in the expected directions, although the quantitative correspondence is less than exact.

With respect to granulated sugar, (Table 4-8) it appears that during the years for which we have planned data (on production from beets only), the imports took place after shortfalls and in something approximating amounts of the shortfalls. The imports were, in any case, of raw sugar, the extraction rate of which is not known to the writer. And, even though the Soviet statistics allegedly include re-exports, as we noted earlier, no exports of sugar in any form appear. Some skepticism on this point may be warranted.

No clear pattern is discernible with regard to cotton. The trade statistics do not show any imports and exports of raw cotton—only of cotton fiber. But targets are available only for the former. However, it is possible to estimate the planned output of fiber by applying to the planned raw cotton figures the extraction rate actually achieved during the years for which statistics are available (1971 and 1972) and by assuming that the rate remained the same in 1973 and 1974. The necessary data are given in *Narodnoye Khozyaistvo SSSR v 1973 g.*[26] Production was apparently over-plan in all four years for which data are available. The planned output was rising, while imports have fallen and exports risen steadily over the years in question. Exports to socialist countries have fallen from 88 percent of total exports in 1970 to 56 percent in 1973 and

Table 4-8
Granulated Sugar from Beets, Ninth Five-Year Plan (Million Metric Tons)

Year	Plan	Actual	Shortfall	Imports	Exports
1971	8.9	7.8	1.1	1.5	–
1972	9.0	7.3	1.7	1.7	–
1973	10.1	8.4	1.7	2.5	–
1974	10.9	7.8	3.1	1.9	–

Sources: Plan: *Ninth Plan,* p. 346. Actual: *Narkhoz* 1974, p. 285.

Exports and Imports: *Vneshnaya Torgovlya,* appropriate years.

61 percent in 1974, while remaining at approximately the same absolute level. This suggests that the USSR, possibly based on its experiences with Egyptian cotton in the sixties, is developing an expanding market in industrialized European countries and Japan and that it is planning accordingly. It can be calculated from the data in Table 4-5 that the annual increase in the export balance from 1971 to 1972 was twice that from 1972 to 1973, roughly paralleling the increase in planned and actual output of raw cotton and (if our estimates are correct) of cotton fiber. But in 1974, the trade balance was virtually identical with that in 1973, with imports and exports both increasing by the same amount. The actual output of fiber was also virtually the same as in 1973, though planned production of raw cotton was up over the previous year by the same quantity as in 1973, even though the harvest was considerably above plan. On our assumptions, the planned extraction rate would have fallen from 32 to 29 percent, but it is by no means certain that this was the case. If, as may well have happened, the planners anticipated roughly the same availabilities as in the previous year, their behavior would be explained; on the evidence we have, this seems the most likely hypothesis. We do not know enough about the timing of the changes in Soviet plans, whether of production, procurement, or foreign trade, to make a judgment. This would appear, then, to be a case in which Soviet exports are based on planned surpluses above domestic needs.

Finally, we look at steel pipe production and trade. Overfulfillments have been small; 100 thousand to 200 thousand tons against production of 13 to 14 million. But both total imports and the import balance have grown steadily, with, in most years, an annual increase in imports from two to five times the overproduction. It is probable that there were differences among types of pipe produced, but the breakdown among types in the output statistics (e.g., in *Narodnoye Khozyaistvo SSSR v 1972 g*[27] does not permit more detailed examination.

The only other output target figures that the author has been able to find since the war are given in *Narodnoye Khozyaistvo SSSR v 1959 god*[28]. Table 4-9 shows the seven-year plan targets and results for the commodities we are

Table 4-9

Goals, Fulfillment, and Net Imports, 1965, Seven-Year Plan (1958-1965)

	Plan[a]	Actual[b]	Trade Balance[c]
Cotton Cloth (mil. running meters)	7.7-8.0	7.081	−176.8 thousand
Wool Cloth (mil. running meters)	500	365	+9
Granulated Sugar (million mt)	9.25-10.0	11.0 (8.9 from beets)	2.331
Grain (procurements, million mt)	"Somewhat higher than 1958" (1958-56.9)	36.3	2.1
Raw Cotton (million mt)	5.7-6.1	5.66	−
Cotton Fiber (calculated) (000 mt)	1,824	1,835	274.8
Wool (000 mt)	540	368	26.4

[a]*Narkhoz* 1959, pp. 323 and 132.

[b]*Narkhoz* 1972, p. 174.

[c]*Vneshnaya Torgovlya* 1918-1966. Calculated. Exports −, imports +.

considering, when given, and also for certain related products, together with exports, imports, and the trade balance. The figures are somewhat surprising. With respect to grain, where procurements fell at least 20 million tons short of plan, net imports were only 2 million tons, and gross imports only 6 million (the latter figure may be significant, if sales to other communist states, which accounted for three-fourths of Soviet exports, were contemplated in the plan.) It seems most likely that the operational planning figures were revised downward sharply at a date nearer to 1965.

On the other hand, raw cotton purchases virtually attained the lower limit set by in the 1965 target. No target figures are available for cotton fiber, but the rate of extraction of fiber from raw cotton remains about constant at 31 to 33 percent. Hence, there should have been a shortfall in supplies for the cotton textile industry, and indeed output of cotton cloth was some 600,000 linear meters short of plan. However, there were net exports of about 177,000 meters, where under our theory there should have been imports. The difference of nearly 800,000 meters is about 10 percent of the high 1965 target. One can only conclude that given the generally low priority accorded to consumer goods in the USSR, the decision was made to export principally to developing countries and import from socialist ones, which is the pattern actually appearing in the statistics. Some of the exports may have been intended as foreign assistance, while the imports are presumably those agreed to in advance.

Thus, the evidence from 1965 fails to support our basic hypothesis, although there is a plausible explanation, the quantities involved are not extraordinarily large, and the control figures may be being pushed beyond the limits of their probable precision.

The wool figures, similarly, support our hypothesis, but, again, should be interpreted with reservations as to the precision of the control figures. The shortfall in wool production was greater than the shortfall in the output of woolen cloth, and there were net wool imports of 26.4 thousand tons. If the proportion of cloth output to wool production is calculated from the plan data, and the proportion applied to the actual results, the shortfall is precisely made up by net imports. This probably an accident.

Production of granulated sugar was 10 percent above the top limit of the 1965 plan range, while procurements of sugar beets were 17 percent short of plan. As it took about 10 tons of beets in 1958 to yield 1 ton of sugar (based on the gross outputs of both in *Narodnoye Khozyaistvo SSSR v 1959 g.*), the shortage of 13.5 million tons of beets should have caused a loss of about 1.4 million tons of sugar. In the absence of imports, it is hard to see where the over-plan production would have come from; with raw sugar imports of 2.3 million tons, the over-plan production becomes explicable, at least assuming that the conversion of raw sugar into granulated does not materially lessen its weight.

Our investigations of the very limited material available, then, do not contradict and, to the degree that they are reliable, support the hypothesis that the USSR imports to cover expected or unexpected shortfalls of its own production.

It would be possible to extend this investigation back into periods for which we have no prognoses. We could assume that the actual growth rate for a five-year plan period was close to that expected, and measure imports against deviations from the trend. But it seems doubtful that the results would be of any significance, since it would be impossible to distinguish expected from surprising shortages. We might, again, apply statistical tests to the series we have here developed. But the series are so short as to make the calculations of dubious significance.

We turn next to the question of the degree to which the USSR balances its trade on an annual basis and to the extent it does, precisely how. In view of the comparative insignificance, at least until recent years, of capital movements and other invisibles, we would expect Soviet trade accounts to balance more exactly than those of market economies. But there is no obvious reason why this balancing should take place over precisely a one-year period, except that, as is well known, Soviet planning does operate largely within a one-year horizon.

Even so, there are alternative, but not mutually exclusive, strategies that the USSR could follow. It could pay for imports with simultaneous exports; it could spend last year's export earnings on this year's imports; or it could export this year to pay for last year's imports. We now examine the Soviet-Western statistics to see whether they offer a clue as to prevailing Soviet practice.

Linear regressions were run to test these hypotheses, regressing Soviet exports on imports, on imports lagged one year, and on current year imports plus lagged imports. Imports were also regressed on exports, similarly lagged and combined. The precise figures are available on request from the author; as will appear, they do not seem to be of sufficient value to merit reproduction in this book. Because it is conceivable that Soviet policies, or their execution, have changed with changes of leadership, similar regressions were run for the subperiods 1950-1954, 1955-1965, and 1965-1973. (We took the year after the leadership change as the last of the preceding period, on the theory that at least that much time would have been required for major policy changes to appear in the statistics.) We also examined total Soviet trade, Soviet trade with developed countries, and Soviet trade with underdeveloped countries and base our examination on Soviet trade statistics. Also, for comparison, we looked at data collected by the U.S. Department of Commerce on Soviet trade with all free world countries and with COCOM countries.

It is possible, of course, that the outcome, if not the intention, of Soviet trading activity differs as between Soviet trade with all countries, with the socialist countries (which are presumably equally interested in annually balanced accounts) and with our major area of concern, the developed industrial countries.

The t-values were markedly lower when two-year lags are used and are seldom significant at the 95 percent confidence level, which suggests that it is annual, not cumulated, figures that best explain the outcome of Soviet trading activity, as we suspected. We, therefore, excluded them from consideration. Moreover, as expected, with one noticeable exception, all the coefficients of determination were quite high: less than 0.9 in only 10 of 72 cases and above 0.95 in most. Similarly, and disregarding the two-year lag cases, the slopes of most of the regression lines were quite close to 45 degrees.

With undifferenced data, as might be expected, the correlations are all very high. There are no known significance tests that will allow us to say definitely that one fit is markedly superior to another, in those cases where the t-statistic shows significance for both lagged and unlagged figures. The Soviet figures for trade with all countries over the years 1950 to 1973 show a slightly better fit for the equation that explains current year imports by previous year exports, which appears to be the result of the fact that Soviet trade with the socialist countries shows a marginal superiority of explanatory power for this equation over the expected annually balanced trade equation. Soviet trade with developed countries appears to be best explained by the hypothesis that the USSR exports this year to pay for its imports of the previous year. This conclusion is reinforced by observation of the U.S. data, which do not include socialist countries but do show, for both the whole free world and for the COCOM countries, the closest fit on that basis.

It seems likely, however, that the data were pushed beyond the degree of discrimination that they will support, as the regressions of the Soviet data for the three subperiods all indicate annually balanced overall trade as the best hypothesis. In the first two periods, the same indication appeared both for developed and socialist country trade, though in the last, trade with the developed countries is best explained by the "buy now, pay later" hypothesis and that with the socialist countries on the "spend last year's income" one. The differences in the latter case, however, are so small that the results cannot be said to invalidate the general assumption that socialist countries do balance their trade annually.

Next, the trend effect was removed from the calculations by regressing annual changes in imports and exports on one another, with the same lag patterns. As expected, the correlation coefficients and t-values dropped considerably. The "balanced" hypothesis presents slightly higher correlations than "buy now, pay later," but the fits of the latter are markedly better than those of the "spend what you earned" equations. This suggestion—for it is little more than that—shows up clearly with respect to the developed countries on Soviet data, though the U.S. numbers show the balanced hypothesis as much stronger. This, however, may be explicable on the basis that the U.S. numbers give c.i.f. data for imports from the Soviet Union, whereas the Soviet ones are f.o.b. for both imports and exports.

If we look at the subperiods, we should disregard the earliest (1950-1954), since differencing reduces the number of observations to three. The U.S. data all turn out to be statistically insignificant; and, perhaps surprisingly, so do the Soviet numbers for the period 1955-1965. It is possible that the impact of wheat imports and of growing Western credits has obscured any possible correlation; but both phenomena were present in the later (1966-1973) period, when the data show substantial support for the "buy now" hypothesis.

The data, then, do not permit the drawing of any very firm conclusions with respect to the question of Soviet intentions and successes in balancing their trade accounts on an annual basis. They do not disprove, but do offer some support for, the suggestion that with developed countries at least the tendency may be to take last year's import bill as this year's export target. And, although the observation is not directly relevant to our main theme, it is at least of interest to note that in the most recent (post-Khrushchev) period, the USSR seems to have tended to adjust its imports from its socialist partners to fit the results of previous years. Given the importance of the role of the USSR as a raw materials supplier to the other socialist countries, this may suggest some (probably unpleasant, from the Soviet point of view) tendency to have to look harder than formerly for things they can usefully import from the Bloc.

The view that the USSR tries to balance its trade, not only overall, but with individual countries is less frequently met with in the literature than the proposition asserting an attempt at overall, or overall hard currency, balancing. It was, however, generally held in the American Department of State, at least through the 1960s, though the belief was tempered by the realization that Western trading partners of the Soviet Union were at least equally concerned to maintain a balance.

The annual trade balances of the USSR with France, Italy, West Germany, Japan, and the U.K. have been compiled both from the Soviet and from Department of Commerce data. (The figures are also available from the author. They do not seem to be significant enough to warrant reproduction.) They show no discernible consistency, except that the USSR has on the whole had a positive balance of trade with all, until the early seventies. The balance was relatively larger with the U.K., which is usually explained as the result of Soviet surpluses with that country running deliberately in order to pay for raw materials purchases through London from the overseas sterling area. No doubt the Soviet surpluses with Italy, and perhaps those with France, are connected with rumored Soviet financing for the communist parties of those two countries. Soviet deficits since the early seventies reflect Western credits, the amount of which is unknown, despite vigorous American efforts throughout the sixties to obtain agreement from other COCOM countries for their regular reporting.

In any case, there is no reason except for Soviet administrative convenience why annual figures should balance on a country-by-country basis, when the currencies in question are convertible. And, obviously the operative numbers are those from the balance of payments, not the balance of trade. However, as is well known, these figures are not available.

In summary, then, we may conclude that to the extent the statistical data can be interpreted as indicating any firm conclusions, they are consistent with the received view of Soviet trade policy.

Notes

1. Alexander Baykov, *Soviet Foreign Trade* (Princeton, N.J.: Princeton University Press, 1946).

2. Glen Alden Smith, *Soviet Foreign Trade Organization, Operations, and Policy, 1918-1971* (New York, Praeger Publishers, 1973), p. 16. See also Franklyn D. Holzman, "Foreign Trade," in Abram Bergson and Simon Kuznets, eds., *Economic Trends in the Soviet Union* (Cambridge, Mass.: Harvard University Press, 1963), pp. 297-98, where the share of imports in domestic consumption of machinery is highlighted.

3. Ibid., pp. 18-19.

4. *Vneshnaya Torgovlya SSSR 1918-1936, Statisticheskii Sbornik* (Moscow: Mezhdunarodnye Otnosheniya, 1967), p. 9.

5. *Vneshnaya Torgovlya SSSR za 20 Let, 1918-1936,* cited in Nauchno-

Issledovatelskii Konyunkturny Institut MVT SSR, *Vneshnaya Torgovlya SSR s Kapitalisticheskimi Stranami* (Moscow: Vneshtorgizdat, 1957), p. 10.

6. Oskar Morgenstern, *On the Accuracy of Economic Observations* (Princeton, N.J.: Princeton University Press, 1963), p. 163. ff.

7. *Vneshnaya Torgovlya SSSR za 1973 god* (Methodological Explanations), (Moscow: Mezhdunarodnye Otnosheniya, 1974), p. 5.

8. See, e.g., U.S. Department of State: *Battle Act Report* (Washington, D.C.: U.S. Government Printing Office, 1972), p. 60.

9. Cf. P.J.D. Wiles, *Communist International Economics* (Oxford: Basil Blackwell, 1968), p. 130: "Its (*scilicet* the valuta ruble's) principal functions are, to translate the prices of exports and imports *settled in capitalist currencies,* into a single convenient unit with a patriotic name; and to enable similar prices to be attached to goods traded with other STEs. It is the valuta ruble that has the official rate of exchange [italics added]."

10. *Vneshnaya Torgovlya SSSR za 1971 god* (Moscow: Mezhdunarodnye Otnosheniya, 1972), p. 10, computed.

11. Milton Gilbert and Irving B. Kravis, *An International Comparison of National Products and the Purchasing Power of Currencies* (Paris: Organization for European Economic Cooperation, 1954 [?]).

12. Abraham Becker, *Comparisons of United States and U.S.S.R. National Output: Some Rules of the Game* (Santa Monica, Calif.: The Rand Corporation, 1960), passim.

13. Peter Wiles, "The Theory of International Comparisons of Economic Volume," in Jane Degras and Alex Nove, eds., *Soviet Planning: Essays in Honour of Naum Jasny* (Oxford: Basil Blackwell, 1964), pp. 99-115.

14. See the Appendix to this volume: U.S. Embassy Despatch 574, April 24, 1958.

15. Tsentralnoye Statisticheskoye Upravleniye pri Sovete Ministrov SSSR, *Narodnoye Khozyaistva SSSR v 1972 g.* (Moscow: Statistika, 1973), pp. 764-765.

16. Yu. Ivanov, "Matrichnoye Opisaniye Sistemy Natsionalnykh Shchetov i Balansa Narodnogo Khozyaistva," *Vestnik Statistiki,* no. 5 (1968), pp. 51-60.

17. Abraham Becker, "National Income Accounting in the USSR," in Valdimir G. Treml and John P. Hardt, eds., *Soviet Economic Statistics,* (Durham, N.C.: Duke University Press, 1972), p. 80.

18. Franklyn D. Holzman, *Foreign Trade under Central Planning* (Cambridge, Mass.: Harvard University Press), pp. 324-25.

19. Ivanov, "Matrichnoye Opisaniye," pp. 59-60.

20. Tsentralnoye Statisticheskoye Upravlyeniye SSSR, *Strana Sovietov za 50 Let* (Moscow: Statistika, 1967).

21. Tsentralnoye Statisticheskoye Upravleniya SSSR, *Narodnoye Khozyaistvo SSSR v 1969 g.* (Moscow: Statistika 1970), p. 42.

22. Tsentralnoye Statisticheskoye Upravleniye SSSR, *Narodnoye Khozyaistvo SSSR v 1972 g.* (Moscow: Statistika, 1973), p. 534.

23. Holzman, *Trade under Central Planning,* p. 327.

24. Paul Marer, *Soviet and East European Foreign Trade 1946-1969* (Bloominton and London: Indiana University Press, 1972), p. 343.

25. Ibid., pp. 294 and 370.

26. Ibid., pp. 322-323.

27. Ibid., p. 213.

28. Tsentralnoye Statisticheskoye Upravleniye, *Narodnoye Khozyaistvo SSSR v 1959 godu.* (Moscow: Gosstatizdat Ts SU SSSR, 1960), pp. 322-323.

5

Organizational and Operational Peculiarities of the Soviet Foreign Trading System

Our discussion of the "received" view of the place and function of foreign trade within the Soviet system of planned operation of the economy shows that foreign trade is a different animal in that system from what it is in market economies. "One could say that there is no trade between M[arket] E[conomie]s, only between enterprises within ME's."[1] "The central questions about international trade deal simply with exchange between *traders* in two national markets."[2] The implication is that the primary movers in trade among citizens of market economy polities are enterprises or traders—that is, private consumers and businessmen.

The classical theory starts from the fact that in international trade, as in all other economic activities, it is the individual economic subject who buys and sells, pays and is paid, grants and receives loans, and, in short, carries on the activities which, taken as a whole constitute international trade. It is not, for example, Germany and England, but individual firms located in Germany and England, who carry on trade with one another.[3]

This recognition does not involve us in

... the absurdity of constructing international trade theory in terms which abstract from national governments .... Governments exist. They cannot be treated as a series of intersections between second differentials and the x-axis. Their very existence affects comparative costs and advantages; for example, they are large spenders and large employers and in either capacity they are not normally dominated by a single-minded enthusiasm for maximization, etc.[4]

It does remind us that the role of governments in international trade is, normally, a regulatory one, arising from the fact of boundaries and exclusive jurisdictions. The government of a market economy state is not usually itself a direct participant in the foreign trading process; it encourages or it interferes with that process for policy reasons of one sort or another, but it is above and outside the daily business of buying and selling that is carried on by its subjects and their foreign partners.

It might be thought that we are misleading ourselves in this matter, since the Soviet foreign trade corporations (V/Os) are state owned (a fact which in itself might not have the consequences to which we are pointing). There are state-owned corporations in most if not all market economies that function in a manner not significantly different from other, private corporations.

It is, however, not only the case that ". . . in fact, a [foreign trading] corporation is not an ordinary business enterprise guided merely by commercial considerations, but a State instrumentality required to implement its government's policy."[5] The important point is that it is the state itself that trades in a command economy and does so through its own subordinate agencies; the state, not the corporations, is the proper subject of our attention.

We shall have occasion to trace the parallel general difference in governmental roles in market and in command economies later, when we shall see that this difference has important implications for the future course of Soviet foreign trade strategy and practice. Here it is sufficient to note that when a government makes itself responsible for the whole of the operations of the national economy, when it undertakes itself to answer in detail all of the "fundamental economic questions" of which economic principles textbooks speak, it undertakes a vastly different assignment from what it does in market economies in establishing and enforcing compliance with the legal framework of economic activity and in regulating the level (but not the detailed shape and direction) of activity in the economy. Indeed, as Wiles points out, ". . . the STE more closely resembles a large firm than a country."[6] It is itself a player in the game; it does not stand above it, directing it and controlling it. But we should not conclude that it is a profit maximizer in the pattern of textbook models of the firm. Recent research in that area, indeed, suggests that treating the capitalist firm on the analogy of the STE as a trader on world markets might make a valuable contribution to our understanding of the motivation of the politics of the Western corporation.[7]

As we have seen, the Soviet government, through the Ministry of Foreign Trade, exercises a monopoly of foreign trade and payment relations. It does so in order that trade further the purposes of the Soviet government with respect to the economy, that it serve the politicoeconomic end of "building socialism." It is not surprising, then, that the legal and operational apparatus it has constructed has certain specifiable and unusual characteristics. We turn now to the examination of the apparatus.

We do not contend that the arrangements that the USSR has established and used are the only possible, or logically necessary, consequence of the basic policies we have already examined. But we shall see that they offer certain advantages for the pursuit of those policies; and we shall have to inquire whether and how much they can be changed while many, if not most, elements of those policies remain as they are.

Soviet and Western authorities agree that the nationalization of foreign trade is the cornerstone of the Soviet foreign trading system, as we saw earlier.[8]

Because of its implications for the future development of Soviet foreign trade administration, it is important to distinguish between the nationalization and the monopolization of foreign trade. While the first is a prerequisite for the second, it does not entail it and did not definitively do so in the Soviet

Union until the foreign trading system took on its present form in the early thirties. Before that, several forms of decentalized participation in foreign trade—under the formal control, at least, of the trade commissariat—were permitted.[9] There is, thus, precedent for permitting direct contact between enterprises and foreign customers, as is permitted in other eastern European countries.[10]

Again, it is worth noting that Yugoslavia has since the early fifties combined nationalized enterprises with decentralized trading, while, of course, capitalist economies have been known to control overall foreign trade through licensing, while permitting decentralized transactions.

The changes of the early thirties, which were climaxed by the decree of the Council of People's Commissars of July 27, 1935,[11] had two primary objectives: the strengthening of central control over all foreign trading operations and the divorce of individual transactions from the direct responsibility of the Soviet state. The solution was found in the liquidation of the former stock companies, in which producers and end-users were joint owners of the foreign trading enterprise, and their transformation into "All-Union Foreign-Trade Monopolies" (*Vsesoyuznyie Vneshnetorgovye Obyedineniya,* abbreviated V/O). Normally specialized by commodity and separated as to export or import functions, these organizations are regarded in Soviet law as formally independent of the Soviet state. The importance of the separation of these concerns from the state was originally, it would seem, the freeing of the state and its foreign relations from direct responsibility for commercial debts and disputes. In the not uncelebrated case of *Israel* vs. *Soyuznefteeksport* (1957), however, this convenient doctrine enabled a Moscow arbitration court to hold for the Soviet defendant on the grounds that its faulure to deliver oil to Israel after the Suez affair was the result of *force majeure,* a finding which would have been impossible had the court agreed with the Israeli submission that a constituent part of a Soviet ministry cannot be held to have been the victim of an outside force when it obeys a ministry export control order.[12]

Thus, by 1935 the present Soviet foreign trading system in all its essentials was in place.[13] No major change took place until the establishment in 1955 of the Chief Administration for Matters of Economic Connections with the countries of People's Democracy, which was renamed in 1957 the State Committee of the Council of Ministers of the USSR for External Economic Ties.[14] This group, however, is primarily concerned with relations with other than developed capitalist countries—that is, with aid and with intra-Bloc transactions.

It remains to remark that external foreign trade representations, normally attached to Soviet embassies, which played or were intended to play an important part in Soviet foreign commercial transactions, have apparently lost their importance. Soviet commercial attachés now play, ostensibly at least, primarily the normal facilitative role of commercial attachés of other countries, though it would be rash to assume normality in every respect.[15]

There is no need to reproduce here a detailed description of the Ministry of

Foreign Trade or to list the forty-three V/Os[16] under its jurisdiction (which handle 90 percent of Soviet foreign trade) or the seven foreign aid organizations under the State Committee for Foreign Economic Relations or the eight under other state committees. These last handle such specialized areas as transport, tourism, meat and cattle, literature, technical aid, and movies. Details can be found in Pozdnyakov, Smith, and other authorities. Suffice it to say that the ministry has the expected assortment of chief administrations for groups of product lines and others for such functional fields as planning, administration, legal matters, finance, and so forth.[17]

We should, however, note the complexity and bureaucratization that this apparatus has arrived at. A remarkably frank treatment of this subject is to be found in a recent (1975) work on "The Administration of Foreign Trade."[18] The author, Gruzinov, says he is basing his views on material collected directly in the trading organizations and acknowledges the assistance of several colleagues.[19] This work deserves, then, special attention.

Gruzinov criticizes forcefully the existing pattern of specialization among the existing V/Os by pointing out the absurdity of separating export from import trade in similar commodities, but also argues that the existing organizations have even so to deal with far too broad a range of products. Thus seven V/Os are charged with purchasing industrial equipment for more than 120 industrial ministries and other agencies.[20]

Moreover, within the V/Os the pattern of organization has anomalies: Some are organized along product lines, some by geographical regions, with the result that coordination is difficult and the whole process unnecessarily time consuming.[21] Responsibility is thus diffused; in particular, whatever the theoretical lines of authority, Gruzinov asserts that the presidents of the V/Os report in fact directly to the Minister of Foreign Trade or his first deputy, so that the central apparatus of the ministry, including, presumably, the six chief administrations that, as Gruzinov has just indicated, are responsible for the major coordinating functions of the ministry, is effectively bypassed.[22]

In general, according to Gruzinov, the apparatus of the ministry at all levels is "complicated enough."[23]

With the effectiveness of the apparatus for achieving the purposes of the Soviet trading system we shall be concerned in Chapter 9.

Our major concern here is with the relationship of this bureaucracy to the rest of the Soviet economic apparatus and with its role and function. The evidence we have surveyed thus far leads to the conclusion that the function of the ministry, like that of foreign trade, is facilitative and auxiliary to the fundamental economic objective of the Soviet Union, the development of its economic power.

The anatomy of the Ministry of Foreign Trade, like most bureaucratic structural descriptions, tells us very little. Indeed, we do not even know its size; we know much less about the course of papers, or of decisions, through its machinery. But if we trace out what is known about the process of planning foreign trade (and remember that *planirovaniye* includes the execution of plans as well as their formulation) we may gain some insight into the way the trading function is carried out by the Soviet monopoly, and how that body relates to the economic processes it is there to serve.

The foreign trade planning process is primarily in the hands of the Ministry of Foreign Trade, although the State Committee on Foreign Economic Relations "and some other institutions" (unspecified) have a role.[24] The "plan of the development of foreign trade" consists of the following subplans:

The import plan;

The distribution plan for imports;

The export plan;

The foreign exchange plan for commercial operations;

The transport plan for foreign-trade commodities;

The plan for incomes and expenditures of the V/Os.[25]

The V/Os are responsible for drafting the plans in the first instance; after the necessary coordination with transport and "other" ministries, presumably including the finance and customer and supplier ministries, they are passed on by the "glavki and administrations" of the MFT, to Gosplan USSR after which they are confirmed by the council of ministers. Tens of thousands of economic organizations are involved, which makes the process exceedingly complicated, says a Soviet source, and doubtless exceedingly time consuming as well.[26]

The confirmed plan, as is the case with all Soviet plans, places a legal obligation upon recipients of plan directives to do what they are instructed—that is, the plans are not "indicative" or predictive, but operational instructions to produce or to receive specific goods. The initial responsibility for fulfilling these import and export plans lies with the V/Os, who issue appropriate instructions to suppliers or customers, domestic or foreign.[27] But, of course, the plans can always be changed to conform to market conditions or other factors.

This technique fits neatly into the Soviet planning practice for the domestic economy. In one sense, the "plan" is a set of targets, known officially as "indicators" (*pokazatelyi*) for the institution planned. Wherever possible, these are specified in physical terms; in such cases as machine tools, totals are given in rubles, but these totals are composed of fixed product prices and are intended to be equivalent to output targets in natural units. The difficulties that an attempt to plan outputs in physical terms have caused are the subject of a voluminous Soviet literature, much of which would read like satire if it were not so well authenticated. One of these difficulties is the sheer number of "indicators," each of which reflects a necessary decision. Another is constant conflicts between indicators and a desired effect; this problem may be illustrated by the steady diminution in the width of Soviet textiles (the "indicator" was linear meters) until square measure was substituted.[28]

Once the targets are set, the supply-sales organization of Gosplan or of the industrial ministry involved, issues requisitions (*zayavki*) and delivery orders (*naryady*) to the appropriate producing and consuming enterprises. These establish "funds" and the basis for contracts between producing and consuming enterprises, which are then required, at least in theory, to conclude contracts specifying the details of the deliveries ordered, within the scope of the planners' directives.[29] The contracts also provide for fines for noncompliance or faulty compliance, the effect of which is at least questionable.

Where foreign purchasers or sellers are concerned, however, Gosplan's authority is limited.[30] But the powers granted to the V/Os are binding on their Soviet suppliers and customers.[31]

It will not have escaped attention that nothing has been said as to the locus of the initiative in this current planning process. Soviet organizations wishing to acquire raw materials or equipment from abroad present *zayavki* to the Ministry of Foreign Trade; these have to be approved by Gosplan. An article in *The Economist*, May 11, 1974, refers to a "shopping list that describes the projects written into each Soviet five-year plan;" such a list is unknown to the U.S. Department of Commerce, but it may be assumed to exist and to reflect highest level decisions on the major investment projects for the plan period. It would seem a reasonable inference that general permission for particular projects is embodied in the five-year plan and in more detail in the annual plans.

Formally, at least, the import plans take their origin in the normal working of the Soviet planning system, for both current and "perspective" plans, through the "method of balances."[32] Balances have been used from the earliest days of the Soviet regime;[33] the operationally significant ones are "material"—that is, physical, accounts of production and disposition of a given commodity for the planning period. Their dispositions are further refined in the "basic conditions of deliveries,"[34] which when confirmed by the government, serve "as a basis, together with the Plan, for economic contracts." They "establish conditions and time of deliveries, give the dates when the purchaser's specifications are due, the conditions (both of assortment and of quality) under which delivery will be taken, and the material (financial) liability for breach of contract."[35] There is some evidence[36] that this part of the description, the planning system, is a counsel of perfection and that the actual operation of the Soviet system is considerably more *ad hoc*, as would be expected from the generally weak bargaining position of a buyer in the tightly stretched Soviet economy.[37]

The typical form of a balance, which has not altered very much over the years, is:

Resources	Distribution of Resources
Total	Total
Of which:	Of which:
Production	Production needs and construction
Imports	The market fund
Other deliveries	Exports
Reserves	Other items of expenditure
Supplies with suppliers at beginning of year	Supplies with suppliers at end of year

Forms for providing the basic information of this sort at enterprise level are sent down to enterprises by their superior organizations; they are filled out to give reports for the previous year and estimates of the final outturn for the current year, together with proposed inputs and outputs for the planned period.[38]

For the foreign trade plans, the V/Os are responsible for initial drafting of plans for the commodities that they coordinate, in response to government orders giving the planning timetable; the proposals are normally due by mid-year of the year before the planning period.[39] The proposals are based on plans already established, trade agreements, and instructions from the government regarding foreign economic ties (i.e., government commitments to other socialist countries or for aid, which do not concern us). With respect to imports from countries with which the USSR does not have trade agreements—which for practical purposes means for the trade that we are dealing with—since the inability of capitalist governments to make those firm commitments of which the Soviet Union is understandably fond is a cause of evident annoyance to the Soviet foreign trade administrators,[40] other considerations become more important. Reliance is planced on the "traditional" desirability of spreading Soviet business around among suppliers,[41] which might surprise many Western businessmen who, to judge from their conversation, believe that the Soviets prefer doing business with people whom they are used to. There is, it should be noted, some evidence for this view.[42]

The draft plans proceed to the Plan-economic Administration of the Foreign Trade Ministry and simultaneously to the appropriate import or export administration—that is, the one supervising the products the V/O deals in. The next stage is the geographic administrations of the ministry. The Plan-economic Administration is the coordinating authority for all these agencies and has particular responsibility for balancing imports and exports. After approval by the Collegium of the Foreign Trade Ministry, the draft goes to Gosplan, which, in consultation with the ministry, works out a final version or versions to submit to the Council of Ministers. Upon approval, this becomes the official, legally binding, and operative "plan"–subject to "changes in conditions of the foreign and other factors."[43] Moreover, "in the process of execution of the plans, recognized by all authorities as a part of the planning process equally important to the formulation of the documents, the Ministry and its organs study the market conditions, especially of capitalist countries, and adjust the timing and directions of their operations to take advantage of opportunities."[44]

This description of the Soviet planning methodology and organization leaves two important questions untouched. The first is the relationship between current (quarterly and annual) plans and perspective (five-year and longer-period) plans, a distinction that occupies much less space in contemporary descriptions of the planning process than it formerly did. The second is the role of prices in the domestic and external prices.

The famous Soviet plans are "perspective"–that is, normally five-year plans (one was curtailed, however, because of the German invasion and one was an exceptional seven-year plan) though longer-term plans are drawn up for certain branches of the economy[45] and the XXII Party Congress issued general targets for the period 1961-1980.[46] But it appears from the voluminous, if unspecific, literature that the annual and even quarterly plans are of most immediate consequence for decision making at enterprise level. Perspective plans, on the other hand, "establish as their main goal the securing of the maximum satisfaction of the constantly growing material and cultural needs of the whole of society by an unbroken growth and perfecting of socialist production on the basis of higher technique."[47]

Thus, the primary concern of five-year plans is the reaching of suitably higher levels of output, chiefly by means of investment in new and expanded production facilities, while the substance of annual and quarterly plans is the exploitation of existing capacity. In a command-powered economy, the latter implies that the current planners must extract maximum output from existing enterprises and see to its distribution to other producing or sales enterprises in such a way that the productive process goes on. It follows that the current plan is of direct and immediate concern to enterprise managers and their superiors in the industrial hierarchy; the indicators are laid down for them in the plans and are the operative expression of their economic responsibilities. In the command economy, the plans serve in the place occupied by costs, sales prices, and profits in the market economy.

Although the literature does not describe precisely the distinction between current and perspective plans, this analysis suggests, and available information on Soviet practice confirms, that overall investment policy is the substance of the perspective plans and that these are based on party directives and decided on at Council of Ministers level.

The literature stresses[48] the necessity of "uninterruptedness" (nepreryvnost) in planning. In practice, this means that plans are subject to constant change.

With respect to the investment decisions embodied in perspective plans, this possibility, indeed necessity, of constant change stands in visible contradiction to repeated Soviet assertions of the inevitability of planning decisions (since they are based on scientific laws).[49] We need mention only such incidents as the supercession of the 1955-1960 five-year plan by Khrushchev's seven-year plan in 1959, or his calls for increased chemicalization of Soviet industry in the middle of that plan (in 1957 and 1958), or his offer of vastly expanded trade with the United States in his letter to President Eisenhower of May 1958. The prospective results of the Nixon-Brezhnev *détente* in the trade field, too, would vastly affect the development of Soviet industry and cannot be confidently included in current long-term plans.[50] In particular, with respect to trade with capitalist countries, clearly détente must introduce a highly unwelcome degree of uncertainty into Soviet plans, perhaps best illustrated by the West German large-diameter pipe embargo of 1962.[51]

Notes

1. P. J. D. Wiles, *Communist International Economics* (Oxford: Basil Blackwell, 1968), p. 211.

2. Richard E. Caves and Ronald W. Jones, *World Trade and Payments: An Introduction* (Boston: Little, Brown, 1973), p. 3, with shift of emphasis from "exchange" to "traders."

3. Gottfried von Haberler, *The Theory of International Trade, with Its Applications to Commercial Policy,* translated by Alfred Stonier and Frederic Benham (New York: MacMillan, 1936), p. 3.

4. A. K. Cairncross, "Comments on the Papers by Goran Ohlin and André Marchal," in Paul A. Samuelson, ed., *International Economic Relations: Proceedings of the Third Congress of the International Economic Association* (London: Macmillan; New York: St. Martin's Press, 1969), p. 218.

5. Jozef Wilczynski, *The Economics and Politics of East-West Trade* (New York and Washington: Frederick A. Praeger, 1969), p. 170.

6. Wiles, *Communist International Economics,* p. 40.

7. C. J. Hawkins, *Theory of the Firm* (London and Basingstoke: The MacMillan Press, Ltd., 1973), especially pp. 60-77.

8. P. I. Lyashchenko, *Istoriya Narodnogo Khozyaistva SSR, Tom III, Sotsializm* (Moscow: Gosudarstvennoe Izdatel stvo Politicheskoi Literatury, 1956), p. 22.

9. Ibid., p. 73.

10. Professor Imre Vajda, summary of comments on his paper delivered to the Third Congress of the International Economic Association, in Samuelson,

International Economic Relations, p. 148: "He had helped to prepare the Hungarian law creating the monopoly of foreign trade. The clear intention was to declare that the monopoly of foreign trade meant neither more nor less than that private companies and persons could not participate in foreign trade. It had not been intended to invest this monopoly in a certain number of public institutions. There was no provision for monopoly within the monopoly . . . socialist enterprises must have free access to the world market, both as exporters and importers—as buyers, sellers, or partners."

11. V. S. Pozdnyakov. *Gosudarstvennya Monopoliya Vneshnei Torgovlyi v SSR* (Moscow: Mezhdunarodnye Otnosheniya, 1969), p. 67.

12. American Embassy, Moscow, Despatch No. 752, June 23, 1958.

13. "These most important characteristics of the organization of Soviet foreign trade remained unchanged for nearly twenty years," Pozdnyakov, *Gosudarstvennya Monopoliya*, p. 66. The changes since 1955, noted below, have mostly to do with relations with CEMA countries and with LDCs.

14. Ibid., p. 67.

15. Cf. Glen Alden Smith, *Soviet Foreign Trade Organization, Operations, and Policy, 1918-1971* (New York: Praeger Publishers, 1973), p. 74; and E. Usenko, "Sushchnost i Formy Sotsialisticheskoi Monopolii Vneshnei Torgovlyi," *Vneshnaya Torgovlya*, no. 6 (1967), p. 36.

16. V. P. Gruzinov, *Upravleniye Vneshnei Torgovlyi* (Moscow: Mezhdunarodnye Otnosheniya, 1975), p. 23. On p. 71, a chart shows only 41.

17. Pozdnyakov, *Gosudarstvennya Monopoliya*, p. 78.

18. Gruzinov, *Upravleniye Vneshnei Torgovlyi.*

19. Ibid., p. 7.

20. Ibid., p. 26.

21. Ibid., p. 29.

22. Ibid., p. 78.

23. Ibid., p. 84.

24. Pozdnyakov, *Gosudarstvennya Monopoliya*, p. 67.

25. Ibid., p. 133. Also V. S. Vagonov, ed., *Vneshnaya Torgovlya Sotsialisticheskikh Stran* (Moscow: Mezhdunarodnye Otnosheniya, 1966), p. 63.

26. Ibid., p. 134.

27. A. Ishchenko, M. Rozenberg, and B. Zatsepnin, "O Vzaimootnoshenii Vneshnetorgovykh Obedinyenii s Sovietskim Postavshchikami Tovarov dlya Eksporta," *Vneshneya Torgovlya* no. 6 (1969), p. 37.

28. V. Kontorovich in *Promyshlenno-Ekonomicheskaya Gazeta,* October 3, 1956; A. I. Kostousov, president of the Moscow Oblast Sovnarkhoz, reported in *Moskovskaya Pravda,* July 26, 1957, both reported in American Embassy Moscow,

Despatch No. 121, August 18, 1958. Similar examples are innumerable; for one, see N. Galperin, "Sovershenstvovanie Materialno-tekhnicheskogo Snabzheniya i Borba protiv Mestnicheskikh Tendentsii," *Voprosy Ekonomiki,* no. 7 (1958), p. 49.

29. See for a detailed description of the entire process: P. A. Shein, *Materialno-tekhnicheskoye Snabzheniye Sotsialisticheskogo Promyshlennogo Predpriyatiya* (Moscow: Gospolitizdat, 1959), esp. *Materialno-tekhnicheskogo Snabzheniya* (Moscow: Gosudarstvennoe Izdatelstvo Politicheskoi Literatury, 1960), especially Chapter V. Also Herbert Levine, "The Centralized Planning of Supply in Soviet Industry," in U.S. Congress, Joint Economic Committee, *Comparisons of the United States and Soviet Economies* (Washington, D.C.: U.S. Government Printing Office, 1959), pp. 151-76.

30. Pozdnyakov, *Gosudarstvennya Monopoliya,* p. 140.

31. Ishchenko et al., "O Vzaimootnoshenii," p. 38.

32. Vaganov, *Vneshnaya Torgovlya,* pp. 97-98.

33. Sh. Ya. Turetski, "Balansovye Problemy Narodno-khozyaistvenogo Planirovaniya," *Planovoye Khozyaistvo*, no. 2 (1936), p. 149.

34. Cf. E. Lokshin, "Voprosy Planirovaniya Materialno-tekhnicheskogo Snabzheniya Narodnogo Khozyaistva SSSR," *Planovoye Khozyaistvo,* no. 2 (1950), p. 47.

35. Eg., ibid.; Vaganov, *Vneshnaya Torgovlya,* pp. 98-99; Shein, *Materialno-tekhnicheskoye,* pp. 180-81, with modifications appropriate to the then prevailing *sovnarkhoz* organizational system.

36. *Planovoye Khozhaistvo,* no. 1 (1955), p. 95 (letter to editor).

37. Joseph Berliner, " 'Blat' Is Higher than Stalin," *Problems of Communism,* vol. III, no. 1 (January-February 1954), p. 22.

38. Shein, *Materialno-teknicheskoye,* p. 174.

39. Vaganov, *Vneshnaya Torgovlya,* p. 100.

40. This theme regularly appears in Soviet comments on trade with capitalist states.

41. Vaganov, *Vneshnaya Torgovlya,* p. 101.

42. Anthony C. Sutton, *Western Technology and Soviet Economic Development,* Vol. I, 1917 to 1930 (Stanford Calif.: Hoover Institution on War, Revolution, and Peace, Stanford University Press, 1968), pp. 285-86.

43. Pozdnyakov, *Gosudarstvennya Monopoliya,* p. 135.

44. Vaganov, *Vneshnaya Torgovlya,* pp. 112-13.

45. M. A. Zavilovich, *Osnovy Metodologii Planirovaniya Narodnogo Khozyaistva* (Moscow: Gosudarstvennoe Izdatl stvo Politicheskoi Literatury, 1958), p. 53.

46. "Perspective plans can be real only when they are made concrete in

current plans." Moskovskii . . . Institut Narodnogo Khozyaistva im. G.V. Plekhanova, *Planirovaniye Narodnogo Khzyaistva SSSR* (Moscow: Izdatel stvo Ekonomicheskoi Literatury, 1963), p. 53.

47. Ibid., pp. 7-50.

48. G. M. Sorokin, "Perspektivnoe planirovaniye Narodnogo Khozyaistva SSSR," *Planovoye Khozyaistvo,* no. 1 (1956), p. 34.

49. Zavilovich, *Osnovy Metodologii,* p. 51.

50. See *The Washington Post,* May 28, 1974, p. 1.

51. Alexander Bykov, *Untapped Reserves of World Trade* (n.p.: Novosti Publishing House, n.d.; presumably New Delhi, about 1972).

6 Prices

We have seen above that the fundamental purpose of the Soviet monopoly of foreign trade was the insulation of the Soviet economy from external influences. We have also seen that the main motive power of economic activity in the Soviet Union is the orders for the production and delivery of prescribed quantities of specific commodities (the plan indicators) to producing units (both industrial and agricultural) and the other orders (allocations) of goods to their destinations. We have noted the crucial and rather crude "method of balances" by which rough consistency among these directives is maintained. We have emphasized that these orders are issued and their execution judged in terms of physical units of output or in ruble totals that amount to the same things.

But this is not to say that money and prices do not exist in the Soviet Union, or that they entirely are without influence. It is to argue that they are not, that they do not embody, the primary forces moving economic activity; but they are there and have a definite, though limited, importance.

Moreover, external prices, the prices at which the Soviet Union buys and sells from its capitalist trading partners, do have power. (This may well not be true among the socialist countries, where, in any case, the quantities and only very secondarily prices matter.[1])

Hence, we are dealing with an interface between two disparate systems. It is implicit in all that has been said thus far that prices within the Soviet system are not the basis for decisions, nor can they seriously influence major decisions. Yet in relation with the world outside, with market economies, they do matter; more importantly, from the point of view of the Soviet foreign trading system, they are outside the control of the planners; if not criteria, they are parameters.

Not only does much of the literature and much of the popular discussion of the future of East-West trade center on the degree to which the Soviet economy is or might be operated on "rational" principles, but much of the justification for the policy of "détente" is based on the assumption that it is or will be and that the influence of this economic rationality will spill over into the political and security areas. It is also assumed that Soviet efforts at internal economic reform are pushing in this direction (correctly, in the author's opinion) and are succeeding (falsely, we believe) and that they can be materially expedited by proper treatment from the West, specifically from the United States (again, in our view, erroneously). It is, therefore, critical to our examination of the methodology of Soviet foreign trade operation that we examine the interface between these systems. We shall first analyze the present Soviet methods of establishing internal prices, and then produce what evidence can be found as to the way those prices are translated into foreign trade prices.

It is notorious that Soviet prices are not determined by the interaction of supply and demand on the, or a, market. The chairman of the State Committee on Prices has said so categorically. "Market prices are, in our view, alien to our economy and contradict the task of strengthening centralized planning. In our view, it is also totally incorrect to imagine that prices should balance supply and demand."[2] As prices are, officially, "the monetary expression of value," and since value for Marxists is embodied labor,[3] there is no theoretical place for the determination of prices by supply and demand. "The truth is that there is no Marxist micro-economics."[4] This does not, however, mean that Soviet economists have not debated the role of "the law of value in planning," or entirely ignored market factors either in theory or in practice. The "law of value" debate of 1956-1958 gave rise to a large body of theoretical—and polemical—writing on the subject.[5] One fundamental question, which appears to have been settled (affirmatively) by 1964, was whether the "law of value" holds under socialism.

We need not here trace the abstruse arguments revolving around the nature of commodity production and its continuation, forms, and extent under socialism. The literature is extensive and its intention is obscure. In summary, the major concerns of the participants apparently were (1) to produce a justification for the continuing existence of money and buying and selling under socialism, which was in the process of becoming communism; (2) to make respectably Marxist greater use of prices and money and either (a) to strengthen centralized control over the economy and help the territorial decentralization then in process to eliminate some of the more glaring disadvantages of the existing ministerial system of control or (b) to lay the groundwork for shifting some of the operational problems of the Soviet economy to market forces. A third desideratum may have been the desire of Soviet economists to make use of some of the progress in economic thought since Marx's time, specifically notions of subjective demand and even of marginal analysis, with which, in conversation if not in print, they showed themselves to be acquainted.[6]

By the early sixties, to judge from a compendium of presentations at the second expanded session of the Scientific Council on Price Formation Problems of March 26-30, 1963,[7] the continued existence of the "categories" of prices and money under socialism was taken for granted. Under certain conditions, of course, the main outlines of which were made explicit during the law of value controversy. "As is known," to quote a very general formulation by a leading Soviet economist:

. . . basic economic and political problems are expressed in the system of prices: distribution of national income and the formation of funds of popular consumption, socialist accumulation and reserves, the organization of planned social connections in the economy, the increase of the purchasing power of money, and many others.[8]

It should be noted that in this formulation, and in the statements we are about to examine, no mention is made of any role for prices in distributing productive resources among competing claims. Rather, "under socialism the law of value cannot be the regulator of production, since production develops under the regulating control of society, which is the owner of the means of production,"[9] or again:

And so, the law of value, which is a law the sphere of activity of which is limited by social property, by planning, and by the whole economic policy of the socialist state, and which does not regulate production, shows its effects in the process of socialistic reproduction, and subserves the realization of the demands of the economic laws of socialism.[10]

In short, as the author of an authoritative study of price formation put it, prices are one economic category that

. . . the Communist party and Soviet Government, in their economic-organizational activity, taking account of the operations of the objective economic laws of socialism, use . . . for the purposes of the development of the economy.[11]

Thus, the primacy of government and party policy over any reliance on market forces (which are normally characterized by the highly pejorative term "*stikhinie*," or spontaneous, in the Soviet literature) is taken for granted at least implicitly by all sides in the debate. The problem explicitly being discussed is not one of how to arrive at prices that are in some sense rational or sensible, but how to use the State's price-fixing mechanism to bring about actions the party and government want to achieve.

Some techniques are obvious, widely used, and generally agreed upon. For example, all Soviet authors note that vodka and tobacco are and should be "priced above their value," or, in simple terms, taxed highly to discourage their use. On the other side, books, phonograph records, and children's clothing are sold "below their value," and, quite possible, below their cost. Observation suggests that there is another category of goods sold relatively cheaply: cameras, television and radio sets, watches, and perhaps other goods produced by factories whose military importance is obvious and that, no doubt, have excess capacity in peacetime. Soviet sources, not surprisingly, are silent on this possibility. The author has suggested in another place the possibility that the cheap, possibly eventually free, distribution of such consumer durables might well take the form of the first steps (beyond housing, which is assigned on a similar basis today) of a future "communist" distribution of goods "according to need" as determined by the Communist Party.[12]   References to the desirability of distributing consumers' goods according to "scientifically based norms" strengthens the case for the view that the Soviet ideal of abundance means, in practice, to each as the Community Party sees fit.[13]

Despite the Marxist piety and the not inconsiderable dialectical skill displayed in the "price controversy" of the late fifties, however (notwithstanding the fact that even before Stalin's death less tendentious economic thinking had not only surfaced, but had secured official recognition of the need for some sort of investment criterion, which turned out to be the reciprocal of an—admittedly notional—rate of interest[14]) and even in the face of a considerable body of mathematical economic writing that was both logical and practical,[15] the level of Soviet economic analysis remained relatively low. It may be true, as Moshe Lewin says that

... when in the late fifties and early sixties, in a considerably changed climate, economists were asked to come forth and propose remedies for the troubles of the economy, they discovered the wide range of amazing dysfunctions and imbalances— including the capacity of the government not only to build but also to wreck and squander—with which the first *piatiletka* had saddled the national economy.[16]

But the economists have not been allowed to say so, at least not in print. The climate has changed; it is no longer the case, as Molotov explicitly and in detail said in 1938, that economists may not discuss price formation because "prices concern politics and not economics."[17]   But they still are bound to Marxist concepts and limited in what they can say; the impact of what they do, say, or practice is still more limited.

However, by 1964 it had become possible to discuss supply and demand, at least in very macro terms and without any suggestion that major planning decisions should be taken with regard to these factors. The justification put forward in the papers presented at the second extended session of the Scientific Council on Problems of Price Formation (March 26-30, 1963),[18] center on the problem of unsalable stocks of consumers' goods, which the authors think should be solved by changing the mix through revising the orders issued under the plan in response to bare shelves and queues, or, more especially, rising unsalable stock. The total volume of consumption, they agree, is not to be altered:

In socialist conditions, supply and demand do not incorporate antagonistic contradictions between classes, between production and consumption, but represent one of the important economic proportions determined by the State plan.[19]

The relation of demand and supply in its most general form measures the relation between the purchasing powers of enterprises, institutions, and the population, on one hand, and the total of prices of goods sold on the other.

However, with a general equality of the sum of prices of the whole collection of goods destined for sale, with the effective monetary demand, in the practice of planning it not infrequently happens that the market funds of certain goods exceed the demand which appears for them (at a given level of prices) and the supplies of other goods do not meet the demand. This indicates a disproportion between the value and the material-physical structures of social production.[20]

The author goes on to reject Stalin's concept that demand under socialist conditions must always outrun supply.

The conclusions drawn by the participants in the conference go, perhaps surprisingly, beyond the suggestion that production plans should be tailored to actual demand as determined by shortages and surpluses. It is even suggested that at least for standardized investment goods (by implication both capital equipment and semifabricates), results on the market should influence output. Always the implication is, so to speak, the reverse of Henry Ford's famous dictum: They can have any color they like so long as it's black—that is, the Soviet economists would allow consumer desires to specify sizes, colors, models, and so forth within overall plan targets. (This may sound elementary; yet as recently as the late fifties, Soviet consumers queued up for anything that happened to be on sale, often before finding out what the queuing was for, as this author observed. In fact, one Embassy colleague saw people buying shoes without regard to style or color, or even size, and swapping around among themselves afterwards.) Moreover, Soviet economists emphasized constantly that the best way of resolving the problem of shortages and surpluses is more production.

And even suggestions for the calculation of demand, still on a macro basis, by groups of consumers and by elasticities of the products each group chiefly wants, are carefully guarded. The groups concerned are primarily differentiated by income; yet urban and rural demands differ considerably. Soviet authorities recognize that peasants are unlike city folk; Academician K. Ostrovityanov remarked in a public lecture in Moscow that "of course" the abolition of machine-tractor stations and the sale of agricultural machinery to the kolkhozes would call for "more theoretical work" on revising the Textbook of Political Economy with obvious reference to this distinction.[21] The author was repeatedly told by economic journalists and sovnarkhoz officials that the peasants would refuse to buy overpriced or inefficient machinery from the MTS: Their traditional canniness was openly recognized, but no such reluctance was ever mentioned in print.

But in the proposed calculation of consumer demand no consideration is given to these social and psychological differences. Nor, indeed, is too much attention to be paid to demand factors of any sort:

The necessity of calculating demand and supply in establishing prices does not mean that state prices can be subordinated to fluctuations under the influence of short-term disturbances of the relation of supply and demand. One must distinguish short-term, market factors not influencing the level of state prices from factors of a longer-term nature, calling forth the necessity of changing planned prices. [22]

In sum, Soviet economists are prepared to recognize that the production of things nobody wants is stupid, and to assert that it is anti-Marxist.

Marx indicated that if under capitalist conditions a certain good is produced in a quantity exceeding the existing social need (by which he implied effective demand), then the good in question must inevitably be sold below its market value. That means, wrote Marx, that "part of the social labor time is shown to have been expended in vain, and the whole mass of goods then represents on the market a much smaller quantity of social labor, than what is really included in it." In other words, the part of the mass of goods exceeding effective demand does not receive social recognition, and labor spent making it ceases to be socially necessary.[23]

But they do not draw the conclusion that the market should therefore regulate production. The higher wisdom of the planners must prevail. But still, they open the way to market and consumer influence on assortment if not on quantity.

The actual process—that is, the operating rules by which wholesale and retail prices are formed in the Soviet Union—is the next thing we should examine. The basic rule is "cost (*sebestoimost*) plus planned profit" for the delivery prices of industry,[24] and this rule prevails with slight modifications today.[25] (The modifications pertain to the nature of, and the method of calculating, the planned profit.) In agriculture, there was, previously, no explicit system of price-fixing principles; compulsory deliveries at low prices and "voluntary" sales of over-plan supplies at higher ones, were at completely arbitrary rates.[26] Since the "reforms" of 1965, and specifically the March (1965) plenum of the Central Committee,[27] agricultural prices are based on costs plus planned accumulation. This is now possible, as it was not under the old system of *ex post* payment by labor days, since the March plenum adopted the principle of paying kolkhoz workers on the basis of the wage scales of the sovkhozes.[28]

With respect to industrial prices, the system remains basically as it has been since the early days of the Plan Era. Alec Nove is quite right in attaching to the Liberman reforms and the rest of the mouse brought forth by the mountainous reform discussions of the mid-sixties the lable, "The Reform that Never Was."[29] From 1932 until 1938, prices were fixed by ministries; after 1938, they were the responsibility of the Economic Council of the Council of People's Commissars, and since its liquidation in 1939 of the Bureau of the Council of Ministers of the USSR.[30] In postwar years, price fixing and revision were the responsibility of Gosplan or Gosekonomkomisiya; after the "reforms," they have been transferred to a State Committee on Prices,[31] working under the Council of Ministers, which retains final authority over union-wide prices. Republican Councils of Ministers and oblast executive committees have similar authority for industry under their jurisdiction;[32] ministries can set many internal transfer prices and prices on semi-fabricates.[33]

The components of *sebestoimost*, before and after the reforms, are shown in Tables 6-1, 6-2, and 6-3. It will be noted that in the prereform version, depreciation (amortization) is explicitly included; in the postreform example, which is said to be "simplified," it is not. However, it is listed as an element by the same author,[34] although it is not entirely clear that processing industry, as well as extractive, is intended.

The major change in the method of price formation introduced by the price reform of July 1, 1967,[35] was the change in the method of calculating profit. Formerly, the rule was 4 to 5 percent of *sebestoimost*;[36] the reform introduced the principle of 15 percent of the value of "productive funds" (*anglice* invested

Table 6-1
Elements of *Sebestoimost* **in the Shoe Industry, 1956** (100 Pairs Identical Shoes)

		Percent of Total Factory Cost
Raw and basic materials	26,438.35	
Value of waste products	93.11	
Raw and basic materials, deducting value of waste	23,345.24	89.57
Auxiliary materials	930.65	3.16
Electricity and steam	67.74	neg.
Wages	1,290.72	4.38
Expenditures connected with the operation of equipment	232.31	.78
Amortization	33.43	neg.
Shop expenses	230.34	.78
General factory expenses	147.77	neg.
Administrative expenses	121.82	.39
Losses from scrap	10.41	neg.
Factory sebestoimost	29,410.43	
Sales expenses	16.59	
Full sebestoimost	29,427.02	

Source: D.D. Kondrashev, *Tsenoobrazovaniye v Promyshlennosti SSSR* (Moscow: Gosfinizdat, 1956), p. 107.

Note: Ruble expenses for three factories totaled and each category calculated as percentage of total factory cost.

Table 6-2
Form for Calculating *Sebestoimost,* **Postreform**

Ministry (Department)
Enterprise
Address, telephone

Calculation of the *Sebestoimost* of Production

(Designation of product, article)
Article_____State Standard or TU(?)_____by whom and when confirmed.

Unit of Calculation
Sebestoimost per unit, rub. and kopeks

Indication of the item of calculation and of other indicators	Plan	Calcu-lated	By the enterprise, ministry without con-sideration of raised or lowered prices	Pro-jected	By the supervising organization with and without price changes
1	2	3	4	5	6
Raw materials, semifabricates and basic materials					
Auxiliary materials					
Fuel, electricity, and steam for technological purposes					
Supplementary wages					
Deductions for social insurance					
Shop expenses					
General factory expenses					
Factory *sebestoimost*					
Nonproduction expenses[a]					
Profit					
Wholesale price of the enterprise					
Turnover tax					
Commercial markup					
Sales markup					
Retail price					
Output of product in physical terms					

Source: A.G. Zavyalkov, *Tseny i Tsenoobrazovaniye v SSSR* (Minsk: Izdatelstvo Vyushaya Shkola, 1971), p. 125.

[a]Mostly fines, according to D.D. Kondrashev, *Tsenoobrazovaniye,* p. 98.

Table 6-3

The Structure of Outlays for Production of Industrial Output by Branches, 1961
(In current prices of 1961: In percent of the total of all production outlays)

Class of Outlay	All Industry	Production of Electricity and Heat	Coal Mining	Petroleum Extraction	Machine Building and Metalworking	Textiles	Meal Production	Sugar Production
Raw and basic materials	64.5				59.4	52.7	87.7	93.4	92.8
Auxiliary materials	4.7	4.7	17.0	7.6	6.2	4.3	2.1	1.4	2.9
Fuel	3.2	54.7	0.9	1.6	11.6	1.7	0.4	0.4	4.2
Electricity	1.8	0.3	3.2	8.9	2.6	2.1	0.6	0.4	0.2
Amortization	3.6	20.4	7.7	46.8	6.1	3.8	0.9	0.5	2.2
Wages and social insurance deductions	18.9	15.2	62.5	23.0	20.0	31.3	7.6	3.1	6.1
Other outlays, not distributed by elements	3.3	4.7	8.7	12.1	3.1	4.1	0.7	0.8	1.6

Source: Moskovskii Institut Narodnogo Khozyaistva imeni G.V. Plekhanova, *Planirovaniye Narodnogo Khozyaistva SSSR* (Moscow: Izdatelstvo Ekonomicheskoi Literatury, 1963), p. 531.

capital) at the latest revaluation, of which 6 percent "constituted profit for paying off the productive funds."[37] This implies a uniform rate of depreciation, which has long been urged by some Soviet economists,[38] and also the separation of depreciation funds from *sebestoimost*. As a practical matter, enterprises are not free to use their depreciation funds without permission from higher authority and hence overspend on current maintenance account.[39] Removal of depreciation from costs, while leaving in operating expenses, may strengthen the tendency to overstate the expense of repairs.

It is important to note, however, that the 15 percent rule is only an aspiration, not a fact;[40] the necessity of maintaining retail and agricultural purchase prices unchanged; differences in retail prices caused by turnover tax, which was now largely transformed into profit (this is a deduction from some exceedingly mysterious language of Zavyalkov,[44] although profit and turnover tax have long been recognized as equivalent methods of "capturing surplus value"); some consumer goods branches or products having high and others low rates of budget payments; the impossibility of equating profitability rates between, say, oil and peat production; and the differing efficiencies of capital goods among branches (obviously not compensated in their valuations) prevented its general adoption without differentiation by industrial branches.

Clearly the most obvious characteristic of these principles of Soviet price formation is that they are arbitrary. Moreover, they are persistent—in principle planned for "a series of years"[42] and in practice seldom changed. Their relationship to supply and demand is sketchy; high prices are sometimes charged on new products to discourage demand,[43] and the (exceptional) use of the turnover tax together with differential rent charges and other adjustments on electricity, oil, and gas is expressly for the purpose of keeping coal and peat competitive.[44] Prices of vodka and tobacco products are high, as noted above, and those of books, records, and children's clothing are low. And total supply and total demand, expressed in money terms, are in principle kept equal, with the slack taken up either by savings,[45] the turnover tax,[46] or the kolkhoz market.

The capture by the state of surplus value, however carried out, is to be carefully distinguished from the recovery by the state of its initial budget investment, which is done under the rubric of "amortization." Soviet authors never seem to say so, but it would seem to follow from the logic of Marxist economics that the transfer of value "embodied" in the means of production to newly produced commodities occurs when the capital good is amortized. As will be seen from Table 6-1, the proportion of the value at least of shoes that amortization represents is exceedingly low, even if material and overhead costs are execluded from the reckoning. In the example there given, the average of amortization as a percentage of wage costs was only 2.6. This peculiarity of Soviet accounting is attributable to low prices of capital goods and, no doubt, to the results of periodic revaluations of the capital stock.

What is important, however, about this system of price formation is that it is completely—with one possible exception—arbitrary. It has, in particular, no relation whatever to scarcity values or opportunity costs expressed through market relationships. As we noted above, a primary objective of Soviet price formation policy is precisely the elimination of such *stikhiny* (natural) influences.

The exception is the result of the fact that the basic element in costs, Soviet style, is labor, either wages or "embodied labor," the instruments or the objects of production, to use Soviet terminology, which means, respectively, capital goods and raw materials and semifabricates. Table 6-3 may appear to contradict this assertion, but when it is remembered that the "raw materials" that make up 70 percent of the costs there analyzed in their turn embody wage costs, as do the "capital funds" being depreciated, the statement appears to stand.

Now, Soviet wages are "planned"—that is, fixed—by government in terms of staffing patterns (seven levels of wages and numbers of employees in each category approved by the Ministry of Finance,[47] although direct allocation of labor (with the exception of graduates of higher educational institutions) has ceased.[48] Labor costs are thus officially under state control. But it is notorious that the state's hand is weak in this area. During the first five-year plan, for instance, wages rose by 70 percent, while productivity grew only by 41 percent—not exactly as intended.[49] True, there have been no such wholesale repudiations of the currency as took place after the Second World War since then, and retail price indices have been held comparatively stable, while total incomes have gone up. But these generalizations tell us nothing to answer the question. Are relative wage rates the result of the (more or less) free interplay of supply and demand on a genuine labor market? Considering the difficulty—which cannot be detailed here—of answering that question definitively for a capitalist economy or, indeed, or defining the question with real precision, we cannot attempt a conclusive answer for the Soviet Union. We may note, however, that since product prices are formed on the basis of summing wage costs through the stages of production, it is impossible to argue that Soviet wages reflect marginal labor productivity. Observation of the activities of government personnel departments in justifying the assignment of grade levels to particular jobs in the US government does not give one much confidence that the process is especially scientific or the justifications very convincing. But at least American officials have private industry to look to as a model and a check; by definition, this approach is impossible for their Soviet counterparts. And it is not entirely impossible that the housing problems in the Soviet Union, coupled with a strong preference (freely expressed to any visitor) for living in Moscow or Leningrad, reduces the mobility of labor even more than nontransferable pensions and local loyalties restrict it in the United States or in other market economies. It is also not impossible that Soviet labor is more specialized and less easily adaptable to different lines of work than American or European labor—though the Soviets are probably not so bound to one employer as the Japanese are.

Nevertheless, it seems not too risky an inference that if indeed, under the rigidities of the Soviet system, wages are the outcome of some sort of quasi-market process, it is one that works only at long term. As a basis for cost determination, then, it would seem to be somewhat questionable.

Postreform Soviet discussions of price formation[50] seem to be tending in the direction of admitting that the utility of a product has some bearing on its "value" and should therefore have some on its price. But their recommendation and urging is in the direction of having the price-fixing organs take demand into account in their decisions; they explicitly reject the notion that prices should be "free." This being the case, one is forced to conclude that the prices of goods in the Soviet Union are, in essence, fixed as the government chooses. They approximate only distantly to those a market would have produced. This conclusion, which was accepted by a group of leading Soviet economists in the field in a discussion with the author in Moscow in 1958, appears to be still valid.[51] Their last line of defense against a charge of circularity was that they had not started in a vacuum; they agreed that to understand Soviet prices, one must consider the prices of 1928 and the whole series of policy modifications of them since.

This question of the basis for Soviet price formation will concern us at a later stage, when we consider the rationale of Soviet prices and their transformation into foreign trade prices. It also lies at the heart of the question, first raised in 1953 by Peter Wiles, "Are Adjusted Rubles Rational?" with its implications for the correction of Soviet output and other indices à la Bergson and his followers.[52]

Notes

1. P.J.D. Wiles, *Communist International Economics* (Oxford: Basil Blackwell, 1968), p. 162.

2. V. Sitnin in *Ekonomicheskaya Gazata 6,* 1968, pp. 10-11, quoted by A. Nove, "East West Trade," in Samuelson, ed., *International Economic Relations,* p. 114.

3. Moskovskii . . . Institut Narodnogo Khozyaistva im. G.V. Plekhanova, *Planirovaniye Narodnogo Khoyaistva SSSR* (Moscow: Isdatelstvo Ekonomicheskoi Literatury, 1963), p. 20; G.A. Kozlov and S.P. Pervishin, *Kratkii Ekonomicheskii Slovar* (Moscow: Gosudarstvennoye Izdatelstvo Politicheskoi Literatury, 1958), p. 370, etc. The formulation by Marx and Engels (*Collected Works,* 2nd ed., Vol. 16, p. 128), quoted by S.G. Stolyarov, *O Tsenakh i Tsenoobrazovanii v SSSR* (Moscow: Statistika, 1969), is: "Price taken just by itself is nothing other than the monetary expression of value."

4. P.J.D. Wiles, "Scarcity, Marxism, and Gosplan," *Oxford Economic Papers,* New Series, vol. 5, no. 3, p. 291. Cf. also Howard J. Sherman, *Soviet Studies,* vol. XVIII, no. 2, (October 1966), p. 168: "Marxists would do best to admit that Marx had no theory of shortrun prices and outputs at the firm level because he was not interested in these issues."

5. See, for example, A. Zauberman, "The Soviet Debate on the Law of Value and Price Formation," in G. Grossman, ed., *Value and Plan: Economic Calculation and Organization in Eastern Europe* (Berkeley and Los Angeles: University of California Press, 1960); Grossman, "New Winds in Soviet Planning," *Soviet Studies,* vol. XII, no. 1, (July 1960), p. 2; Appendix to this volume; U.S. Embassy Moscow Despatches No. 206, October 24, 1957; No. 451, March 4, 1958; No. 2, July 2, 1958; and 121, August 18, 1958.

6. See the Appendix to this volume.

7. V.P. Dyachenko, ed., *Uchet Sootnosheniya Sprosa i Predlozheniya v Tsenoobrazovanii* (Moscow: Akademiya Nauk SSSR, Otdeleniye Ekonomiki, Izdatelstvo Nauka, 1964).

8. Sh. Ya Turetsky, "O Voprosye Otpusknykh Tsen Na Sredstvakh Proizvodstva," *Promyshlenno-Ekonomicheskaya Gazeta,* February 10, 1957.

9. M. Bor, "Zakon Stoimosti i Tsenoobrazovanye v Proizvodstve Promyshlennosti SSSR," *Voprosy Ekonomiki,* no. 3 (1957), p. 106.

10. Ya A. Kronrod, *Sotsialisticheskoe Vosproizvodstvo* (Moscow: Gospolitizdat, 1955), p. 98.

11. D.D. Kondrashev, *Tsenoobrazovaniye v Promyshlennosti SSSR* (Moscow: Gosfinizdat, 1956), p. 3.

12. William N. Turpin, "The Outlook for the Soviet Consumer," *Problems of Communism,* vol. IX, no. 6, (November-December 1960), p. 30.

13. See G.A. Dikhtar, "Otnosheniya Sprosa i Predlozheniya kak Faktory Tsenoobrazovanii," in Dyachenko, *Uchet Sootnosheniya,* p. 12.

14. For a summary of the "investment criterion controversy" see Wiles, "Scarcity, Marxism, and Gosplan" pp. 301-12, and sources there cited.

15. Cf. the discussion of the optimizers school in John P. Hardt, *Economic Insights on Current Soviet Policy and Strategy* (McLean, Va.: Research Analysis Corporation, 1969), pp. 52-54.

16. "The Disappearance of Planning in the Plan," *Slavic Review,* June 1973, p. 287.

17. Quoted in Jozef Wilczynski, *The Economics and Politics of East-West Trade* (New York: Frederick A. Praeger, 1969), p. 91, citing *Ekonomicheskaya Gazeta,* June 13, 1964.

18. Dyachenko, *Uchet Sootnosheniya.*

19. Dikhtar, "Otnosheniya Sprosa," p. 6.

20. Ibid., p. 9.

21. American Embassy Moscow Despatch No. 451, March 4, 1958.

22. Dikhtar, "Otnosheniya Sprosa," p. 19.

23. Ibid., p. 13.

24. Kondrashev, *Tsenoobrazovaniye,* p. 102.

25. A.G. Zavyalkov, *Tseny i Tsenoobrazovaniye v SSSR* (Minsk: Isdatelstvo Vyeishaya Shkhola, 1971), p. 121.

26. Cf. the famous Stalin story quoted in Wiles, "Scarcity, Marxism, and Gosplan," p. 296, on the relative prices of wheat and cotton (citing *Bolshevik,* 18, 1952).

27. Zavyalkov, *Tseny i Tsenoobrazovaniye,* p. 248.

28. Ibid., p. 214.

29. In L.A.D. Dellin and Hermann Gross, eds., *Reforms in the Soviet and Eastern European Economies* (Lexington, Mass.: D.C. Heath & Co., 1972).

30. Kondrashev, *Tsenoobrazovaniye,* p. 102.

31. Zavyalkov, *Tseny i Tsenoobrazovaniye,* p. 98.

32. Ibid., pp. 98, 101.

33. Ibid.

34. Ibid., pp. 124, 126.

35. Ibid., p. 123.

36. Kondrashev, *Tsenoobrazovaniye*, p. 84.

37. Zavyalkov, *Tseny i Tsenoobrazovaniye*, p. 130.

38. Cf. V.D. Belkin, *Tseny Edinogo Urovnya i Ekonomicheskie Izmereniya na ikh Osnov* (Moscow: Izdatelstvo Ekonomicheskoi Literatury, 1963), pp. 30-34, and authorities there cited.

39. Kondrashev, *Tsenoobrazovaniye*, p. 100.

40. Zavyalkov, *Tseny i Tsenoobrazovaniye*, p. 131.

41. Ibid.

42. Ibid., p. 123.

43. Ibid., p. 139.

44. Ibid., Chapter VI.

45. A. Aleksandrov, *Finansovaya Sistema SSSR* (Moscow: Gosfinizdat, 1956), p. 53.

46. Maurice Dobb, "Soviet Price Policy," *Soviet Studies,* XII, no. 1 (July 1960), p. 87, quotes Turetsky: "It is not the level of retail prices that depends on the turnover tax, but the turnover tax, its magnitude, depends on the distribution of the social product, on the structure of prices." Sh. Ya. Turetsky, *Ocherki Planovogo Tsenoobrazovaniya v SSSR* (Moscow: Gosudarstvennoye Isdatelstvo Politicheskoi Literatury, 1959), p. 29.

47. Reference undiscoverable.

48. I.M. Levin, *Planirovaniye Truda i Zarabotnoi Platy na Promyshlennykh Predpriyatiakh* (Moscow: Gospolitzdat, 1958), pp. 103-39.

49. P.A. Belousov, *Obshchestvenno Neobkhodimye Zatraty Truda i Uroven Optovykh Tsen* (Moscow: Izdatelstvo "Mysl," 1969), p. 55.

50. Ibid., Dyachenko, *Uchet Sootnosheniya,* and Belkin, *Tseny Edinogo.*

51. See the Appendix to this volume.

52. In *Soviet Studies,* vol. VII, no. 2 (October 1955), p. 143.

7

Consequences

By adopting the point of view that the Soviet Union, in its relationship to foreign trade, is properly to be regarded less as a government than as "U.S.S.R., Inc.," an entity for which foreign trade is a staff function subordinated to more fundamental purposes, we can proceed to trace certain consequences—some logical and empirical manifestations—of this unusual state of affairs.

Perhaps the most important, at least logically, is the separation of production from trade.[1] As we have seen, neither maximizing the monetary or commercial gains from trade nor maximizing the volume of trade is the purpose for which the Soviet Union trades. Since the time of Adam Smith, it has been the firm belief of Western economists that the commonwealth would be most effectively maximized if private traders "truck," to use Smith's word, for their own account as profitably as possible. They, and most Western governments, have believed that free trade is so effective an instrument of economic improvement that the removal of barriers to international trade has itself become an objective of government policy. We shall have occasion later to consider the matter of the objective function of the USSR in more detail; for the moment, we may accept "the maximization of national production capacity and of national output" as convenient shorthand. And the USSR has never accepted the argument that free trade is the best way to achieve that goal.

While the USSR is clearly not mercantilist in the sense that it actively seeks a positive balance of trade, it seems to be pursuing the same ultimate ends as the mercantilists aimed at. "The ends of mercantilist policy were national autarchy and the expansion of state power."[2] If, then, mercantilist purposes were the accumulation of "treasure" as an instrument for hiring mercenaries and otherwise expanding the power of the prince—*pecunia nervus belli*, or wealth, the sinew of war[3]—then there is an analogy to Soviet objectives. The USSR, however, seeks these objectives, first, by making its import decisions in real terms and buying so far as possible goods that will directly contribute to its productive power and, secondly, by participating directly in trade as a state, rather than achieving its goals by regulation. The operations of the Ministry of Foreign Trade, which can be viewed as the procurement branch or purchasing office of the enterprise, have the beneficial effect of preventing the uncontrollable and, hence, distracting influence of foreign demand from affecting domestic production in all its forms. "In a strictly centralized planned economy one expects from imports no competition and no stimulus to achievement for the domestic economy, rather only the acquisition of commodities of vital importance which either cannot be produced at home or can be produced only in insufficient quantities."[4]

One reason why Western countries encourage exports is, of course, their impact on employment levels. The export multiplier is as good a Keynesian tool as the budget deficit, and Germany, France, and Japan, to take only the most obvious examples, have consciously used exports as a macro-economic policy instrument. The risks that this policy involves are obvious; and the Soviet Union not only has no need of it for employment-policy reasons,[5] but is actively opposed to reliance on such *stikhiinye* influences as those of the market.[6]

One manifestation of this separation of production from trade, as it is one technique for attaining it, is the inconvertibility of Soviet currency. It is useful to distinguish, following Altman,[7] between currency convertibility and commodity convertibility. The former exists, in trivial ways: A foreigner who has bought rubles for foreign currency can convert them back; Soviet tourists are allowed to buy foreign currency for rubles for their trips.[8] Even among the socialist states, convertibility is not permitted, with minor exceptions: Noncommercial transactions are carried on in "transferable rubles," which are carefully segregated from domestic currency.[9]

Specifically, the rules are:

First, the circulation of foreign currency on the territory of the U.S.S.R. is not permitted. All foreign exchange in the possession of individuals must be sold either to the Bank for Foreign Trade or the State Bank of the U.S.S.R. Foreigners in the U.S.S.R. exchange their foreign currency for Soviet money if they need to buy Soviet goods or pay for services. Citizens of the U.S.S.R. returning to the homeland after a stay abroad, are obliged to sell the Vneshtorgbank or the State bank any foreign exchange they have.

Secondly, all payments received by state enterprises and organizations from the sale of goods abroad or for the performance of various sorts of services must be turned over to the Vneshtorgbank of the U.S.S.R. Consequently, all foreign exchange payments are at the disposition of the state, which uses them as it sees fit.

Thirdly, the import into the U.S.S.R. of foreign currency and other foreign exchange instruments (gold, silver, platinum and metals of the platinum group) is permitted without any sort of limitation; the free transfer into the U.S.S.R. of foreign exchange through banks is also permitted.

Fourth, the export of foreign exchange and other things realizable in foreign exchange by foreigners and by Soviet citizens is permitted with the permission of the Ministry of Finances of the U.S.S.R. It is not necessary to receive permission, if foreign exchange deposited in the Vneshtorgbank in free foreign exchange accounts (Type A accounts) or foreign exchange brought in from other countries and registered with Soviet customs, provided that no more than two months have lapsed since the day of importation, is being exported . . . .

Accounts between the Soviet Union and capitalist countries are maintained, not in rubles but in foreign currency. [With the exception of foreign trade accounts with Finland, which are kept in rubles on a clearing account.] [10]

But there is no general right for a foreign owner of ruble balances to exchange his claim for a claim against a non-Soviet economy. Except for foreign authors, a few of whom have had ruble royalty accounts established in their names that they can make use of only on visits to the Soviet Union and even then only for tourist-type expenses, as one surprised American writer told this author in Moscow, foreigners cannot accumulate ruble claims. As we noted earlier, the Soviet Union makes its foreign payments in foreign currencies; it was, indeed, the holding of dollar balances in non-U.S. banks that led to the invention of the Eurodollar, when the Soviet State Bank found it profitable to earn interest by lending these balances out at short term.

What is significant is the absence of commodity convertibility, the impossibility of acquiring and using general claims on the Soviet economy. From the point of view of the Soviet planners, it is inconceivable that persons not under their control should be allowed to place orders—that is, issue binding directives—to the Soviet productive apparatus. It is in this sense that Wiles' remark that "money has no influence there" (i.e., in a planned economy) is true and relevant.[11] From the point of view of a foreigner, he can find nothing to buy, since by definition he has been preempted by the directives of the Plan. The interposition of the foreign trading organizations, with whom alone he is allowed contact, insures that there is no way in which considerations of the demands of foreign markets can be brought directly to bear on Soviet producers. Theoretically, of course, these demand pressures could be transmitted by the V/Os; but foreign businessmen often chafe at the difficulty, amounting to the impossibility, of the effective and timely use of that mechanism. The U.S.-Soviet commercial agreements of 1972 contain no provision for direct contact between foreign businessmen and Soviet suppliers or final users, and indeed the agreements refer specifically to transactions between U.S. companies and Soviet *foreign trade organizations.*[12]

One consequence of this state of affairs is the irrelevance of tariffs in Soviet trade relations. "In the past, tariffs have not been used as instruments for providing protection to domestic industry in the CEMA countries but have been important in their external trade, insofar as they tend to influence the importing organization's choice of foreign suppliers."[13]

There is no evidence that the latter half of this statement is applicable to the Soviet Union. Indeed, there is no logical place for such a policy instrument in the Soviet system: Why discourage when you can simply forbid? "Because foreign trade is run by a state monopoly, tariffs are redundant, trade is controlled by implicit export and import quotas. The decisions to trade are made directly by the government, often without the mediation of price comparison."[14] The USSR has often made it plain that it maintains the appearance of a tariff apparatus purely in order to have a bargaining weapon to use in negotiations with foreign states that "discriminate" against it by denying it most-favored-nation treatment. (It does use tariffs on private package shipments in order to discourage them. But this matter is much less significant for the USSR than for other East European countries that have larger emigrations.) We shall consider below the significance of this problem for the possible integration of the Soviet economy into the world trading system. From our present point of view, it is important merely as a symptom of the distinctive nature of the way the USSR participates in the international trade process.

Although the intention to balance trade bilaterally by countries is frequently ascribed to the Soviet Union by Western negotiators and scholars, it does not appear explicitly in Soviet foreign trade theory. Rather, the emphasis there is customarily on "nondiscrimination" and mutual advantage, whether the reference is to intra-Bloc or to East-West trade, and on "aid" with respect to the developing countries. Before 1940, the USSR traded multilaterally under a foreign trade regime essentially identical to its present one.[15] Moreover, as Wiles correctly notes,[16] bilaterialism with Western countries was imposed on the USSR by the latter; before 1958, trade negotiations between Western European countries and the USSR always involved an effort on the part of the former to secure inclusion in the lists of goods to be exchanged of commodities—normally consumer goods—which the latter was urged to agree to take, in order to secure permission to buy the machinery items in which it was really interested. Anyone who was involved, however peripherally, in reporting on these negotiations and in the COCOM process by which the West undertook to prevent trade from contributing to Soviet military power will have vivid memories of that aspect of the matter.

More recently, according to U.S. Department of Commerce officials interviewed in the summer of 1974, Soviet trade agreements with Western countries have seldom referred to bilateral balancing (goods lists are a thing of the past). The department's unpublished compilation of trade treaties between Western countries and the USSR shows only nine agreements in force that provide for bilateral balancing of trade to the extent possible. All of these countries, except Jordan, are Latin American. There is no indication of the side from which the initiative for the inclusion of this clause came, except that the similarity of wording may suggest, weakly, that it was a Soviet proposal.

The contrast with the situation before the attainment of convertibility by the major Western trading nations is marked, even though the United Kingdom and Germany had begun to abandon quota lists and strict bilateral balancing even before that event.[17] "There were approximately 240 bilateral trade and/or payments agreements between Free World and Sino-Soviet bloc countries in operation in 1957."[18]

The reasons ascribed for the alleged Soviet penchant for bilaterial balancing in trade with market economies by such writers as Boltho, Wiles, Wilczynski, Familton, Holzman, and Wyczalkowski[19] can be briefly summarized. Wiles is perhaps a bit too flip when he puts the continuation of the practice down to "sheer intellectual error,"[20] and while this may find some support in Holzman's "analogy with domestic practices,"[21] it seems more likely that the basic reason is administrative convenience or, as Holzman puts it, "The easiest way to achieve overall balance in the latter case (i.e., under central planning) is undoubtedly by planning for a high degree of bilateral balance."[22] The other principal reason adduced, the possibility of improving the terms of trade, shades off into the problem of trade discrimination, which we examine in detail below.

It is fair to conclude, however, that the tendency to trade bilaterally with industrialized market economies, which as we saw earlier is not strongly evident from the statistical results of this trade, need not be a permanent feature of the Soviet trading system, although one should not underestimate the administrative convenience of the practice. What is apparent, however, is that bilateralism is not an insuperable obstacle to change. One might indeed argue that if the other changes necessary to integrate the USSR into the world trading system are made, bilaterialism as such will cease to be a major problem.

Discrimination is a highly emotive word in Soviet treatments of foreign trade; there is perhaps no area in which indignation is more frequently or more fervently expressed. The refusal until recently of the United States and the EEC to give the USSR most-favored-nation status as a matter of right clearly rankles, even though it is generally conceded that the actual effect of its denial is minimal. Similarly, the USSR has often expressed anger at strategic embargoes, even while asserting that they have not prevented it from becoming a major industrial power. Yet an effort to point out to a Soviet diplomat that the Soviet state trading system is 100 percent discriminatory meets with blank and apparently genuine incomprehension.

In normal usage, discrimination means interference with the making of foreign trade decisions, as between trading partners of different nationalities, on grounds other than normal commercial conditions—price, quality, delivery dates, credit arrangements, and so forth—by means of differential tariffs or other government measures. Discrimination is usually practiced by a government in the exercise of its regulatory functions, and rules prescribing permitted and illegitimate discriminatory practices have been formulated and continue to evolve among the governments of market economy countries. There is perhaps no area of the foreign trade field in which it is more apparent, or more often forgotten, that the institution of state trading, as distinguished from state regulation of trade, makes the concept inapplicable. There is simply no way of ascertaining, much less of proving, that a government trader is discriminating illegitimately, except by demonstrating that an identical good was available under identical conditions from another supplier at a lower price. And it would be a poor advocate who could not adduce reasons for his client's decision that could be made to look respectable, if the entire decision-making process goes on within a single, closed bosom.

In sum, discrimination for noncommercial reasons is built into the Soviet foreign trading system and cannot be expunged from it by promises of nondiscriminatory behavior or by expressions of good intentions. Indeed, when it suits their purposes the Soviet authorities hold out promises of discrimination in favor of chosen partners, as in the Khruschev letter to President Eisenhower of May 1958, or in the Nixon-Brezhnev exchanges of the early seventies. There is no obvious reason why the USSR should give up this advantage, and no obvious way in which it could do so without major changes in its foreign trading system and, indeed, in its internal economic administration. The treatment of non-discrimination in the U.S.-Soviet agreements of 1972 goes no further than the provision of MFN treatment with respect to tariffs, internal taxes, charges on payments and "rules and formalities."[23]

Closely connected with the question of discrimination is the oligopolist-oligopsonist power of the Soviet Ministry of Foreign Trade, which is most graphically demonstrated by the famous wheat deal. The advantages this power confers on the Soviet authorities are obvious, although apparently not to those Western corporations and governments who are eager to supply the USSR with capital and technology to build up Soviet raw material industries in return for promises of future deliveries. We may usefully distinguish two ways in which this power can be used.

Simply as a very big prospective purchaser, the Soviet government enjoys a favored position as a customer. The belief prevalent in West Germany in the early 1950s, for example, that there was an enormous and profitable market in "the East," from which the Germans were debarred only by American political power in American national and private interests, made quite credible subsequent reports of the degree to which Herr Beitz of Krupp was prepared to satisfy Soviet wishes. And, as a government, its position vis-à-vis private entrepreneurs is further bolstered. Western businessmen, "hard-headed" in their own eyes, accept on occasion treatment from so large and so powerful a customer that they would not think of entertaining from their peers.

Thus, "In negotiation with the Russians, one must reckon that they may copy, modify, or develop any western machine they buy; they seldom recognize foreign patents, though on occasion they have been induced to pay royalties."[24] It is reported, though this author is unable to find a printed direct source, that the USSR dislikes the explicit payment of royalties or of interest at rates above 5 or 6 percent and accordingly force Western sellers to incorporate payment for these costs in the selling prices of their wares. "Interest rates that are too low have, for instance, to be compensated for in the selling price."[25] Western businessmen have been known to recognize in conversation that the extreme difficulty, amounting to impossibility, of getting reliable information on the precise output of goods made under Western licenses or patents by the USSR makes the practice of charging fees on the basis of the number of items produced impractical.

Recent American dealings with the USSR, most notably perhaps the Pepsi-Cola agreement[26] illustrate a growing Soviet (and, indeed, general Eastern European) drive to make self-liquidating or automatically balanced deals on a product-by-product basis. American businessmen who have consulted this author have shown, typically, great reluctance to agree to trade limited by the amount of Soviet goods they can sell or to accept what amounts to a barter deal however disguised. It is useful in this connection to distinguish between the inconvenience of having soft drink sales in the USSR limited to what can be paid for by (additional?) vodka sales in the United States promoted by the pop concern and the uncertainty (which is important on the national level as well as to the private entrepreneur) entailed in making investments in the USSR—and under its control—that can be liquidated only by future deliveries of raw materials. The uncertainty relates, of course, not only to the likelihood that the materials will be delivered, but also to the prices at which they can be sold at a distant date.

It is not the case, it is true, that a tendency to operate in this manner is inextricably built into the Soviet foreign trading system. But it is true that the existence of a government foreign trade monopoly makes this practice at once easier to adopt and more liable to exploitation by the Soviet government. The dangers are clearly shown by the Israeli-Soyuznefteeksport case referred to above.

Any consideration of Soviet foreign trade practices sooner or later gets around to the question of dumping. The principal accusations of dumping levied against the USSR in the postwar period are summarized by Glen A. Smith;[27] they relate to the late fifties and early sixties, and the major cases involved aluminum, tin, and oil.

In 1957-58 the USSR undercut British import prices on aluminum, which thus lead to complaints to the Board of Trade from Alcan Aluminum, Ltd., that the USSR was dumping. The Canadian Embassy in Moscow asked this author for information supporting the charge, and promised a copy of the results of the investigation; the evidence available was, in his belief, far more suggestive of an error, or at worst of competitive price-cutting, than of "sales at less than fair value." Unhappily, however, the Canadians were not allowed to make available their report or Alcan's submission. Similar charges were freely made with respect to tin at about the same time; the view of the American Embassy was at least that the probable reason was Soviet ineptness in face of large imports of tin from China.

In the late fifties and early sixties, the USSR increased its exports of crude petroleum, and there was considerable talk within the U.S. government of a Soviet oil offensive as part of what was then believed to be a more general Soviet economic offensive. Soviet press reports at the time suggested that production had in fact outrun storage capacity, which thus provided a further stimulus to Soviet desire to export, and a genuine concern existed within the American government over the possibility of excessive and dangerous dependence by NATO members on Soviet crude supplies.

It seems reasonable to agree with Smith's conclusion on all three episodes: Price competition, even when inconvenient to firms dominant in a market, is not necessarily ill-intentioned, much less "dumping." The USSR in the first two of these instances, at least, readily agreed to cease selling at "dumping" prices; moreover, in 1958, it agreed with deBeers for the latter to market Soviet gem diamond exports under its well-known cartel arrangements.

With respect to American law, "dumping is defined by act of Congress as the sale or purchase in the United States of foreign goods below their fair market value in the exporting country, or in the absence of such value, below foreign costs of production."[28]

Now, as we have seen, Soviet internal prices cannot be translated into external prices in any consistent or significant way; moreover, internal prices are set by fiat and not by the "market." It follows, and the U.S. Treasury has consistently operated on the assumption, that it is not possible to establish the fact of sales below fair market value or below costs of production, except by "constructing" a fair value based on costs in "comparable" noncentrally planned economies. Discussions with Treasury Department officials and with Tariff Commission personnel over the years have suggested strongly to this author that the practice is not one that carries overwhelming persuasive power, even with the officials who use it. Moreover, it appears clear from our examination of Soviet trading policies that for the USSR to obtain less foreign exchange than it might would run counter to the very purposes for which it exports at all.

It is interesting to ask next whether the policies and the resulting organizational forms and trading practices of the USSR have any influence on the prices received and paid by the Soviet Union in its trade with the industrialized countries. The only available data come from the trade statistics; consequently, the only unit prices that can be extracted are annual averages, which have meaning only for commodities that can be regarded as homogeneous.[29] This, in turn, means that it is exceedingly difficult to make generalizations about the prices paid for Soviet imports of just those items in which the USSR is most interested.

If, as the evidence indicates, the USSR is primarily interested in trade with the developed countries as a means of securing necessary inputs—either to cover emergency shortfalls or to procure advanced capital equipment—and uses exports primarily as a means for paying for those inputs, one would expect the USSR to be a price-taker on both ends of the line. Soviet imports must be bought on oligopolistic markets, in which the sellers are price-makers and quantity-takers, to use Wiles' terminology,[30] and Soviet imports must be sold on (pretty well) competitive markets, where the USSR is a price-taker and quantity-maker.

Does this follow logically from Soviet policies and from their organizational embodiment? Not, of course, inevitably, but on the whole, it would seem, the answer is yes. In fact, on the whole, agricultural and mineral raw materials are sold on competitive, perfect markets, especially on the world level—or were, until the formation of OPEC. Even where, domestically, production is highly concentrated (as in the U.S. steel, aluminum, and copper industries, for example,[31] international competition and the threat of imports, if not their actuality,

have kept prices from being so rigid as they are, typically, in manufacturing industry. And, however unwilling economists have normally been to recognize
the fact, it is the common experience that industrialists are in very many cases
oligopolists and normally react to a change in demand by reducing, not prices,
but output.[32] Which is to say that they are price-makers, quantity-takers.

Tables 7-1 and 7-2 show Soviet imports from and exports to western
Europe, 1965-1968, as given in Marer,[33] with adjustment to make the classes
fit more precisely into the categories of "competitive" and "market-power"
markets, respectively. The adjustment consists of adding to Marer's "primary"
import category SITC classes 5 (chemicals) and 6 (manufactured goods classified chiefly by materials). Without adjustment, it will be seen, Soviet exports
to Western Europe consist, to the extent of about three-quarters, of primary
products; after adjustment, the proportion goes to 95 percent. Imports of
manufactured goods bought on "market-power" markets increase from 78 to
89 percent over the four years in question; after adjustment, the percentage
drops to a range of 46 to 53 percent. But one may think it not improbable

Table 7-1
West European "Competitive" Imports from USSR, 1965-1968 (SITC Groupings,
Millions of Current Dollars, c.i.f.)

Year	Total Imports	Primary	Percent	Primary + SITC Classes 5 & 6	Percent
1965	1488.90	1104.81	72	1710.63	95
1966	1639.01	1208.64	75	1670.50	95
1967	1758.99	1319.37	74	1565.40	96
1968	1902.51	1301.37	74	1420.06	95

Source: Paul Marer, *Soviet and East European Foreign Trade, 1946-1969* (Bloomington and
London, Indiana University Press, 1972) p. 224, Table IV STIC M.U.

Table 7-2
Soviet "Market Power" Imports from Western Europe, 1965-1968

Year	Total Imports	Total Manufactured	Percent	Mfg.-SITC Classes 5 & 6	Percent
1965	944.65	740.18	78	432.81	46
1966	923.65	748.86	81	436.47	53
1967	1280.98	1090.61	85	638.13	50
1968	1591.02	1416.67	89	852.41	53

Source: Marer, *Foreign Trade*, p. 232, Table IV SITC X.U.

that, for example, Soviet imports of chemicals are in the main bought from Western firms with considerable market power, as they probably do not consist primarily of bulk chemicals. A glance at the appropriate, though rather sketchy, Soviet data on imports from the major European countries confirms the impression and gives a similar idea with respect to other manufactures,

This being the case, it is not unlikely that the Soviets should be the marginal suppliers of western imports in many cases, and that they should also have to pay higher prices than others for their own imports. Another factor in the situation is the ability of the Soviet trading corporations to function as monopsonistic buyers. There is ample evidence[34] that they do this; but in the nature of the case, when they are contracting for special items, it is to be expected that they pay the price of the tailor-made commodity. Moreover, the existence since 1950 of export controls in most of the major suppliers of advanced technology has meant, according to frequent if undocumentable reports, that the USSR has had to pay exceedingly high prices for embargoed technology.

The available statistical, as distinguished from anecdotal, evidence is difficult to compile with precision. However, the German, British, and French foreign trade statistics for the year 1972 have been combed in an effort to see the extent to which the Soviets have received less-than-average prices for their exports. The survey is admittedly somewhat impressionistic: The USSR does not always figure as customer or supplier in the trade lists; the articles are not always of sufficient uniformity to make averaging possible; and in some cases the quantities are derisory. Nothing similar was possible on the import side because of lack of homogeneity. In trade with the U.K., of the 22 commodity groups in which the USSR accounted for a significant share of imports, it received the lowest average prices in 14 cases, second lowest in 5, and third lowest in the remaining 3. For France, the numbers are 21, with lowest prices in 15 cases, second in 4, and third and fourth in 1 each. For Germany, of 58 cases, the USSR received lowest average prices in 36, second lowest in 9, third in 11, and fourth in 2. And as the European data are c.i.f., it is not impossible that were freight costs eliminated, even more instances of bottom-dollar prices would be apparent.[35]

These, then, appear to be the principal consequences of the Soviet foreign trading system, of its organization and its policies, for foreign trade and its pricing: the insulation of internal economic policy and operations from external influences; commodity inconvertibility, as a result of which the possessor of claims against the Soviet economy is able to exercise them only as and insofar as the Soviet authorities choose; separation of seller from customer; the irrelevance of tariffs; a tendency towards bilateralism, if only for administrative convenience; total trade discrimination, built into the system and very difficult to separate from it, even conceptually; monosony power and potential monopoly power, vitiated only by the nature of the markets for the commodities that the Soviet Union exports; practices with respect to licenses, patents, copyrights, and interest that differ from those customary in trade among market economies; a strong desire for capital imports that will pay for themselves directly; the possibility of (probably unintentional) dumping, together with extreme difficulty in identifying or proving it; the Soviet Union's status as a price-taker as both exporter and importer; and an apparent tendency to receive relatively low prices for such of her exports as can be examined from this point of view.

Notes

1. Adam Zwass, *Die Waehrung im Aussenhandel der RGW Laendern* (Vienna: Wiener Institut fuer Wirtschaftsvergleiche, 1973), p. 6.

2. M. Blaug, *Economic Theory in Retrospect* (Homewood, Ill.: Richard D. Irwin, 1962), p. 12.

3. Frederic C. Lane, *Venice and History* (Baltimore, Md.: The Johns Hopkins University Press, 1966), p. 311; cf. Erich Roll, *A History of Economic Thought* (London: Faber and Faber, Ltd., 1938), especially pp. 63-70; and H. M. Robertson, *Aspects of the Rise of Economic Individualism* (Cambridge: The University Press, 1933), pp. 58-59.

4. Zwass, *Die Waehrung*, p. 4.

5. Cf. P. J. D. Wiles, *Communist International Economics* (Oxford: Basil Blackwell, 1968), p. 59; and F. D. Holzman "Foreign Trade Behavior of Centrally Planned Economies," in Henry Rosovsky, ed., *Industrialization in Two Systems: Essays in Honor of Alexander Gerschenkron.* (New York: John Wiley & Sons, 1966), p. 241.

6. Cf. Moskovskii . . . Institut Narodnogo Khozyaistva im. G. V. Plekhanova, *Planirovaniye Narodnogo Khyzyaistva SSSR* (Moscow: Izdatel'stvo Ekonomicheskoi Literatury, 1963), p. 10: "There, where anarchy and competition rule, the necessity of proportional development of production builds itself a road only by means of constant and innumerable violations and crises and functions as a blind law of nature."

7. Oscar Altman, "Russian Gold and the Ruble," *IMF Staff Papers,* vol. VII (1959-1960), pp. 430-35.

8. Zwass, *Die Waehrung,* p. 14; and V. S. Gerashchenko, *Denezhnoe Obrashcheniye i Kredit SSSR* (Moscow: Finansy, 1966), p. 372-73.

9. Details are given in K. A. Larionov, *Dva Mira—Dve Valyutnye Sistemye* (Moscow: Finansiye, 1973), pp. 39-40.

10. Gerashchenko, *Denezhnoe,*

11. Wiles, *Communist International Economics,* p. 62.

12. U.S. Department of Commerce, *U.S.-Soviet Commercial Agreements 1972: Texts, Summaries and Supporting Papers,* Washington, D.C., January 1973, pp. 75-94, especially p. 89. Emphasis added.

13. R. J. Familton, "East-West Trade and Payments Relations," *IMF Staff Papers*, vol. XVII, no. 1 (March 1970), p. 182.

14. Holzman, "Foreign Trade Behavior," p. 240. We shall consider the question of price comparisons later.

15. Robert F. Dernberger, "Prices, the Exchange Rate, and Economic Efficiency in the Foreign Trade of Communist China," in Alan A. Brown and Egon Neuberger, *International Trade and Central Planning: An Analysis of Economic Interactions* (Berkeley and Los Angeles: University of California Press, 1968), p. 205, quoting Raymond F. Mikesell and Jack N. Behrman, *Financing Free World Trade with the Sino-Soviet Bloc* (Princeton, N.J.: Princeton University Press, 1958).

16. Wiles, *Communist International Economics*, p. 40.

17. Mikesell and Behrman, *Financing Free World Trade*, p. 97.

18. Ibid., p. 12.

19. Andrea Boltho, *Foreign Trade Criteria in Socialist Economies* (Cambridge: The University Press, 1971), pp. 92-95; Wiles, *Communist International Economics*, p. 40 and pp. 254-86; Jozef Wilczynski, *The Economics and Politics of East-West Trade* (New York: Frederick A. Praeger, 1969), pp. 203-07; Familton, "East-West Trade and Payments Relations," pp. 189-92; Holzman, passim, but especially in "Foreign Trade Behavior," pp. 247-50; Marcin R. Wyczalkowski, "Communist Economics and Currency Convertibility," *IMF Staff Papers*, vol. XII, no. 2 (July 1966), pp. 166-69.

20. Wiles, *Communist International Economics*, p. 40.

21. Holzman, p. 250.

22. Ibid., p. 249.

23. U.S. Department of Commerce, *U.S.-Soviet Commercial Agreements 1972. Texts, Summaries and Supporting Papers.* Washington D.C.: U.S. Government Printing Office, 1973, p. 88.

24. *The Economist*, July 12, 1958, p. 144, quoting "one British businessman . . . tempered with asides from another whose experiences in Moscow were much more frustrating." It is doubtful that Soviet accession to the Paris Convention on Patents will make a major difference in this regard.

25. *The Economist*, "East-West Trade Survey," January 6, 1973, p. 9.

26. See *The Wall Street Journal*, November 17, 1972, p. 3.

27. Glen Alden Smith, *Soviet Foreign Trade Organization, Operations, and Policy, 1918-1971* (New York: Praeger Publishers, 1973), pp. 20-29.

28. U.S. Senate, Committee on Foreign Relations, *A Background Study on East-West Trade* (Washington, D.C.: U.S. Government Printing Office, 1965), p. 49.

29. Cf. Horst Mendershausen, *Terms of Trade between the Soviet Union and Smaller Communist Countries, 1955 to 1957* (Santa Monica, Calif.: The Rand Corp., 1959); and Mendershausen, *The Terms of Soviet-Satellite Trade, 1955-1959* (Santa Monica, Calif.: The Rand Corporation, 1962).

30. P. J. D. Wiles, *Price, Cost and Output* (Oxford: Basil Blackwell, 1956), p. 19.

31. Cf. John M. Blair, *Economic Concentration: Structure, Behavior, and Public Policy* (New York: Harcourt Brace Jovanovich, 1972), pp. 3-22.

32. Cf. A. D. H. Kaplan, Joel B. Dirlam, and Robert F. Langellotti, *Pricing in Big Business: A Case Approach* (Washington, D.C.: The Brookings Institution, 1958), p. 24: "The regularity of steel prices through marked changes in operating levels occurring since 1947 seems to bear out the traditional tendency to resist price revisions in steel until action is unavoidable."

33. Paul Marer, *Soviet and East European Foreign Trade 1946-1969*. (Bloomington and London: Indiana University Press, 1972), p. 224, Table IV SITC M. U. and p. 232, Table IV SITC X. U.

34. For example, James Trager, *Amber Waves of Grain* (New York: Arthur Fields Books, 1973), passim; and *The Wall Street Journal*, August 22, 1974, p. 25.

35. The tabulations and calculated average prices are available on request from the author. The figures are drawn from: *Annual Statement of the Overseas Trade of the United Kingdom, 1972, Vol. II, Imports of Commodities Analyzed by Country* (London: HM Stationery Office, 1973); Statistisches Bundesamt, *Der Aussenhandel der Bundesrepublik Deuschlands, Reihe 2, Spezialhandel nach Waren and Laendern, 1972* (Wiesbaden: W. Kohlhammer GMBH, 1973); *Statistiques du Commerce Extérieure de la France: Importations, Exportations en m.g.p., Annee 1973* (Paris: Ministère de l'Economie et des Finances, Direction Générale des Douanes and Droits Indirects, 1974).

8

Soviet Foreign Trade Administration and Pricing in the Seventies and Beyond

Our examination of the operation of the Soviet foreign trading system as its has functioned since the inception of the monopoly of foreign trade in the early 1920s has confirmed, documented, and given precision to the view of its purposes and methods commonly accepted in the West by those scholars who have examined it closely. We have seen that it does indeed have certain fundamental (and intentional) differences from the regime prevailing in market economics, whose laws and characteristics are studied by economists in the international economic field, and often believed by policy-making government officials to apply to the Soviet system as well.[1]

These peculiarities of the Soviet system stem from the complete and intentional subordination of foreign trade to the demands of the national economic plan, with the result that foreign trade is not an activity carried on by a collection of individuals free to buy and sell abroad—or not—as they choose. It is rather a staff function, a procurement operation whose primary purpose is the acquisition of foreign goods demanded by the plan, either to cover unforeseen shortfalls or to provide capital equipment and technology needed for the longer-range purposes of the Soviet government.[2] We have seen that as one result the USSR is ordinarily a price-taker, both as importer and as exporter; as another, the interface between a system relying on prices arbitrarily (which does not mean randomly) set by central authority and one using prices formed, or at least influenced, by "market forces" is an area of friction. We have seen the reasons why it is in principle and in practice impossible for Soviet domestic ruble prices to form the basis of rational intelligent decisions.

The accuracy of this judgment is explicitly confirmed by most if not all Soviet writers on foreign trade. For example, "Analysis shows that our actual prices cannot be a sufficiently reliable basis for judging the economic effectiveness of foreign trade."[3] Again:

This means that [the problem of the effectiveness of foreign trade] can be solved correctly and finally only under the condition of the preliminary or concurrent solution of a series of other economic problems, and, in particular, those of the effectiveness of capital investments and of prices.[4]

Further:

Calculation of the economic effectiveness of foreign trade on the basis of existing prices leads to mistaken conclusions which do not give a picture of the size of the real social expenditures and sometimes entirely fail to correspond with the relations of expenditures on the production of goods.[5]

Again:

But such a comparison [of domestic with foreign prices] because of the deficiencies of wholesale prices does not always express with sufficient accuracy the actual level of the effectiveness of exporting.[6]

And for a final example:

. . . one must have definite value indicators in which the full macroeconomic expenditures for the production of all goods connected with foreign trade would be expressed with the requisite accuracy.
   The wholesale prices of industrial goods and the procurement prices for agricultural production existing in the Soviet Union, and also the transport tariffs on freight shipments cannot be recognized as fully meeting the demands set out above.[7]

These observations are apparently made by people directly and operationally concerned with foreign trade, so far as their positions are identified. A confirming, if slightly more optimistic, view is that of a professor who is in charge of the section for relations with developing countries in the Academy of Sciences:

For many goods these [full macroeconomic] costs have already found expression in the wholesale delivery prices *(optovykh otpusknykh tsenakh)* introduced in the USSR in the middle of 1967. The perfection of wholesale prices in the USSR and other socialist countries is going on in the direction of their getting closer to real value.[8]

It should be borne in mind, however, that even the revised "full macroeconomic costs," while they admittedly include charges for capital and for economic rents, are still essentially arbitrary, in the sense that none of their elements is the result of a market process (except to the debatable degree that Soviet wages represent an approximation to the results of bargaining). We shall consider the Soviet criticisms of the concept by Gosplan Sector Chief Probst later.
   Indeed, the consideration we are about to embark on with respect to indicators of the effectiveness of foreign trade can not improperly be regarded as an examination of Soviet attempts to compensate for the inadequacy of their pricing system as an indicator of opportunity cost or relative scarcities.
   The organizational and operational peculiarities of which we are speaking have caused and are causing major difficulties for Western governments and for Western businessmen; these are well-known and sufficiently documented. It is perhaps worth noting that for the U.S. government, at least, the hope of changing some of these anomalies and easing some of the limitations has been a major objective of its efforts to expand and normalize East West trade under Democratic and Republican administrations alike.[9]

These hoped-for changes, however, were never very clearly specified either in the public pronouncements cited in the previous footnote nor in the internal discussions in the government. The basic strategy of the proposed legislation of the late sixties was that the President should be granted authority to negotiate trade agreements with the communist countries excluded from MFN treatment by law, these agreements to extend MFN in return for 'equivalent benefits' for the United States. The officials concerned were reluctant to go beyond giving examples of the equivalent benefits, which usually included patent and copyright protection, permission for American firms to open offices in Moscow, and, vaguely, "improved access" to Soviet final users. The hope was that increased business contacts between American and Soviet citizens would modify Soviet attitudes and practices; the basis for the hope was never very clearly stated. With the other East European countries, of course, the objective of making possible and supporting aspirations and efforts toward greater economic independence of the Soviet Union was explicitly stated, though seldom publicly mentioned.

It was also impossible to get American officials to concentrate on attempting some measure of equivalence or on the difficulties of putting numbers on relative marginal utilities of either the concessions each side would make or on the results of any expansion of trade which might take place.

Subsequent experience with the Jackson Amendment, which made MFN treatment dependent on Soviet concessions with respect to emigration, may suggest that any attempt to influence the Soviet Union in the direction of modifications of its internals system in return for trade benefits is necessarily futile. It may be argued, however, on the other hand, that that experiment was vitiated by the open disunity between the Congress and the President and the Secretary of State, a breach that may well have given the USSR the impression that the Americans didn't know what they wanted and would not insist on their demands. Our examination of the Soviet system, however, would seem to suggest that it is designed to secure for the Soviet political authorities complete control over external commercial relations, and thus precisely to thwart any external attempts to exert political influence on the Soviet state or the Soviet society.

From the Soviet point of view, then, one might well conclude that the foreign trade monopoly effectively secures the degree of protection from outside influence that it is designed to attain. And one might wonder whether, under these circumstances, American efforts to secure either commercial or political benefits from trade concessions to the USSR are necessarily vain, or whether, perhaps, some might be secured if the Americans were clearer on their objectives and more subtle in their negotiating tactics.

But our present concern is the degree to which Soviet arrangements and practices meet Soviet needs. We have now to look at the suitability of the present Soviet system of foreign trade administration and pricing as well as the present techniques of decision making in this field, in a world where it is widely believed (or at least officially asserted) that the Cold War is over, negotiation has replaced confrontation, and *détente* is the catchword of the day. We shall

look specifically at the methods, both those proposed and those in use, by the
Soviet authorities in deciding on what and where and how much to trade, note
both Soviet and Western criticisms of the process, and try to arrive at our own
judgment of the success with which present Soviet needs are being met. For it
is only if present methods are inadequate that we can reasonably expect them
to be changed.

We then raise the question of the future. Soviet writers themselves recognize
that changing times and the results of past changes demand changed approaches
to fundamental questions of economic operation.

Under contemporary conditions the economic connections in our state are
rapidly becoming more complex; the interconnections and interdependencies
of economic, social, and political factors are strengthening themselves in extra-
ordinary degree.[10]

More specifically, the same author says:

The present stage in the economic and social development of the USSR increases
the demands on the methodology, theory, and practice of macroeconomic planning.[11]

Accordingly, the question of the locus and the basis of decision making with
respect to foreign trade is fundamentally different in nature from analogous
questions respecting market economies, with which Western students of international trade are familiar. To take one example:

The pure theory of international trade is concerned with the fundamental relationships which exist between two trading bodies. . . . The questions to be answered are, for example:

1.   What goods enter into international trade?
2.   Why does a country carry on trade with another?
3.   What is the level of a country's trade?
4.   On what terms does a country trade?
5.   What effects do growth, factor distortions, tariffs, quotas, etc., have on the
      volume and terms of trade?[12]

A glance at any textbook on international economics will confirm the observation that this summary indeed typifies the Western economist's approach to
international trade as an object of study. It is at the outset positive; it seeks to
explain what is; and having found that what exists does so for good reason, it
proceeds to normative conclusions and seeks to make policy recommendations
as a result of which the benefits procured unto us by trade can be defended and
expanded. But, as we have seen, in observing that private parties do trade and
assuming that they will continue to do so, Western theory does not contend with
the problem of the existence of trade as a matter of conscious governmental

choice based on considerations having nothing whatever to do with the private and individual desires of a government's subjects.

But we have seen that foreign trade exists for the Soviet Union precisely as a matter of conscious governmental choice. It is organized and run for the benefit and in the interests of the government. Even if the objective function of a linear programming model of foreign trade aims at the maximization of personal consumption over time,[13] and abstracts from the fact that about one-third of Soviet consumption is collective,[14] the objective function is a vector of consumer goods, the composition and size of which depends entirely on the decisions of the Soviet government. So does the division of the national income between present consumption and investment, as well as the degree and the time profile over which the latter will be transmuted into the former. ("Jam yesterday," as the Queen told Alice, "and jam tomorrow, but never jam today.")

Accordingly we turn our attention to the way foreign trading operations are now said to be integrated into the current and perspective plans. It will appear that that integration is done on the basis of judgments and calculations of "the economic effectiveness of foreign trade," which we then examine.

Historically, as we have already established, Soviet planning methodology avoided explicit or implicit references to foreign trade and its integration with the plan and its balances. Klinsky's 1974 study is the first, so far as this author is aware, that deals with the integration of foreign trade in the planning process. Klinsky puts "predictions about the foreign economic ties of the U.S.S.R." and "the long-term development of foreign trade and scientific-technical cooperation with foreign countries" among "the most important economic problems and scientific-technical prognoses needing elaboration for establishing the draft concepts of the long-term perspective plan"—though admittedly they come last on his list.[15]

With respect to the utility of the present system both under present circumstances and under the new conditions in which the world outside the USSR as well as the Soviet Union, seems likely to find itself, we are distinctly handicapped in making judgments by an extreme paucity of hard data.[16] Our conclusions, with respect to present conditions and even more in regard to possibly different ones, must therefore be cautious.

Before proceeding to economic analysis, however, we may usefully take explicit note of an organizational power controversy that may have been going on. The legal scholar on whose historical and organizational discussion of the foreign trade monopoly we have principally relied seems in certain passages to be replying to unnamed proponents of greater organizational freedom for Soviet enterprises from the control of the Ministry of Foreign Trade, in his rather heavy use of citations from Lenin and, even more interestingly, Stalin and Bukharin, to show that the monopoly is the true Leninist line.[17]

Thus he refers to Stalin's proposals for weakening the monopoly and Bukharin's desire to abolish it and quotes Lenin crushingly: "No tariff policy can really exist in the epoch of imperialism and of monstrous differences between beggar and unbelievably rich countries." And he goes on to cite the anchoring of the principle of monopoly in Article XI of the Constitution of 1924, and the institution of an all-union people's commissariat for foreign trade, against the wishes of the Ukrainians, to preserve unity in the face of the outside world. In this he is no doubt also answering proponents of decentralization going beyond what he considers acceptable.

In a similar way, in his more general discussion of the present Soviet trading methods, the author quoted is careful to point out the limitations on the rights of other ministries to engage in foreign relations, so long as they are not commercial—although, somewhat confusingly, he does refer to their power to promote exports.[18]

Again, in discussing the problems connected with transport and credit, he lays heavy stress on the necessity of maintaining unity.[19] The implication seems to be the necessity of the preeminence of the Ministry of Foreign Trade. And in his peroration, having reiterated all the advantages—economic and, even more strongly, political—of the foreign trade monopoly run by the Ministry of Foreign Trade, he concludes on the necessity not merely of its continuation, but of its strengthening.[20]

Criticism of the organization and operations of the ministry has begun to appear in the Soviet literature during the past five years or so, however. V.P. Gruzinov[21] says that his book, published in 1975, is based on extensive research within a number of V/O's and subdivisions of the Ministry of Foreign Trade. His criticisms are directed at operational details rather than major reforms, but like other recent publications we shall notice in a moment, his work shows increased recognition of the importance of foreign trade with capitalist countries and clear recognition of Soviet difficulties in competing on sophisticated markets for manufactured products.

Gruzinov devotes much attention to the necessity of introducing an "automatic system of administration" of foreign trade, in order to cure the many defects he finds in the present system. Sounding like a graduate of the Harvard Business School, decision trees and all, and citing several Western models,[22] he draws attention to the excessive complication of the whole foreign trade apparatus.[23]

Gruzinov's sketch[24] of the organization of the ministry indicates clearly that there is excessive layering, with the not surprising result that higher officials (deputy ministers) are too much concerned with daily operations to take any overall or a long-range view of the course of Soviet foreign trade operations. Lines of responsibility, as shown in his organizational plans, are anything but clear.

Naturally, this structure leads to insufficient delegation of authority,[25] to the avoidance of risks,[26] and to the misuse of technically trained personnel in routine jobs. It also leads to the multiplication of paper: 613,000 incoming and outgoing documents only in the subdivisions of the central apparatus of the ministry in 1972, with the number growing at 7 percent a year. The total number of pieces of paper handled by the ministry in 1972 was 22 million; in 1973, 25 million. Pushing paper took up 70 percent of the working time of "administrators in the central apparatus."[27] As one result, the process of handling correspondence is much slower than Gruzinov considers desirable and necessary.[28]

Gruzinov has a series of organizational changes, straight out of management textbooks, that he recommends for remedying such problems; but he also advances two suggestions of more direct interest.

One of these is increased emphasis on "marketing" (he uses and explains the English term) and on customer satisfaction;[29] the other is a restructuring of the ministry and of the V/O's on the basis of combining export and import activities in the same product area.[30] This latter measure he thinks will end the Soviet habit of taking foreign trade decisions in excessive isolation and will also enable the ministry to use its monopsonistic-monopolistic powers to increase its bargaining power with capitalist firms.

Gruzinov adverts[31] to the problem, which we touched on earlier, of determining what is socially beneficial in the shape in this instance of making what is useful for society profitable for every producer.[32] True, he is more or less assuming that what is socially desirable is known, which we show below to be unlikely under Soviet conditions; but in fact, as we also noted, the ministry is primarily concerned with executing orders based on that assumption. He believes that the answer is to be found in proper, administratively efficient, organization, but it does not appear from his recommendations, which are primarily structural, that he is any closer to the answer, or for that matter to the question, than the U.S. State Department has come in its efforts to solve foreign policy problems by shuffling bureaus and people. In particular, it is not immediately obvious how enlarging the ministry's chief administrations, putting them under *khozraschet*, and making them responsible for imports and exports alike in their fields would really change matters substantially, much less serve as the basis for the future administration of foreign trade.[33]

A deputy minister of foreign trade, in an anecdotal and "literary" article in *Novy Mir*,[34] presents a not dissimilar analysis of present Soviet foreign trade policies, especially as they affect trade with the developed capitalist countries. In particular, he stresses the importance of "marketing" and of follow-up service and readily available spare parts in capturing markets for machinery; he even argues for greater attention to and special training in advertising. He suggests following the examples especially of Japan and West Germany in respect of licensing agreements, to the acquisition of which from the United States he ascribes much of their postwar progress. He even hints at the desirability of importing capital.

But Smelyakov does not go into organizational details; he does, however, make it plain that he regards the present system as something less than adequate for the role he envisions for foreign trade in Soviet economic policy. And for the first time in the Soviet literature, his emphasis is on the benefits of exporting manufactured goods from another point of view than that of prestige.

A hint, if not a suggestion, for further development of Soviet capabilities in the foreign trade area is contained in a 1975 book[35] that, however, is primarily oriented toward trade between the West and the non-Soviet Eastern European countries. Here again, so far as the USSR is concerned, the emphasis is on exporting, "marketing," and, in particular, long-term transfers of capital and technology.[36] However, the book devotes more attention to the Western-imposed obstacles to these developments than to their organizational or policy implications for the USSR.

It would thus seem that there may well have been some sentiment in the Soviet Union, especially in the hey-day of the reform movement in Eastern Europe, which was so strongly influenced by the demands of foreign trade for greater flexibility and decentralization, for movement in that direction in the USSR. We may conclude, however, that the official line remains opposed to any major organizational changes in the Soviet Union's trading methods. This con-clusion is reinforced by the prominence ascribed to Lenin's role in the shaping of Soviet foreign trade organizational forms, with special mention of the early prac-tice of allowing certain enterprises to trade abroad on their own account and the subsequent decision to concentrate control in the People's Commissariat (later Ministry) of Foreign Trade, in an article in that ministry's house organ in 1964.[37]

The ninth five-year plan document[38] devotes two pages to a discussion of economic ties with developed capitalist countries, two each to consideration of trade with socialist and with developing countries, and two to the structure of foreign trade; Kosygin's report[39] devotes most of its foreign trade section to pronouncing the doom of capitalism, as shown in the latest recession in the developed world. In neither place are any useful figures or specific details given. Nor do "results" of foreign trade appear among the plan results.

However, with the publication in 1974 of a massive (787-page) volume on planning methodology, the silence of Soviet sources on the planning of foreign trade has been bent, if not broken.[40] Just over ten pages of this volume deal with the planning of foreign trade and foreign exchange operations,[41] the summary foreign exchange plan, and the effectiveness of foreign trade.[42] The section also contains a brief passage dealing with deliveries for complete plants being built out-side the Soviet Union, which does not touch on our primary concern of Soviet trade with developed countries.

Perhaps the most curious feature of this planning directive is that it does not discuss in any general sense the process by which it is decided what goods are to be procured abroad or what the parameters that delimit the range and volume of possible imports may be. As we shall see, criteria are provided for deciding whether a proposed import can and should be produced within the USSR, but the directives appear to assume that the problem is one of selecting item by item from a presumably long, indeed endless, list of proposed imports those that can and should be included in the final procurement orders. But the planning process itself does not deal with the question of the initiative to buy, or to sell, abroad.

The directives indicate rather clearly that the process of developing the foreign trade is one of negotiation and compromise:

The elaboration of the perspective and annual plans of foreign economic relations will usually proceed in two stages:
Elaboration of the basic directions (control figures) for the period being planned;
Elaboration on that basis of the developed plan.[43]

Gosplan is in charge, with the Ministry of Foreign Trade, the State Committee on Foreign Economic Relations, and "certain other," unspecified, "participating" agencies. All other government organs involved in one way or another with foreign trade or foreign exchange operations are "involved."[44] (It is interesting to speculate that among these "other agencies" are, presumably, the KGB and other intelligence agencies working abroad, the Soviet defense ministry, and those agencies of the party that earn and spend foreign exchange.)

The overall foreign activity plan, if we may call it that, consists of a commodity trade plan (the plan for the export and import of goods, to use the Soviet title), a complete projects plan, and the foreign exchange plan, always characterized in parentheses as "the balance of payments of the U.S.S.R."[45] Notably, and in keeping with the general thrust of the volume, emphasis is placed on "perspective" (five-year and longer) plans as well as on the heretofore more operationally significant annual plans. It remains, of course, to be seen whether this attempt to revive long-term planning will be more successful than previous efforts, or whether, as in the past, the shorter-range plans will be those that really count.

The emphasis in the commodity plan is on trading partners; the plan is drawn up by countries, grouped, as is the case with Soviet foreign trade statistics,[46] into socialist countries (with a subdivision for CEMA countries), developed capitalist countries, and developing countries. These groups are, however, further subdivided according to payments arrangements. The discussion[47] is not very illuminating, but suggests that developed capitalist countries and developing countries with convertible currencies are grouped together, followed by individual country tables, which are then grouped according to (less desirable) types of payment arrangements: clearing, state credits, commercial credits, blocked currency, and "other" types of accounts. This appears to relate to the general part of the plan, for developed capitalist countries are then grouped in two subdivisions, one including convertible and convertible-clearing countries, and the other those with blocked clearing accounts. Developing countries are then grouped in the same way. Those developing countries important for Soviet trade are given a separate listing.

The commodity trade plan then proceeds to specify in detail how requisitions for goods to be exported and imported are to be assembled and passed to Gosplan; there is an overall plan of deliveries for exports from ministries at all-Union and Union-republican level, and a similar overall plan for imports. There is also, curiously, a separate set of "assignments" to "basic" ministries "for developing products for sale for freely convertible currencies," which suggests that Gosplan and/or the Ministry of Foreign Trade mobilizes a sort of reserve of commodities for sale outside the predominately bilateral structure of trade agreements.

The basic guideline contained in the planning directives with respect to decisions of what to import reads as follows:

The basic requirement for the plan for the import of machinery and equipment is that equipment, machines, apparatus, and ships must be bought on foreign markets only when it is more economically profitable to buy them abroad than to produce them at home or when domestic production cannot be organized in the necessary time frame in the necessary quantities and reliable quality.[48]

Specifically, capital goods imports are to be planned in accordance with party and government decisions on priority branches of the economy, and on the basis of proposals from the appropriate agencies with "justifications." Some idea of the mass of documentation that is involved emerges from the following list of papers to be submitted:

Technical-economic justifications for the purchase of equipment, machines, apparatus, and ships with their technical description, and also with citation of the place of installation of the equipment and the period of their putting into use; conclusions of the appropriate machine-building ministries regarding the suitability of the equipment, machines, apparatus, and ships to be bought, given the contemporary levels of the development of technology and testifying that the equipment cannot be produced in the necessary timeframe and with reliable quality by domestic industry; calculations on the provision of raw materials needed for the output of products with the imported equipment; calculations as to the necessary means (in Soviet rubles) for obtaining and installing the equipment, machines, and apparatus, and for obtaining the ships with confirmation of the availability of the necessary capital investment [funds] for the purpose cited.[49]

One is inevitably reminded of the astonishment shown by the then Romanian vice-premier in charge of planning and his delegation on a visit to a major American investment banking firm in the late 1960s, when they were shown the handful of pages on the basis of which the bankers undertook the financing of a major expansion of an American steel company. They referred explicitly to the mass of documentation they required for similar investment decisions, and the vice-premier, asking for a copy of the prospectus, said, "We've got to introduce this in our country."

All this paperwork and all the interministerial arguments and jealousies that it must inevitably arouse are, it should be noted, merely the groundwork for the preliminary consideration of the feasibility of an import. We turn now to a discussion of the basis on which the Soviets determine its desirability and of the ways in which they decide on the best way of paying for it.

The Soviet rubric for this problem is "determining the economic effectiveness of foreign trade." As an authoritative author puts it: "the problem of evaluating, that is, of the quantitative determination, of the economic effectiveness of foreign trade comes down to comparing the results received by society from foreign trade with its expenditures on foreign trade operations."[50]

As we shall see, effectiveness is measured both *ex ante* and *ex post.* Concentration on effectiveness precludes, or replaces, consideration of the best ways to price exports and evaluate imports. It illustrates and furnishes further evidence of the point we have observed earlier from the numbers, that the Soviet authorities are price-takers both as buyers and as sellers. This direction of their theoretical and practical attention shows that they recognize the fact that foreign market prices are parametric.

After some years of theoretical discussion of the problem of evaluating effectiveness, an official "Temporary Methodology for Determining the Economic Effectiveness of Foreign Trade" was issued by Gosplan USSR in 1968.[51] (This work is unknown to the Soviet economic researchers in the Department of State and the CIA, according to telephone interviews in the summer of 1975, and is not listed in the Library of Congress catalogue, but a copy was kindly made available to the author by Dr. Murray Feshbach of the Department of Commerce, who obtained it on a visit to Moscow in 1974.) That the "Methodology" is still in use, and its importance, is indicated by the statement in the "Directives" that it is "intended for practical use in the economic justification of annual and perspective plans, and for individual decisions in the area of foreign trade as well."[52] The "Directives" echo, amplify, and make official the author cited above:

The economic effectiveness of foreign trade is determined by means of comparing the expenditures on the production of exported goods with the expenditures which the country would have to bear if the imported goods bought for foreign exchange earnings from exports had been produced in the country, and not imported.[53]

The object of the exercise is put in the "Methodology" as follows:

In the interests of securing the most rational commodity and geographic structure of foreign trade, and of increasing the economic effectiveness of foreign trade as a whole, it is necessary to take into account in putting together the drafts of the plans the maximum possible expansion of the production of those goods for export which will be most profitable from a macroeconomic point of view, that is, those which demand the smallest current and capital outlays for production and transport, which enjoy the greatest demand on the external market, and which secure the receipt of the maximum foreign exchange earnings.

In planning imports, it is necessary to strive toward the goal that foreign exchange earnings received from the sale of our wares abroad be spent on the purchase only of those goods which are essential for the increase of the economic and technical level of the development of production in the country and for increasing the level of living of the Soviet people.

Foreign trade must also solve the problem of supplying the needs of the economy for those goods which it is economically more profitable to buy abroad than to carry out the production at home. Under these circumstances, the economic outlays occasioned by the export of goods sold for the purchase of imports must be less than the expenditures for the domestic production of the imported goods or their substitutes.[54]

It would appear from this statement of tasks that the formulation of a single objective function for foreign trade has by no means been achieved. The criterion for listing possible exports in order of profitability, by the use of the qualifying term that we have translated as "macroeconomic" (the Russian is *narodnokhozyaistvennye*), expressly entails, as its expansion shows, the inclusion of capital charges in the "indicators," as recommended by several writers whose views we shall examine below. But the "Methodology" does not prescribe, as one might expect, the ranking of possible export goods according to their marginal net excesses of foreign exchange receipts over domestic production costs. It is true that, as we have seen in Chapter 6, Soviet domestic prices, even adjusted for capital costs, are not valid indicators of relative Soviet scarcities, not even if it were assumed that the planners' preferences could in some way substitute for consumer demand in forming a demand curve. The necessary assumption that is needed in order for Soviet prices to be "rational" in Wiles' sense—that is, "so as best to solve the scarcity problem"[55] —is that present and past wage payments, or more generally labor costs, in fact accurately reflect present planners' demand. Soviet writers do not advance the argument that relative wages reflect relative scarcities, except to the degree that the modification "socially necessary" is applied to "labor costs."

The rationale for the "Methodology," and its formulas, are laid out most extensively in G.M. Tuchkin's *Ekonomicheskaya Effektivnost Vneshnei Torgovlyi*,[56] signed to the press in February 1969. But Tuchkin is prepared to go somewhat further. He is more concerned than other authors with the interface with foreign markets and with the significance of foreign prices and hence of exchange rates.

Tuchkin has made it plain that for intelligent decisions the operative prices

must be the "prices of a single level," advocated by Bel'kin[57] and other economists, that Tuchkin calls "ideal, abstract rubles having a uniform purchasing
power."[58]   These prices correspond with the "socially necessary outlays of labor"
that, it may be argued, are a theologically acceptable Marxist camouflage for
rational shadow prices, especially those derived from linear programming
analyses of the Soviet economy. He then faces the problem of using these ideal
prices in an equation with world market prices or any prices expressed in
foreign currency. If exchange rates, Tuchkin says, are based on the whole
national output of a country and express the world market's judgment of labor
socially necessary in that country, then they can be translated into abstract
rubles and the obvious difficulty with the coefficients of effectiveness—that
numerator and denominator are in noncomparable units—disappears. But just
how this is possible, without knowing what the "true" exchange rate is even
between these two "ideal" units (of which the ideal unit of foreign exchange
appears to be in Tuchkin's mind much nearer to real world currencies than his
"abstract" ruble is to Soviet currency) is by no means clear. Presumably he
thinks that the 1:1.1 ratio between the dollar and the ruble given by the
official exchange rate is close enough to make his formula functional, and
equally, one assumes, he would translate marks or francs into dollars at the
official IMF parities obtaining at the time of his writing, this is, before floating
exchange rates became common.

   His more interesting observations have to do with the combined effectiveness of exports and imports to and from a single country, which are dealt with
under the rubric of import equivalents. Here the average domestic (ideal) ruble
value of the goods imported, which is equivalent, or should be, to what it would
cost in ideal rubles to produce it domestically, is used to value the foreign
exchange received from the export of a specific commodity. When this product
is divided by the (ideal) costs of the export in question, the result expresses the
effectiveness of an export in domestic rubles. By a similar process, the absolute
effectiveness of imports can be established. And, in a further stroke, Tuchkin
proposes multiplying each ordered absolute coefficient by the average coefficient
of the other side of the trading process—that is, exports by the average effectiveness of imports, imports by the average effectiveness of exports. In this way,
the trading of $2,000 cats for $5,000 dogs can be reduced to sanity.

   The "Methodology" notes, more or less in passing, that purely for the
purpose of the accounting of the V/Os an indicator of "budget effectiveness"
(also called the "profitability [*rentabel'nost*] of foreign trade") of imports
and exports is calculated. In each case the domestic receipts or expenditures
from the transaction is compared with the foreign exchange expenditures or
receipts, presumably reduced to or expressed in valuta rubles. The purpose is to
give an indication of the subsidies or profits in domestic rubles which are being
generated by current V/O operations; it is not suggested that these are of any
particular importance.[59]

While, as we have seen, the "Methodology" does not prescribe a single criterion for determining what and how much is to be exported, its discussion of the indicator of export effectiveness and the other considerations bearing on export decisions seem to imply a rank ordering. With respect to imports, there seems to be a clear distinction between two different types of requirements: There appears to be one set of goods whose importation is "essential" either for raising productive efficiency or for consumption purposes, and another, which we might by contrast designate as "optional," which "it is economically more profitable to buy abroad than to produce at home."[60] Where the locus of decision lies between, as well as within, these categories is not specified, nor is it clear where the initiative is to come from in examining possibilities of the second type. Presumably a production ministry or the Ministry of Trade pushes its requisition through its own hierarchy, Gossnab, Gosplan, and ultimately the Council of Ministers, whereupon the order becomes binding on the Ministry of Foreign Trade, in the case of some component, process, machine, or lot of consumption goods. But it is not obvious who has an interest in arguing that while no doubt product X can be produced at home, money, or "socially necessary labor," can be saved by buying it abroad. Within CEMA, the matter may come up chiefly in the course of trade negotiations; with respect to capitalist countries, one might expect salesmen for potential suppliers to be a major source of this sort of innovation, but this possibility is precluded by the Soviet isolation of end users from suppliers. The question must remain open. But in the absence of evidence that there is some group within the Soviet economic apparatus that has a strong direct interest in searching out economies from comparative advantage, it must be our suspicion that opportunities for real savings are often if not generally overlooked. The penchant for "autarky" that we have already noted, together with Pryor's suggestion that the socialist countries systematically undertrade, may be taken as partial confirmation of this suggestion.[61]

The calculation of these indicators of the effectiveness of imports and exports is carried out on the basis of countries and groups of countries, the latter being, for this purpose, countries whose currencies are freely exchangeable with one another. One has the impression, however, that in addition to the institutional tendency toward bilateralism we have already noted, the Soviets even in 1968 were pushed further in that direction because of the differences in purchasing power of foreign exchange receipts—which could only be important, in those prefloating days, in terms of the export prices of the trading partner. This feature of the system makes it difficult if not impossible for the Soviets to buy in the cheapest market and sell in the dearest, and must seriously reduce the utility of money, even of foreign currencies, as an information system.[62]

The indicators prescribed for practical use by the "Methodology" seem in fact to have been in use in Soviet planning practice for only a comparatively brief period, and to have been adapted, in part through the CEMA mechanism, from the practice of other Eastern European countries. True, in one of the earliest published discussions of the effectiveness of foreign trade, the author takes to task "the well-known bourgeois economist Ch. Kindleberger" for writing:

... that in the Soviet Union in the prewar years the planning of foreign trade was carried out only "by means of material balances," without any value calculations whatever, "without taking into account relative expenditures and profits from using capital and labor in exporting and import-competing branches."
    The author here displays ignorance of the concrete facts from the planning practice of the Soviet Union. But the facts bear witness to the fact that in the prewar period for many years the foreign trade organs of our country calculated indicators of the effectiveness of exports and imports, permitting a comparison of the internal and foreign trade prices of imported and exported goods. These indicators were used in forming the structure of the foreign trade of the Soviet Union.[63]

What these indicators may have been, and what period is referred to, Shagalov does not tell us. He specifically does not suggest that any such indicators were in general use at the time he wrote (1965). Another author, writing in *Vneshnaya Torgovlya* a few months earlier, offers further testimony, not only to previous Soviet neglect of the topic, but to its inadequate current treatment:

Up to now, in the economic literature, we have not been given a sufficiently precise delineation and delimitation of the concepts of effectiveness and profitability of foreign trade. ... Ordinarily no explanation whatever is given exposing the substance of these concepts.[64]

He refers to three articles, all from the early sixties. And he points out that in all comparisons of expenditures with results, or as we might say cost-benefit analyses, the costs and benefits are not given in units that permit actual comparisons.
    A Western author not unsympathetic to the Soviet Union, in one of the few Western surveys of foreign trade efficiency criteria in Eastern Europe, says that "the original Soviet doctrine of foreign trade, carried to its logical conclusion equated autarchy [*sic*] with socialism. It is therefore hardly surprising that for years Soviet theory was signally unconcerned about criteria for policy choices involving foreign trade."[65]
    More to the immediate point, the same author, writing in 1964, observes: "This is indeed a field in the economics of socialism in which Soviet students and Soviet practice avowedly look today to Central Europe for theoretical enlightenment and empirical lessons."[66] And indeed Zauberman's observation is illustrated by all the Soviet discussions of criteria of effectiveness of the midsixties and confirmed by the fact that the "Methodology" did not go beyond

the more elementary stages of sophistication, as compared with Polish, East German, and Hungarian work, and was still in official use in 1974.[67]

The first serious attempt to prescribe measures of foreign trade effectiveness in the USSR appears to have been a joint product of Shagalov, G. Smirnov, and B. Zotov in *Planovoye Khozyaistvo* in 1964,[68] where an indicator was proposed in this form:

$$K_{vt} = \frac{\Sigma Z_i}{D_i} \cdot \frac{D_e}{\Sigma Z_e} \, ,$$

where K_{vt} is the required coefficient, the Zs are expenditures on exports and "anti-import production" —that is, the cost of what would have had to be produced at home, except for the imports, and the Ds are foreign exchange earnings and costs. (There is no suggestion as to what should be done when the import in question cannot be produced within the Soviet Union. It may be that, as we have suggested earlier, "essential" imports of this sort are not regarded as subjects for decision by the foreign trade officials, whose task then is to buy them and to procure the necessary foreign exchange as efficiently as possible.) As $K_{vt} = K_i \cdot K_e$, indicators of export and import effectiveness are reckoned at the same time. These, the authors remark, would be sufficient for policy purposes if one but knew what imports were being exchanged for which exports. But as that is not the case, the calculations should be done in terms of the average value of imports being obtained from a given country or group of countries.

The authors are also careful to point out that the existing system of wholesale prices, and to a somewhat lesser but still significant degree the production costs reckoned on the standard system, distorts the effectiveness of exports as compared with their "full macroeconomic cost" calculations.[69] The trouble comes from the neglect of most of the indirect capital costs of raw materials and, though they do not say so, from the low-price policy followed with respect to basic raw materials throughout the plan era. By means of an input-output table from which they quote, they show that it is possible to compute the overall capital costs of raw material production and that when this is done, what appeared to be profitable exports of iron ore lose their attractiveness in comparison with sales of more highly processed goods. This problem, however, concerns for the most part the pricing of Soviet exports to other socialist countries and is more involved with Soviet proposals that the other Eastern European countries share in the capital investments needed to meet their raw material requirements than with Soviet trade patterns with the industrialized West—though it clearly has a bearing on proposals for foreign investment in Soviet raw material supplies to be repaid in kind.

It is difficult to comprehend just what decisions might be facilitated or improved by these computations, which are rightly characterized by Zauberman as "the oldest tool, and a rather crude tool."[70] Zauberman says that the East Germans were ranking potential exports in order of foreign-exchange earning power calculated on this basis, despite the "marginalist flavor" of doing so. There is no indication that the Soviets do such a ranking. But if the domestic prices used for comparison are meaningless, the result must be equally so.

Matters did not improve much when Shagalov published his piece cited above. Indeed, by ascribing the discovery of the advantages of trade to Marx, and by going through an elementary textbook model of comparative advantage theory, he appears to be trying to argue against autarky and for more trade. But it is interesting to note that after doing a demonstration based on labor time, he shifts to a similar one based on "international value" and more than hints that world market prices, in implied contrast to socialist domestic ones, reflect real values in the Marxist sense.

Much of Shagalov's essay is devoted to a distinction between the "direct" and the "indirect" effects of trade. The direct effects are just those under static conditions, which are our concern at the moment, while the indirect effects include dynamic results to which we turn later. Shagalov says roundly:

At the present time it does not appear possible to determine precisely the total economic effect (not only the direct, but also the indirect) from foreign trade and divide out of the general sum of the growth of the national income planned for a long perspective that part of it which is functionally connected with foreign trade and progressive movements in the economy brought about by it.[71]

Nonetheless, he argues, measurement of the direct impact of foreign trade, by calculating its foreign-exchange effectiveness, is sufficiently reliable and covers enough of the matter to be useful (he may be implying, better than none). And here he is arguing primarily for the inclusion of capital costs in the domestic-ruble outlays that are to be divided by the valuta earnings or costs to provide the required indicator. Accordingly, he recommends adoption by the Soviet Union of a CEMA formula of the following type:

$$K_{e(i)} = \frac{S + E_n K}{D_{e(i)}},$$

where $K_{e(i)}$ is the indicator of the effectiveness of an export (import) [one assumes that an individual commodity is here in question, though obviously commodities could be summed over a country or over the whole of Soviet foreign trade], S is the cost of production [*sebestoimost*] of the exported (imported) production, K is the necessary capital investment for the production of a unit of output, E_n is the normal coefficient of effectiveness [of investment], taken as uniform for all branches, $D_{e(i)}$ is the foreign exchange earnings from the export of a product (D_e) or the foreign exchange expenditure for obtaining the imported product (D_i).[72]

Shagalov knows that this formula does not take into account indirect capital costs, but argues that it can do so, by means of the coefficients of the interbranch balance, a matrix formulation where he presumably has in mind the input-output tables then becoming available for the Soviet Union. He recommends also that "full" labor costs be used instead of the more commonly employed notion of *sebestoimost*—that is, that indirect labor costs be included from the same coefficient matrices and that raw material costs be "cleaned" (the Russian text also uses quotation marks) of profits at preceding stages of production. In these suggestions, he is following eastern European practices, as reported by Boltho and Zauberman.

G. Smirnov opposes the view that capital costs should be taken into account in computing the value of exports. His exposition appears to shy consciously away from using explicitly the bourgeois notion of marginal costs, yet to imply it. He says:

One may ask, would it not be better in the given case to compare the result of importing (goods not produced internally) not with the value at internal prices of exported goods, but with the macroeconomic expenditures for their production? Obviously, such a comparison would be in most cases mistaken. In the cases we are considering, we are talking about the export of goods from current production, which existing basic funds make possible. Society has already paid the costs of creating these funds and they should be accounted for, in determining their general effectiveness for the economy, regardless of whether the capital of the given branch is being used for the production of goods for export or for the domestic market, or is even not being used at all. The price of the given commodity should be fixed considering the degree of utilization of the basic funds and the need of society for the commodity itself (taking into account the possibility of substituting other goods).[73]

Clearly the point in question here is analogous to the proposition familiar in elementary microeconomics that firms maximize profits or minimize losses by producing until marginal costs equal marginal revenue and suggests the well-known economic principle that bygones are forever bygones. And the choice between the two points of view depends on whether one is looking at the matter from a long-run or short-run standpoint. But the discussion does point up the problem with which all commentators on indicators of effectiveness seem to be grappling, and which the "Methodology" and the planning "Directives" leave open by enumerating the "other considerations" than the indicator that must be "taken into account." This is the question of how, in the absence of a set of internal prices that can be used as indicators of relative scarcities, it is possible to determine what it pays to import and to export in the long term or short. In fact, the entire discussion of indicators of effectiveness can not improperly be read as a search for objectively valid substitutes for arbitrary prices.

It is in reading Soviet lucubrations of this sort that one becomes impressed with the utility of certain tools of the Western economist, in particular the distinction between average and marginal. A Gosplan sector chief, writing in 1965, demonstrates beautifully how Soviet economic writing, and thinking, suffers from Soviet unwillingness to use them. He recognizes that it is perfectly possible to make a sensible judgment on the desirability of new technology by comparing the results of its introduction (assuming these, and the corresponding costs, can be measured with sufficient accuracy) with average branch costs. But he quite properly (and explicitly) points out that where (what he is not allowed to call) marginal costs vary as widely as they do in extractive industry and in agriculture, operating on the basis of average costs distorts the picture of the real burden to the USSR of exporting certain products. He says:

A socialist country, in expanding the internal production of raw materials or fuels for export, cannot but count in the deteriorating economic indicators (especially the increase in the cost of production) which result from the necessity of the supplementary putting into exploitation fields and ore deposits with less favorable geological-production and economic-geographical conditions.[74]

And, he argues, if the export of cheap (Ural-Volga) oil means extra investments and extra costs, which may make other fuels fifteen times as expensive, then the indicator of profitability from exporting it is "baseless." He applies the same reasoning to Caucasian cotton and to residual oil. He also notes that in evaluating the import of Polish coal into the central and northwestern regions of the USSR, one should not take as a basis the average cost of mining and transporting Pechora, Moscow Basin, and Donets coal to these regions, but the capital and transport costs of the coal for which the imported fuel is a substitute.[75] Smirnov, Zotov, and Shagalov's treatment of the indirect capital costs, neglected under the then prevailing practice, and their effect on the profitability of exports, are relevant in this context.[76]

A more serious criticism of the "full macroeconomic cost" approach that the Gosplan official stresses is the impossibility of treating indirect capital costs as a given in the equation. He points out: "Under given concrete circumstances, the use of 'imputed costs' does not ease, it makes more difficult the proper resolution of the problem, since in 'imputed costs' one presupposes a previously determined coefficient of economic effectiveness as a given quantity."[77] And, as we have seen, this given parameter, at the rate of 15 percent, is retained in the current official methodology. Probst also points out, correctly, that the effectiveness problem for foreign trade is intimately connected, logically, with that of determining the effectiveness of investment, but that while a uniform coefficient for foreign trade may well be desirable, it is not necessarily the case that this needs to be identical with the coefficient of profitability (in the sense of return on, and hence indicator of the efficiency of, capital investment in industry). He admits, however, that there is no obvious solution to the question of how to determine the appropriate level of profitability, and recommends a not entirely clear process of reliance on calculating the economies of social labor with respect to capital expenditures in each individual case.

It would seem that this approach requires the comparison of the effects of imports with their costs in export goods, which is impossible unless, as other writers imply should be done, trade is to be balanced on a strictly bilateral basis and judged country by country. Even then, we do not escape the problem of a criterion of scarcity or of opportunity cost measurement from the point of view of the Soviet economy as a whole.

Such a possibility is opened up by one proposal for a real mathematical approach to the problem of effectiveness, contained in a 1972 article by Shagalov.[78] His suggestion is fundamentally the use of an input-output table in which all the "imputed" or indirect costs of investment will be worked out. (Although all the other articles and books on foreign trade effectiveness make extensive use of mathematical formulations, with one exception, none performs or suggests the performance of any mathematical manipulations or indeed computations beyond the level of Lenin's famous "four rules of arithmetic.")

Shagalov is aware that "in theory" the model for optimization should be dynamic, but holds that simplifications (which among other things reduce the types of foreign activity to two: trade, which he seems to define to include only cash transactions, and credit operations, which he regards as a separate sort of activity) are essential and for practical purposes negligible.[79]

Shagalov takes the individual and social consumption function as his objective function and recognizes as he does so that existing data do not permit the inclusion of such social outlays as those for education, health, and so forth as endogenous factors in the model. These are taken as given, based on the plan. Available "reproducible" and "nonreproducible" "means of production" (i.e., capital and raw material capacities) are treated as restrictions, while the model requires a balance on commercial trade account with any discrepancy treated as credit expended or received.

It would be pointless to reproduce here Shagalov's system of equations, which he describes as constraints. It is a Leontieff input-output system and is made up of the following vectors and one matrix, each dated for one year of the planned period and all expressed in prices, presumably wholesale, of the base year: (1) a vector of gross outputs of i commodities produced by s techniques: (2) a matrix of input coefficients multiplying a vector of intermediate outputs; (3) vectors of exports and imports of the i's to r different markets, divided between cash and credit transactions; (4) vectors of the i's needed for investment and for personal consumption; and (5) a residual vector, giving the quantities of the i's planned for social consumption and changes in stocks. It appears to be more precise to characterize items (1) through (3) as sums of vectors over the productive techniques (the s's); it is not immediately obvious what the addition of this complication adds to the input-output table in general or indeed even what the different "techniques" referred to may mean, unless the idea is to gross up the table (which Shagalov elsewhere says has been done) so that the number of i's is sharply reduced and, for example, final products of a similar type are lumped together as one form of output but are treated in the model according to the ministries that produce them. We may leave out of consideration here the constraints, as Shagalov calls them, that permit making investment endogenous to the model. The other significant constraints are inequalities specifying that the amount of labor and the amount of raw materials needed for the production of intermediate products must be available, and the foreign exchange constraints, which we now consider.

A balance is to be worked out for each country (market) and summed to give, despite what was said earlier, a balance of cash and of credit transactions over the total of exports and imports valued in foreign exchange prices. In a footnote, Shagalov remarks that these balances can be modified by including interest charges on credits. But it is noteworthy that these foreign exchange balances are not included in the overall model, which leads one to conclude that in all probability they are worked out separately and the domestic ruble values of imports and exports, cash and credit, are parameters for the input-output calculations. Constraints are also calculated for the maximum limits of possible purchases from and by the Soviet Union on each of the markets for which trade is planned. How these magnitudes, like the values to be inserted in the foreign exchange equations for prices abroad in future years, are to be calculated Shagalov, perhaps wisely, does not explain. But it is obvious how useful the CEMA practice of (theoretically, anyway) fixed prices for a planning period must be, and one might expect that to the extent that it can reduce fluctuations on world market prices, the Soviet Union would be greatly in favor of commodity agreements among free world countries.

Shagalov indicates that the models have been constructed and used, though he cites results only from 1964. He points out that about 8 billion (presumably domestic) rubles could have been saved by optimal planning of foreign trade in that year, and compares that figure to a total turnover of 13.9 billion valuta rubles.

Of perhaps greater interest is the fact that Shagalov points specifically to the possibility of determining the marginal value of a unit of foreign exchange, as well as to the emergence from the model (through the dual of the linear programming problem) of optimal prices, which are opportunity costs at the margin.[80] (He is, of course, careful not to use the term marginal.) This possibility furnishes, as he indicates, the opportunity to calculate the effectiveness of imports and exports on a realistic and meaningful basis. The determination of the optimal foreign exchange rate—which, Shagalov says, might be obtained from an optimization model (which process, he says, would be less controversial) —can be derived by a "graphic method" that is easier to carry out.

The method requires the ordering of ratios of foreign exchange receipts for different goods with their "socially necessary costs." The ratio of effectiveness (domestic costs/valuta value)—rising for exports, falling for imports—is then plotted against increasing trade turnover with a given country. The most effective export (import) is then multiplied by the quantity the foreign market will take or supply of it; the successive goods are blocked onto the graph, and the points connected by curves, rising for exports, falling for imports. Their intersection gives the optimal exchange rate.

This system, with its emphasis on spending in the customer country what is earned there, is probably much better adapted to trade among the socialist countries, with their inconvertible currencies, than with the West. But if the developed countries are dealt with as a group and if their currencies are believed to have fixed cross rates, it is conceivable that the problems of this sort of computation are manageable. Obviously, since with the graphic method we are back to Soviet internal prices, jiggled as they may be, the actual degree of optimization achieved may be considerably less than Shagalov believes possible, though quite possibly an advance on existing methods.

Despite the adoption and apparent continued use of the official "Methodology," the variety and inconsistency of the "indicators of effectiveness" continues troublesome. The remarks about the necessity of considering other factors, which not only commentators have made but the "Methodology" itself contains, hint strongly enough at this problem. And one writer makes it explicit: "In foreign trade the indicator of effectiveness of imports is essentially deformed, and has become so multifarious in its significance that it is often hard to establish a direct dependence of results on outlays."[81]

It remains to remark that Soviet authorities are aware that their formulas and theories about effectiveness do not come to grips with the dynamic aspects of comparative advantage. They refer to the matter from time to time in passing, usually under the heading of the "other factors" that must be kept in mind in addition to contemplation of indicators of effectiveness. Thus:

It is well known that increasing the effectiveness of social production is closely related to the planned reorganization and perfecting of the branch structure of the economy, at the basis of which lies the objective demands of technical progress. Foreign trade significantly broadens the possibility for progressive movements in the economy, changing the intra-branch and interbranch proportions of production and investment.[82]

And:

In turn, foreign trade exercises a significant influence on the development of production in our country.[83]

Also:

Including the country in the system of the international division of labor making
possible the development of certain export products and curtailing the production
of branches whose output is displaced by imports, increases the share of some
types of production at the expense of others, leads to changes in the proportions
in related branches and thus affects the formation of a certain structure of the
economy . . . . Taking advantage of the benefits of the international division of
labor gives the possibility of narrowing the collection of products put out in the
given country, increasing the scale of their production, cutting their costs and
raising their quality.[84]

Or, as the academic commentator puts it:

Foreign economic ties not only give a direct effect in the form of the growth of
the national income, but also an indirect effect as a result of the active influence
on social production and on economic life in general; and the macroeconomic
importance of the indirect effect may be greater than that of the direct . . . . In
this light it is obvious that an approach to the evaluation of the economic effectiveness of foreign trade which takes as the chief, and often only, criterion the
effectiveness of the capital investments connected with it is insufficient.[85]

In short, Soviet economists are aware of the benefits of specialization and
do not refer to the Stalinist period when the other Eastern European satellites
were forced or permitted to try to develop every possible line of industry. They
are explicitly aware that costs may be reduced as a result of economies of
scale—though it is not necessarily the case that they draw the appropriate conclusions when they might imply a reduction in Soviet production.

They are equally if less vocally conscious of the benefits of importing:

The importation of means of production, in particular of equipment, opens up
the possibility of deep qualitative changes in the whole economy of a country.
The newest technology, meeting the conditions of the highest attainments of
world science and technology, machines, equipment, of foreign trade, significantly hasten technical progress in the country, secure the saving of time and
vast economies of material means.[86]

Soviet economists are aware that their indicators do not permit the quanti-
fication of qualitative differences among imports, especially but not exclusively
of technical innovations; the use of "coefficients" in the formulas is suggested,
but no hint is given of how these might be determined, especially with respect
to the structural changes in the economy that might result over time from the
adoption of innovations.[87]

Finally, Soviet economists are by no means willing to limit the benefits of
trade to comparative advantage under static conditions, but expressly wish to
consider dynamic effects. The possibility that an unprofitable line of exports

may become competitive as output expands (infant industry arguments applied to potential export industries) is mentioned by Tuchkin, among others:

It is possible that precisely broadening production for export establishes the necessary conditions for such an increase in the productivity of a given national branch of industry (as to make the export of a less effective product desirable).[88]

But nowhere in the literature is there a discussion of the basis for deciding on specialization of this sort. We are not here concerned with the method of wrestling with the problem within CEMA, although a casual acquaintance with the progress of that body seems to leave no doubt that the Soviet Union will specialize in everything and the other Eastern European countries will get further and further away from their Stalin-imposed autarky—except, perhaps, for Romania, whose Galati steelworks stands as a proof that Stalin's soul, or at least his economic philosophy, goes marching on.[89] And the opportunities for the USSR to specialize in relation to Western markets are probably limited to raw material extraction for the foreseeable future.

We turn now to a consideration of the views of Western authors on the effectiveness of the Soviet foreign trading system and its criteria for specific and general economic decisions.

Notes

1. An Assistant Secretary of State for Economic Affairs expressed to the author in the late fifties the view that it was absurd and unnecessary for the United States government to concern itself with the impact on the Soviet economy, and hence on the military and economic power of the Soviet Union, of imports of capital goods embodying advanced technology. His argument was that the USSR also gives up resources in return and that so long as the Western trading partner receives a fair price, there is no net advantage to the Soviet Union. The argument assumes, of course, that the prices at both ends of the transaction represent the marginal utility of the goods exchanged. But as we have seen, this is not the case: Soviet prices do not measure the value of the resources used in making Soviet export goods or the value of imported goods to the Soviet economy. Nor do world market prices or American export prices necessarily correspond to the strategic or social utility of the goods exported. Hence there is no reason to conclude that equivalents, in terms of strategic or social utility, are being exchanged.

2. See Chapter 3 of this volume, especially the explicit statement of G. Smirnov.

3. Ibid., p. 96.

4. A. Borisenko, "K Voprosu ob Effektivnosti Sotsialisticheskoi Vneshnei Torgovlyi," *Vneshnaya Torgovlya,* no. 10 (1964), p. 7.

5. A. Probst, "Ob Opredeleniyi Ekonomicheskogo Effekta Vneshnei Torgovlyi," *Planovoye Khozyaistvo,* no. 11, (1965), p. 39.

6. G. Ladygin and I. Motorin, "Raschet Effektivnosti Eksporta Toplivo-Syrivykh Tovarov," *Vneshnaya Torgovlya,* no. 9, 1967, p. 18.

7. G. Smirnov, B. Zotov, and G. Shagalov, "Otsenka Ekonomicheskoi Effektivnosti Vneshnei Torgovlyi," *Planovoye Khozyaistvo,* no. 8 (1964), p. 28.

8. G.M. Prokhorov, *Vneshe-ekonomicheskii Svayzi i Ekonomicheskii Rost Sotsialistisheskikh Stran* (Moscow: Mezhdunarodnye Otnosheniya, 1972), p. 240.

9. See U.S. Department of Commerce, *U.S.-Soviet Commercial Agreements* (Washington, D.C.: Government Printing Office, 1973), pp. 76-77; Letters, Secretary of State Dean Rusk to the Speaker of the House and the President of the Senate, May 11, 1966, transmitting the "East-West Trade Relations Act of 1966;" State Department Press Release No. 107, May 11, 1966; and addresses by Assistant Secretary of State Anthony M. Solomon, October 21, 1965, especially pp. 8 and 9, and March 2, 1967, p. 6, Department of State Press Releases No. 249, October 20, 1965, and No. 43, March 2, 1967.

10. A.I. Klinsky, *Planirovaniye Ekonomicheskogo i Sotsialnogo Razvitiya* (Moscow: Mysl, 1974), p. 12.

11. Ibid., p. 11.

12. R. Shone, *The Pure Theory of International Trade,* Macmillan Studies in Economics (London and Basingstoke: The Macmillan Company, 1972), p. 11.

13. B. Shagalov, "Optimalnoye Planirovaniye Vneshnei Ekonomicheskikh Svyazei," *Voprosy Ekonomiki,* no. 11 (1972), p. 97.

14. G. Smirnov, "K Voprosu ob Otsenki Ekonomicheskoi Effektivnosti Vneshnei Torgovlyi SSSR," *Voprosy Ekonomiki,* no. 12 (1965), p. 97.

15. Klinsky, *Planirovaniye,* p. 34.

16. See the Proposed Research of Joseph Berliner, Robert Campbell, and Herbert Levine for an indication of major areas of ignorance as well as the comments of Marshall Goldman and Paul Marer, in Robert W. Campbell and Paul Marer, eds., *East-West Trade and Technology Transfer* (Bloomington: Indiania University Press, 1974), pp. 25-28 and 45-46. Also see Barry L. Kostinsky, *Description and Analysis of Soviet Foreign Trade Statistics* (Washington, D.C.: U.S. Department of Commerce, FER-No. 5, 1974), for the most recent treatment of obscurities in this field of statistics.

17. V.S. Pozdnyakov, *Gosudarstvennaya Monopoliya Vneshnei Torgovlyi v SSSR* (Moscow: Mezhdunarodnye Otnosheniya, 1969), pp. 31-33, 43, and 49-51.

18. Ibid., pp. 97-98.

19. Ibid., p. 173.

20. Ibid., p. 197.

21. V.P. Gruzinov, *Upravleniye Vneshnei Torgovlyi* (Moscow: Mezhdunarodnoye Otnosheniya, 1975), p. 3.

22. Ibid., p. 84.

23. Ibid., p. 76.

24. Ibid., p. 73ff.

25. Ibid., p. 131 and p. 57.

26. Ibid., p. 59.

27. Ibid., p. 162.

28. Ibid., p. 137-8.

29. Ibid., p. 65-67.

30. Ibid., p. 113 and p. 77.

31. Ibid., p. 95.

32. Cf. Douglas C. North and Robert Paul Thomas, *The Rise of the Western World* (Cambridge: The University Press, 1973), pp. 6-8.

33. Gruzinov, *Upravleniye*, p. 113.

34. N. Smelyakov, "Delovye Vstrechi," *Novy Mir,* 1973, p. 203.

35. A.M. Voinov, V.A. Lokshin, and L.A. Rodina, *Ekonomicheskie Otnosheniya Mezhdu Sotsialisticheskimi i Razvitimi Kapitalisticheskimi Stranami* (Moscow: Nauka, 1975), pp. 192-84.

36. Ibid., pp. 46-47.

37. K. Bakhtov, "Monopoliya Vneshnei Torgovlyi SSSR i Razvitiye ee Organizatsionnykh Form," *Vneshnaya Torgovlya,* no. 10 (1964), p. 46.

38. N.K. Baibakov, ed., *Gosudarstvennyi Plan Razvitiya Narodnogo Khozyaistva SSSR na 1971-1975 gg* (Moscow: Isdatelstvo Politicheskoi Literatury, 1972), pp. 327, 335.

39. Ibid., pp. 52-56.

40. Gosplan SSSR, *Metodicheskie Ukazaniya k Razrabotku Gosudarstvennykh Planov Razvitiya Narodnogo Khozyaistva SSSR* (Moscow: Ekonomika, 1974). Cited hereafter as "Directives."

41. Ibid., pp. 490-96.

42. Ibid., pp. 598-600.

43. Ibid., p. 591.

44. Ibid.

45. Ibid., p. 594.

46. Barry F. Kostinsky, *Description and Analysis of Soviet Foreign Trade Statistics* (Washington, D.C.: U.S. Department of Commerce, 1974), p. 9.

47. "Directives," p. 592.

48. Ibid., p. 595.

49. Ibid.

50. Smirnov, "K Voprosu," p. 94.

51. Gosplan SSSR, *Vremennaya Metodika Opredeleniya Ekonomicheskoi Effektivnosti Vneshnei Torgovlyi,* 1968, mimeographed. Cited hereafter as "Methodology."

52. "Directives," p. 600.

53. Ibid.

54. "Methodology," pp. 1-2.

55. P.D.J. Wiles, "Are Adjusted Rubles Rational?" *Soviet Studies,* vol. VII, no. 2 (October 1955), p. 143.

56. G.M. Tuchkin, *Ekonomicheskaya Effektivnost Vneshnei Torgovlyi,* (Moscow: Mezhdunarodnye Otnosheniya, 1969).

57. V.D. Belkin, *Tseny Yedinogo Vrovnya i Ekonomicheskie Ismereniye naikh Osnov* (Moscow: Izdatelstvo Ekonomicheskoi Literatury, 1963).

58. Tuchkin, *Ekonomiheskaya,* p. 156.

59. "Methodology," p. 2. Cf. Prokhorov, *Vneshe-ekonomicheskii,* p. 242, and Tuchkin, *Ekonomicheskaya,* p. 52.

60. "Methodology," ibid. Cf. Prokhorov, ibid., p. 241: "We may mention that importation, taken preliminarily, is to be divided into two sorts: (1) necessary, including goods which are not produced in the country, and (2) alternative, when the import of goods is dictated by economic advantage, that is, the domestic production of these goods costs more than the export equivalent for paying for them."

61. Frederick L. Pryor, *The Communist Foreign Trade System* (Cambridge, Mass.: MIT Press, 1963); and Abram Bergson, "On Prospects for Communist Foreign Trade," in Alan A. Brown and Egon Neuberger, *International Trade and Central Planning: An Analysis of Economic Interactions* (Berkeley and Los Angeles; University of California Press, 1968), pp. 385-86 and 387-89.

62. K. Brunner and A.H. Meltzer, "The Uses of Money in the Theory of an Exchange Economy," *American Economic Review,* vol. LXI, no. 5 (December 1971), p. 784. Cf. Michael Kaser, *Soviet Economics* (New York: World University Library, McGraw-Hill, 1970), pp. 93-95.

63. G. Shagalov, "Ekonomicheskaya Effektivnost Vneshnei Torgovlyi Sotsialisticheskikh Stran," *Voprosy Ekonomiki,* no. 6 (1965), p. 95.

64. Borisenko, "K Voprosu," p. 8.

65. Alfred Zauberman, "The Criterion of Efficiency of Foreign Trade in Soviet-type Economies," *Economica,* N.S. XXXI, no. 121 (February 1964), p. 5.

66. Ibid.

67. Andrea Boltho, *Foreign Trade Criteria in Socialist Economies* (Cambridge: The University Press, 1971), pp. 62-64, summarizes and criticizes eastern European doctrines and, occasionally, practices through the end of the 1960s.

68. Smirnov, Zotov, and Shagalov, "Otsenka," p. 22.

69. Ibid., p. 31.

70. Zauberman, "The Criterion," p. 6.

71. Shagalov, "Economicheskaya," p. 96.

72. Ibid., p. 98.

73. Smirnov, "K Voprosu," p. 95.

74. Probst, "Ob Opredeleniyi," p. 42.

75. Ibid., p. 42.

76. Smirnov, Zotov, and Shagalov, "Otsenka," p. 28.

77. Probst, "Ob Opredeleniyi," p. 44.

78. G. Shagalov, "Optimalnoye," p. 63.

79. Ibid., p. 65.

80. Ibid., p. 71.

81. Prokhorov, *Vneshe-ekonomicheskii,* p. 229.

82. Smirnov, Zotov, and Shagalov, "Otsenka," p. 26.

83. Smirnov, "K Voprosu," p. 94.

84. Shagalov, "Economicheskaya," p. 93.

85. Prokhorov, *Vneshe-ekonomicheskii,* p. 229.

86. Shagalov, "Economicheskaya," Emphasis added.

87. Prokhorov, *Vneshe-ekonomicheskii,* p. 245.

88. Tuchkin, *Ekonomicheskaya,* p. 165.

89. See John Michael Montias, *Economic Development in Communist Rumania* (Cambridge, Mass., and London, England: MIT Press, 1967), pp. 203-30; Montias, *Background and Origins of the Rumanian Dispute with COMECON, Soviet Studies* XVI, 2 (October 1964); and Michael Kaser, *COMECON: Integration Problems of the Planned Economies,* 2nd ed. (London: Oxford University Press, 1967), pp. 209-14.

How Well is the Soviet Apparatus Doing Its Job?

The indicators of the effectiveness of foreign trade we looked at in the last chapter may be divided into two classes: those that are in actual use and those that are suggested, recommended, or hoped for. These categories correspond to Edward Hewett's division of planning systems into "primitive" and "optimal,"[1] although a better word for the latter class might be "optimizing." The crucial point of the distinction is that primitive systems work on the "method of balances" we discussed earlier, while optimizing systems would, if they existed, be a form of "perfect computation" deriving their parametric directions from a computerized, linear programming model of the economy and making their decisions on the basis of Belkin-type "prices of one level," which are shadow prices resulting from computations of this sort. But this sort of "Π in the sky" remains beyond reach.

The distinction applies at both levels of concern to us: We are primarily interested in the planning of Soviet foreign trade with developed countries, but that planning is a function and an expression of the general economic planning system of which it is a part and to whose purposes it is subservient. And in the case of the Soviet Union, foreign trade is not and has not been, as it has in the more developed CEMA countries, an engine of rationality or, if the term be preferred, of optimality in planning. But the indicators of effectiveness that we have been considering in their Soviet context, as we saw, are derivative from Eastern European efforts to grapple with questions that are different in kind from those the Soviet authorities face. As a preliminary to our consideration of the suitability of these indicators and the planning system for foreign trade that uses them, we should glance at the reasons why the questions they were developed to answer are different from those the Soviet authorities are using them to answer.

Primarily, the differences result from the fact that the European CEMA countries are both economically and historically more involved with foreign trade than the USSR. Their choice is not between trading and autarky; it is between trading with CEMA and trading with the West. Moreover their interests, their traditions, their geographic situation (most markedly with East Germany, but scarcely less so as regards Poland, Czechoslovakia, and Hungary) lead them to hanker for dealings with the West. And the continuing presence of businessmen familiar with pretakeover ways makes the process both easier and more attractive than it is for the USSR.[2] There is no use overlooking, either, the constraint imposed on them, and the longings and aspirations that work against it, by their political and military subordination ot the Soviet Union.

Not surprisingly, this state of affairs gives effectiveness indicators a role in East European planning and trading with a quite different emphasis from its function in the Soviet system. For example, there has been no great concern in the Soviet analyses we have examined with the problem of the foreign exchange costs of exports leading to indicators of net foreign exchange effectiveness. Yet this aspect was crucial—perhaps because it was so readily apparent as a problem and so easily susceptible of measurement—in Eastern Europe.

Some indication of the dimensions of this matter may be gleaned from an early experience of the Yugoslav planners when they tried to introduce a market trading system of foreign trading. They were eager to increase their exports of manufactured products and at the same time (the early fifties) were anxious to build up trading relations with Turkey, a new ally in the now-forgotten Balkan Pact. So they trumpeted as a great achievement the sale of 2,000 railway cars to Turkey. And then it came out—it was frequently talked about in Belgrade—that they had spent more money, in Belgian francs, for brake and coupling systems for the cars than they earned in Turkish lire. And there was no doubt which currency was more valuable, whatever the official exchange rates.

So they took action. They forbade the sale within Yugoslavia of imported goods at foreign prices for foreign currency, unless the currency in question was that in which the goods were bought. And hence this author was not allowed to buy Dunlop tires, a sterling import, for dollars, until the matter reached the attention of the appropriate bureaucrat, whereupon the regulations were changed. This incident, which has never been reported in print, indicates at once the difficulty of foreseeing every contingency and the dangers of oversimplified, mechanical tests of effectiveness.

Peter Wiles[3] quotes Alec Nove's account of Bolivian hyperpoly (overtrading) resulting from subsidizing imports to make manufactures "profitable" and an account from *The Economist*[4] of "profitable" sales of British eggs, the product of subsidized feedstuffs, to Germany—sales that did not in fact bring in as much foreign exchange as had been spent for the chicken feed. Administrative decisions are not silly in centrally planned economies alone.

Hence criticisms of the East European effectiveness indicators that center around their utility for small countries trading extensively—and that is the standpoint of the Western commentators who have dealt with the problem—are irrelevant to the Soviet situation. We shall, therefore, extract from these criticisms only those that apply to a large, nearly self-sufficient country that is not importing raw materials on a large scale for the purpose of processing them and exporting them profitably. Having done that, we shall look at the degree to which these criteria are relevant for decision-making purposes in such an economy and then take note of one or two observations of our own.

Boltho[5] shows that the use of average instead of marginal costs can easily

lead to erroneous specialization, the result of a misreading of where real comparative advantage lies, in the case of decisions to expand the output of manufactured goods under conditions of either increasing or decreasing cost. This
point is that toward which Borisenko was going in his argument against ignoring
rising costs in extractive industries and agriculture.[6] Pryor, who deals largely
with the DDR, makes the same point.[7] Wilczynski touches on it,[8] but is more
concerned with the general difficulty of using irrational internal prices to yield
correct solutions for any efficiency problem. Holzman's discussion of the
problem does little more than rehash Boltho and other authors.[9]

The authorities generally find two other sources of confusion in the system
of efficiency indicators, and as we have seen, Soviet commentators are conscious of both of these. One is the question of properly accounting for capital
costs and for economic rents; the other is the inclusion or exclusion of turnover tax. It is, indeed, the rectification of Soviet errors in these two areas that
is at the heart of Abram Bergson's efforts to "adjust" the rubble.[10] The question
that lies at the bottom of the argument that has gone on for years over the
"rationality" of Soviet pricing—which we cannot deal with here—is quite simply
whether these are the primary sources of difficulty in using Soviet internal
prices, however "adjusted," as satisfactory measures of opportunity costs and
relative scarcities. We concluded in Chapter 6 that this is not possible, and
nothing is to be gained by flogging the problem further.

It would, then, appear to be the consensus of Soviet and Western scholars
alike that the criteria actually in use for judging the effectiveness of Soviet foreign
trade are incapable of producing quantitatively reliable results, even under static
conditions. We would add that the planning and decision-making process, as we
know it from the "methodology" and the "Directives," assume that future prices
and quantities are known and that future receipts and expenditures can be
planned. The assumption doubtless holds with respect to trade with other
socialist countries, especially CEMA members, under long-term agreements with
prices that normally remain fixed. (Although *The Economist* reported[11] that the
USSR is raising the price of its oil exported to CEMA countries by 130 percent.)
But it cannot hold with respect to agricultural imports and exports, as the Soviet
grain deals of 1963, 1972, and 1975 bear witness, even with respect to quantities,
and it is even less tenable with respect to prices. It would be interesting to
calculate annual fluctuations in total receipts and unit prices in Soviet trade
with developed market economies for major commodities, in order to see
whether, and how far, actual outturns deviate from what might have been expected on the basis of simple extrapolations.

If the present "primitive" methods for planning and judging the results of
foreign trade offer, then, little hope that the process makes recognizable sense
from a theoretical point of view (we shall consider the practical implications
later), is there some hope that "perfect computation" may do better?

In view of the fact that despite reams of paper on the subject the Soviet

Union shows no disposition to alter the main lines of its overall planning policies and that there is no evidence it is doing so with respect to foreign trade,[12] the question may seem academic. As we noted in Chapter 6, the "reform" is one that never was.[13] The political obstacles are well-known, but, in the author's opinion, normally underestimated:

What I'm getting at is that organizations, specially large organizations, which are merrily going along their way, making money, being quite successful; these organizations aren't gonna change for the sake of change; they aren't going to change until the pressures on them become so great that they *have* to change.[14]

The question has been asked whether Soviet trade history is consistent with Heckscher-Ohlin theories of factor proportions in international trade.

Boltho[15] points to a "Leontieff paradox" in Soviet foreign trade and cites the assertion of Smirnov, Zotov, and Shagalov:

It is sufficient to note that according to tentative calculations the capital intensity of industrial products exported by the Soviet Union exceeds the capital intensity of industrial imports by almost 1.5 times.[16]

We may overlook the cautious formulation, since the authors give no indication of the calculations on which it is based, and since in any case the measurement of capital intensity (and, indeed, even its meaning) is not an easy problem in market economies and is quite impossible in command ones. We note also that there is no indication that the trade in question is confined to trade with developed economies, and the techniques of negotiating intra-CEMA trade,[17] with their practice of agreeing on quantities before prices (which is, after all, a logical consequence of trading on the basis of the balances of primitive planning) makes the whole concept of prices difficult to apply, as we have amply demonstrated.

Thus the paradox in question may not exist, it may apply only to manufactured goods and thus eliminate a large part of Soviet trade, or it may apply only globally and not with respect to Soviet-free market trade. It is in any case irrelevant to the decisions and judgments the Soviet authorities have to make. For what it may be worth, we may note the elaborate efforts of Rosefielde to demonstrate that Soviet trade with the West does indeed follow Heckscher-Ohlin theory.[18] Whether one wishes to accord much credence to his calculations, considering that he uses per capita GNP as his "factor availabilities proxy"[19] and considering the views expressed by Caves[20] on the meaning of factors of production, is another question.

For whatever the theoretical and statistical arguments, it remains true, as Wiles has remarked, that the USSR does import bananas and export timber. Our problem, then, is not one of the degree to which Western theory explains or justifies Soviet practices, but rather whether those practices do what the Soviets want them to. Or, more precisely, whether the admitted inefficiencies in those practices are sufficient to cause major changes in them.

Consider, for example, the structure of Soviet trade with the West, both from a static-efficiency and a dynamic point of view.

If, as we have argued, the relevant Soviet imports are (1) those made to make up for shortfalls, anticipated or not and (2) high technology goods, while exports consist of whatever is most easily available to cover the costs of imports, then the only efficiency question that arises with respect to foreign trade is: Could these necessities have been obtained at lower costs in exports? If price considerations are secondary (if that), the question is not very important, and, *a fortiori* revelations that better deals might have been made are not likely to cause changes in what is, from every other point of view, obviously a successful operation. Indeed, it is fairly generally believed that in the 1972 grain trans-actions, Soviet traders used their monopsony position and their ability to keep their intentions secret not only to prevent a price rise as they came into the market, but even to extract a government subsidy from the United States. The magnitude of the transaction even suggests that whatever putative losses they may have suffered in earlier years, the gains from that one deal may well have made up for them.

From a slightly different point of view, one may not unreasonably con-clude that the Soviet situation as price-takers on both the import and the export side is perfectly satisfactory. They have been able to profit from such noncommunist oligopolies or monopolies as the diamond cartel and OPEC, and from the Western monetary system, all of which either secured monopoly gains for them when they began to use the Western apparatus or markedly raised their gains, without costing the USSR anything in the way of political ill-will. The fact, which would appear obvious, that these arrangements are irrational from the Western point of view does not imply that they are invidious from a Soviet one.

It would, indeed, appear that the primary obstacle to the attainment of Soviet goals from trade has been the strategic embargo imposed by the West following the outbreak of the Korean War, rather than any deficiencies in the Soviet procurement system. The effectiveness of the embargo—whether one considers it from the point of view of sheer mechanics (did it stop exports considered undesirable?) or from that of its putative goal (did it slow the growth of Soviet military strength?)—is hotly debated. Unfortunately, most of the evidence on both counts is classified information. With respect to the first, it can be said, though somewhat dogmatically, that the Soviets claim to have secured everything they really wanted, and there has been evidence in certain specific instances that bears out the claim, though there is none known to the writer to suggest that in other cases the embargo has not in fact worked. On the second point, all that can be said here is that there have been cases in which Western countries have flatly defied COCOM agreements, and others, much more numerous, in which they have insisted on changes in the rules that were not entirely acceptable to all concerned. What is perhaps more to the point, in this author's view, is the fact that the logic of the embargo system has never been persuasive. It has, to put the matter as succinctly as possible, never faced the question of time as it relates to strategic exchanges. It is much easier to argue for banning the export of a commodity with direct or immediate military applications than to work out the long-term effects of a contribution to the overall economic capacity of the Soviet Union. It is the latter calculation that is of primary importance to Soviet generals and their political masters.[21] In any case, it can be argued that the primary contribution of the West to the Soviet economic system is much less the provision of specific commodities, services, and technology—although the utility of a source of last resort and of technological shortcuts should not be underestimated—than the provision of a model for internal economic development.

From a dynamic point of view, there are two major areas in which change could benefit the Soviet Union. The first has to do with the structure of trade: Simply put, it is the consideration that full participation under normal terms in the world trading system would bring the USSR significant increases in social well-being or, more precisely, in global output through the usual processes of specialization. This argument depends on the notion that free competition on free markets maximizes welfare—a proposition that is much more widely accepted in the West than it is convincingly proved. But it is in any case irrelevant. There is no conceivable way—no way imaginable by this author, at least and none with which he is familiar—in which a planned economy can effectively simulate a market one, and no earthly reason why it should.

Clearly, in the case of foreign trade we have seen ample evidence that trying to make the Soviet economy imitate a market economy, with consumers' demands working through traders' profits to determine the volume and structure of trade in such a way as to maximize consumer satisfaction, is unthinkable without a similar restructuring of the whole economy whose servant foreign trade now is. And there is not only no evidence to suggest that the Soviet Union is going in this direction, but every indication, including the invasion of Czechoslovakia, that it will not permit any such development.

The reasons may be simply and authoritatively stated:

That the social engine has been effective in its primary tasks—industrialization, reconstruction, maximization of military might—few will deny.[22]
    The CPE (centrally planned economy) turns out to be the prime element of rigid Muscovite control in eastern Europe, and of highly centralized control of the USSR by the Soviet Communist Party.[23]

As Solzhenitsyn argued, even if controls are relaxed to some extent:

. . . you [the Soviet leaders] will still have absolute and impregnable power, a separate, strong, and exclusive party, the army, the police force, industry, transport, communications, mineral wealth, a monopolized foreign trade, an artificial rate of exchange for the ruble . . . .[24]

But:

To divest the Communists of their ownership rights would be to abolish them as a class. To compel them to relinquish their other social powers, so that workers may participate in sharing the profits of their work—which capitalists have had to permit as a result of strikes and parliamentary action—would mean that Communists were being deprived of their monopoly over property, ideology, and government.[25]

That is what is at stake. But then:

The urgent political need for improved economic efficiency presents the regime with a terrible dilemma. If they marketize they run the risk of losing control. If they limit reform to the improvement of central planning they must face the dangers of continuing instability.[26]

Why?

The emergence of money as a homogeneous universal medium of exchange goes hand in hand with its reinstatement as a universal standard of value, the essential precondition of rational economic calculation.[27]

What is much more to the point, the use of money as Holesovsky envisions it confers both economic and intellectual power on "outsiders" from the planning mechanism: Their decisions will influence developments once under the control (at the command) of the planners; and the ability to calculate will open the door to independent, scientific questioning of the planners' fiats.

This has been recognized by communists, if not by Soviet ones. A leading Polish economic official argues that the centralized system can only work for "a small number of high-priority projects."[28] More generally, "the existence of a long-term economic plan, with its internal consistency, coordination of ends and means, and balanced structure, could not be acceptable to a despotic government."[29]

Hence either perfect competition or perfect computation (were the former attainable and the latter possible) would destroy the position of the Communist Party in the Soviet Union and the USSR in CEMA, in return for benefits that must be uncertain and are clearly not necessary. The Soviet economic system is not about to collapse; on the contrary, it seems to be certain of salvation from the West if it shows any signs of needing or wanting it. Change of the foreign trading system is impossible, as well as futile, without changes in the system of which it is a part. And that system is not in such straits as to demand the destruction of everything it was built for in order that it be saved.

Notwithstanding all this, it can be argued that there is a second way in which normalization of its foreign trading practices, if that were possible without the consequences we have just looked at, could benefit the Soviet Union. That way would be the full integration of the Soviet, and the other communist, economies into the world trading and financial system on a genuinely equal basis. If the basic philosophy that has guided the United States since World War II in international economic matters is sound, the result would be an increase in world-wide levels of well-being and the strengthening of peace—on updated Cobdenite lines. But there is no visible reason to think that the Soviet rulers would abandon what, as we have seen, is a successful policy of suboptimization at their level for so utopian, and indeed anti-Marxist, an idea.

The conclusion that emerges from our study of the Soviet system of administering and pricing its foreign trade, then, is simple if not very encouraging: That system may make little sense according to the canons of orthodox Western economics, but it is a splendid example of the successful pursuit of mercantilist ends if by nonmercantilist means. Its inefficiencies entail costs, but its structure ensures that those costs are minimal for those in power and are borne by people who have little power to influence their rulers. There is no reason to expect it to change in essentials, and no reason to expect changes in nonessentials to improve matters significantly from the point of view of the Western world.

Notes

1. Edward A. Hewett, *Foreign Trade Prices in the Council for Mutual Economic Assistance* (New York: Cambridge University Press, 1974), p. 155.

2. While the author is not directly acquainted with the fact with respect to other Eastern European countries, it was quite obvious in Yugoslavia in the early fifties that the opportunity to travel to and make purchases in the West was one of the major attractions toward working in foreign trade enterprises. It was equally apparent that the presence of "bourgeois survivals" in the foreign-trading firms made dealing with them much easier for foreigners; no doubt these specialists were invaluable to their communist superiors as well.

3. P. J. D. Wiles, *Communist International Economics* (Oxford: Basil Blackwell, 1968), p. 429.

4. *The Economist*, May 4, 1957.

5. Andrea Boltho, *Foreign Trade Criteria in Socialist Economies* (Cambridge: The University Press, 1971), pp. 73-75.

6. See Chapter 8 of this volume.

7. Frederick L. Pryor, *The Communist Foreign Trade System* (Cambridge, Mass.: MIT Press, 1963), p. 107.

8. Jozef Wilczynski, *The Economics and Politics of East-West Trade* (New York: Frederick A. Praeger, 1969), p. 327.

9. Holzman, *Foreign Trade Under Central Planning* pp. 16-20.

10. A. Bergson, *Soviet National Income and Product in 1937* (New York: Columbia University Press, 1953), Chapter IV.

11. *The Economist*, July 5, 1975, p. 125.

12. Cf. Hewett, *Foreign Trade Prices*, pp. 154-55: "Undue administrative interference will negate the beneficial effects of the entire system, and elegant optimization models or not, there will be no optimum achieved." And his footnote: "Soviet planners are the worst offenders in this area. There is a tremendous overallocation of intellectual resources into the models of optimization with a complete neglect of meaningful systems for securing their implementation. Of course this is a difficult political problem because Gosplan bureaucrats have a strong lobby in the Soviet Union; any Soviet economist who studies optimum management systems is engaging in a very long-term investment if his conclusions are wrong."

13. Cf. Gertrude E. Schroeder, "Soviet Economic Reform at an Impasse," *Problems of Communism*, July-August 1971; Schroeder "Soviet Economic Reforms—A Study in Contradictions," *Soviet Studies*, July 1968; and Radoslav Selucky, *Economic Reforms in Eastern Europe: Political Background and Economic Significance* (New York: Praeger Publishers, 1972). The literature is extensive.

14. Peter Cohen, *The Gospel According to the Harvard Business School* (New York: Penguin Books, 1973), p. 205.

15. Boltho, *Foreign Trade*, p. 76.

16. G. Smirnov, B. Zotov, and G. Shagalov, "Otsenka Ekonomicheskoi Effektivnosti Vneshnei Torgovlyi," *Planovoye Khozyaistvo*, no. 8 (1964), p. 29.

17. Cf. Wiles, *Communist International Economics*, p. 159; and Pryor, *The Communist Foreign Trade System*, p. 135.

18. Steven Rosefielde, *Soviet International Trade in Heckscher-Ohlin Perspective* (Lexington, Mass.: D. C. Heath, 1973), p. 51 ff.

19. Ibid., p. 60.

20. Richard E. Caver, *Trade and Economic Structure: Models and Methods* (Cambridge, Mass.: Harvard University Press, 1963), Chapter IV; 1, pp. 93-101, "The Meaning of Factors of Production."

21. William E. Odom, "Who Controls Whom in Moscow." *Foreign Policy*, no. 19 (Summer 1975), especially pp. 111-13.

22. Gregory Grossman, ed., *Value and Plan: Economic Calculation and Organization in Eastern Europe* (Berkeley and Los Angeles: University of California Press, 1960), p. 1, "Introduction."

23. R. V. Burks, "The Political Implications of Economic Reform," in M. Bornstein, ed., *Plan and Market: Economic Reform in Eastern Europe* (New Haven and London: Yale University Press, 1973), p. 393.

24. Aleksandr Solzhenitsyn, "Letter to the Soviet Leaders," *The Times* (London), March 3, 1974.

25. Milovan Djilas, *The New Class* (New York: Frederick A. Praeger, 1957), p. 45.

26. Burks, "The Political Implications," p. 385.

27. Vaclav Holesovsky, "Financial Aspects of the Czechoslovak Reform," in Gregory Grossman, ed., *Money and Plan–Financial Aspects of East European Economic Reforms* (Berkeley and Los Angeles: University of California Press, 1968), p. 94.

28. Wlodzimierz Brus, *The Economics and Politics of Socialism* (London: Routledge and Kegal Paul, 1973), p. 25.

29. Moshe Lewin, "The Disappearance of Planning in the Plan," *Slavic Review*, June 1973, p. 287.

10

Who Will Bell the Cat—And How?

If the analysis of this book is at least approximately correct, it follows that the Soviet Union has a well-designed capacity for exploiting the world trading system and the market economies of the free world, to use an outmoded but perhaps not altogether misleading designation, to its vast advantage. What conclusions may we accordingly draw for—that is, what policy measures seem to be required of—the United States and its allies? The purpose of this chapter is to suggest some of the possibilities.

The problem, to restate and summarize our conclusions, is this: The Soviet Union, through its concentration in the hands of its state apparatus, under the control of the Communist Party's Central Committee, of all its external economic dealings, is in a position to divide and conquer the outside trading world by playing both nation against nation and company against company. How effectively it does this is another question. It may be true, as a U.S. State Department officer once at least half-seriously argued, that the USSR cannot accurately determine what its real interests are nor decide what specific procurements from the outside will contribute most to their advancement. But it does not appear to follow, as he concluded, that we should simply let the Soviets do what they please, on the assumption that whatever they do will be a mistake.

Even if following that course would do the most damage to the Soviets, moreover, it would still not enable the United States, or the West, to use its economic power effectively in its own interests. And the first step to be taken in trying to assess the policy implications of the present state of affairs is, surely, to specify with some precision and on the proper levels of discourse, what it is that we seek, as distinguished from what we wish for or hope for.

This is not the place to attempt a profound analysis of the differences between the two systems confronting one another in the last quarter of the twentieth century. No more is it to the purpose, or within our compass, to "revise" the hitherto accepted view of who is responsible for the Cold War; nor, on the other hand, is it our object to defend every decision and action of the West since 1945 or 1918. It may, however, be permissible to suggest that however far the West may fall short of its ideals, there does lie at the root of Western society the notion that the ultimate value is the development of the individual personality, that anything that hampers this growth is *pro tanto* wrong, and that the purpose of society and of the state is to promote that growth for all its members to the greatest degree and with the widest variety possible.

It is also clear from the whole corpus of the Marxist-Leninist tradition that that tradition not merely denies this value judgment, but aggressively asserts its opposite. Where the West believes in and, however clumsily, tries to encourage free individuals and independent nations, the Soviet Union tries to build a monolith. If this distinction, this contradiction, is even approximately valid, then the implications for Western and American policy toward the Soviet Union, past, present, and future, are considerable.

It may be the case, as the Secretary of State under Presidents Nixon and Ford is said to believe, that the ultimate victory of the Soviet system is inevitable and that therefore the task of the Western policymaker is to negotiate the best terms of surrender possible. Even if that were more obviously the case than it appears to be, however, it would not necessarily follow that the best Western policy is grudging acquiescence in every Soviet demand and continuing permission for Soviet exploitation of the institutional weaknesses of a world market economy and of national market economies.

It can also be argued that with the "end of ideology," the quarrel between the Soviet Union and the West is simply a matter of national power jockeying. This thesis equates the Soviet Union with other nation-states, and implicity assumes that the Grand Duchy of Moscow, if it had continued in its original form to this day, would behave in much the same way as the USSR now acts. Much of the behavior of the USSR, many of its national attitudes, can no doubt be illuminated by this hypothesis. But, even if one allows the fullest possible play for this instrument of analysis, one does not banish the fact that its foreign trading apparatus is *sui generis* and gives it important advantages, in this chess game, if it may be so termed for our present purposes.

Western, American-led, policy since 1945 has been, it would seem, based on the assumption that the Soviet Union will expand its sphere of control, by force if necessary, in any direction and at every opportunity that appears possible without risking nuclear war—and without even that qualification, if the risk of retaliation is not made unacceptably large. The assumption has also been made that the Soviet Union will if it can bring to power in free countries communist parties under its complete control, which can then so entrench themselves as to make their removal by peaceful means impossible. Accordingly, Western policy has concentrated, in the economic field, on denying "strategic" commodities to the Soviet Union, and on maintaining a visibly higher standard of material life.

At the same time, not without reason, the West has assumed that more intercourse at all levels between Soviet citizens and institutions and Western ones must alter the relationship between the Soviet state and its members, thereby increasing individual freedom in the Soviet Union and reducing the desire, and the ability, of the Soviet state to impose its system on free men and independent nations. A large, if mostly overlooked, element in George Kennan's containment doctrine similarly suggested that if the USSR were contained, internal stresses based on individual and national aspirations incompatible with the existence of a monolith must inevitably split it or erode it. Trade has been seen as one method of increasing those internal strains—of furthering aspirations that the monolith cannot satisfy.

One argument for increasing East-West trade in the sixties, revived in modified form under Secretary Kissinger, was the good trading partners don't go to war with each other; the Kissinger version emphasized tying the USSR into such a network of commercial (and political) arrangements with the West that it would have a vested interest in peace. Later we shall touch on the question whether in fact the Soviet Union is by nature "aggressive" or not; for the moment it is sufficient to observe that good trading relations between, say, England and Germany before both world wars did not prevent hostilities. This neo-Cobdenite argument does not, therefore, appear tenable.

Besides, there is the possiblity—more dreamed of than realized, perhaps—of making economic gains from dealing with the Soviet Union. It was once argued within the U.S. Department of State that expanding trade with the USSR would help the American balance of payments. If our analysis is correct, of course, nothing of the sort is possible except at the cost of other countries, or temporarily: The Soviet Union exports only in order to import, it imports only what it considers that it cannot efficiently produce itself, and it cannot forever run a deficit with all its trading partners. Individual countries, however, can and do see short-term opportunities for gains and so, even more, do individual companies. It used to be argued that the United States might increase its gold reserve by trade with the USSR, but this argument has dissolved with the weaning away of the international monetary order from its base in gold.

Another argument much used in support of increased East-West trade, though not directly relevant to our concern with trade with the Soviet Union, but important in the general discussion because that subsumed Soviet-Western trade, is that it might encourage tendencies toward independence on the part of the East European satrapies of the Soviet Union. The argument is used in support of increased Soviet-Western trade by asserting that the USSR could scarcely object to expanded trade between the satellites and the West if it were itself trading with the West on a large scale. It is hardly necessary to point out that that degree of inconsistency would hardly be a major hobgoblin for Kremlin minds.

Much of the Western attitude toward the Soviet Union, it seems fair to say, is based on the notion that the Soviet Union's political and economic nature is an aberration, which reason and time will inevitably erode. The policy conclusion seems to be, treat them normally and they will become normal. Our analysis of the Soviet economic system, sketchy as it was, gives no color to that belief, and it may be sufficient to assert roundly that there is nothing in the political cards that suggests that a "return to normalcy" is inevitable, likely, or even possible.

On the basis of these notions, Western and American economic policy during the past thirty years has been based, it would seem, on the twin notions of denying "strategic" commodities to the USSR while encouraging, with varying degrees of enthusiasm, "peaceful" trade. The idea used to be expressed as a preference for fat communists to thin ones; the author used on occasion to point out, in a phrase later lifted without attribution by Samuel Pisar,[1] that the difficulty lay in making sure the inputs went to the midriff rather than the biceps. The position seemed to be that although the Soviet Union was undoubtedly antipathetic to the well-being of the West, there was nothing we could do about it, with nuclear war being unthinkable and conventional military strength both insufficient and not easily applicable; so we should hope that something would, in time, turn up. Meanwhile, so far as trade was not directly, visibly, and immediately helpful to the Soviet armed forces, it should be permitted and indeed encouraged.

We argued (Chapter 9) that "strategic" trade controls can be evaded (perhaps more easily than ever nowadays, when the United States is shipping large quantities of highly sophisticated weapons to countries whose internal security arrangements are at least open to skepticism) and are difficult to secure international agreement on. In any case, they take no account of the fungibility of any inputs over a sufficiently long period. Hence they make no sense unless an outbreak of hostilities is expected within some defined period of time.

From what has been said so far, the conclusion would appear to follow that trade between developed capitalist countries and the Soviet Union benefits only the latter, except from the point of view of short-run commercial advantage. The policy question then arises, what can and what should the West do in the present situation?

The atmosphere of the past quarter century has, it seems fair to say, derived from the equation of an "aggressive" Soviet Union with an "aggressive" Nazi Germany; the mind-set of Western policymakers, especially American ones, appears to have been formed in the light of Munich, the Rhineland, and Manchuria and to have resulted in a determination to stop aggression before it starts. Whether or not this mental framework has been useful in the past, there is reason to question whether it fits our present policy needs. Without attempting to argue the point—an effort that would require a book in itself—we may reasonably ask whether either a nuclear assault or a conventional ground attack on Western Europe is any longer, if it ever was, a realistic basis for planning. In fact, as we have hinted, it seems highly unlikely that such an eventuality plays more of a role in the serious decision making of our leaders than the prospect of the Second Coming does in the operations of Christian churches.

It needs, one may suggest, to be replaced by the fruits of another analysis. If war is improbable, how can relations between the two systems, whose fundamental contradictions seem apparent, be so adjusted as to further the development of the kind of society to which the Western tradition is dedicated?

A very simple, indeed simplistic, answer is that since the Soviet Union is determined to further the transformation of the whole world into a Marxist-Leninist monolith, anything it does is inimical to our interests and should, for that reason alone, be opposed. Since there is, as we have seen, no obvious economic advantage on a national-interest level to be gained by letting the USSR trade on our markets, the logical conclusion of this line of thought is total embargo. The political impossibility of this policy, not only as regards American business but even more with respect to the other industrial nations, is obvious: Our allies have shown, repeatedly, over the past quarter-century that any self-denial by the Americans with respect to trade with the USSR will be gratefully accepted, but not reciprocated.

If it be granted that the West has nothing significant of an economic nature to expect from the Soviet Union—and any hopes that the USSR could become a cheap and reliable source of raw materials if only the West would make the necessary investments is, one may assert roundly, unrealistic—there remains the possibility that it could use its undoubted economic leverage to achieve its political ends. The techniques for doing so entail formidable, perhaps insuperable, problems, both at the national and at the international level, but they are at least worth examining.

Accepting the obvious fact that the Soviet Union is not going to disappear and that it is not going to become friendly and cooperative, but accepting also the probability that hot war is unlikely, are there changes in Soviet behavior that could be encouraged, promoted, and agreed on, formally or tacitly, to the West's benefit?

It is easy to draw up lists of desirable Soviet actions; they could range all the way from disarmament agreements through relaxation of Soviet control over the rest of Eastern Europe, including nonintervention in Yugoslavia, to the various social changes aimed at in the Helsinki agreements, and to modifications of the foreign trade monopoly to the benefit of Western businessmen. The problem is, as the American government discovered (or should have) in the late sixties when it was considering a series of trade agreements with Eastern European countries, one of commensurability. The strictly commercial concessions that were then named and considered seemed, to some officials at least, too small to warrant extending MFN treatment (especially on a permanent basis) to the USSR; the kind of thing we would really have liked—agreements on Berlin, for example—were both too large and in another dimension from the concessions we had in mind.

And one does not have to accept the whole of the Soviet position on political concessions for economic gains to comprehend the difficulty the USSR would face if it admitted that it was making such concessions; permitting interference in its internal affairs would be the mildest language it would use. A totalitarian system like that of the USSR could, of course, take such steps and even announce that it was doing so of its own free will, without running the risk of internal disturbances of significant magnitude. Still, doing so would not be easy.

There is also the consideration that most of what the USSR wants from the

West is either institutional—MFN treatment, for example, or an end to export licensing—or one-shot—prototypes or turnkey factories—in character, while its counterconcessions would be much more easily revocable.

Despite the obvious difficulty of the problem, however, the fact that we are going to coexist with the Soviet Union for the foreseeable future—that is, that war is not going to put an end to our problems in dealing with it, and the obvious desirability of getting something political in return for permitting access to our markets suggest a search for a mechanism for getting a political price for what we have been selling and have no prospect of stopping selling, as things stand.

If we cannot break up the Soviet government's monopoly of foreign trade—and we have seen that there is no likelihood of that—the only apparent answer is to fight monopoly with monopoly and to counterbalance government control with a mechanism that allows the public policy interests of the Western community to speak its part in economic decision making. Retrograde as the suggestion may appear, it may be worth considering the desirability of meeting Soviet mercantilism with Western mercantilism, of setting up a countermonopoly that would make its decisions, not on the basis of Western market prices and private commercial interests alone, but with regard to political ends as well.

Merely to set down such a suggestion on paper brings up visions of the enormous political, policy, legal, and technical problems entailed. What follows, then, is not suggested as a panacea, nor as a blueprint, but is presented as one conceivable way in which the West might organize itself to gain political advantage from meeting the economic needs and desires of the Soviet Union.

In the best of all possible worlds, it would be the West as such that would organize for this purpose. And it is not inconceivable that the United States, the European Economic Community, and Japan could find a suitable form of organization and of decision. Short of that and in any case a necessary prerequisite for it, however, an American organization to control and to perform trade with the Soviet Union in the interest of attaining political benefits could be worth considering. We may usefully consider such a national apparatus first; its extension to the industrialized West would follow similar lines, but, obviously, would add another tier of difficulties to the execution of the idea.

The purpose of the operation would be to make certain that all trade with the USSR took place only after a decision that the maximum possible political benefit would accrue to the United States in return. There are at least two possible approaches: either a special organization should be empowered to negotiate specific agreements with the USSR, only in furtherance of which trade would be allowed; or a government corporation could undertake the whole trading process, as a monopoly representing the United States for the purpose. In the former case, the role of the government would be regulatory and permissive only; in the latter, it would trade for its own account, with, one would assume, much less concern for commercial profit and advantage than private traders would show.

In either case, the organization should start from the proposition that trade is to be permitted, or engaged in, if and only if there is clear evidence that it would further American political objectives. This entails that these would need to be defined and placed in order of priority, which in turn means getting the levels of importance and of generality right. Judgment would constantly be required not only with respect to what is desirable, but also with regard to what is negotiable. Mistakes would be inevitable. But putting the burden of proof in the way we have suggested—that is, requiring that it be shown, or the American administrators convinced, that a particular transaction or series of transactions would produce positive benefits—would at least leave the American negotiators in a position to require the Soviets to show cause why the deal should be made, rather than putting the Americans in the position of having to show why it should not be. Thus the Soviets could be made to advance proposals; it need not be American ingenuity alone that is employed.

It would seem highly desirable that private industry be drawn as intimately as possible into this trading process, but that the public rather than private interests predominate. Securing this kind of balance, especially on a long-term basis, would be exceedingly difficult; it might best be obtained if the form of a corporation were used, instead of a commission staffed by permanent and temporary civil servants, aided by industry "advisors."

The basic conceptual difficulty with this proposal, as it seems, is that American government normally operates, at least in principle, in the open and on the basis of clear, definite guidelines and regulations. We have no fondness for admitted reliance on administrative discretion and for secrecy. Indeed, the whole proposal finds its nearest, and not altogether encouraging, parallel in the CIA. Yet it is difficult to think of acceptable alternatives. Certainly intergovernmental agreements negotiated in public, or even published after the fact, would be extraordinarily difficult to reach, if they openly required political in return for commercial concessions. Yet an unaccountable agency operating in the dark by its own lights alone would not sit well with the American people or with the business community; and there is not much in the history of congressional "oversight" to make one think that that technique of supervision would inspire much confidence.

Moreover, the whole notion violates deep-seated American feelings about the beneficent effects of free private trade. We have built for the Western world since 1945 an economic system based on that notion; its basic principles are as old and as deep as the Constitution. Yet the suggestion is being made that we should revert to mercantilism, which is derided in every economics textbook, that we should do so in imitation of communist Russia.

Besides, if the notion is proposed for the United States alone, it will rightly be scorned as merely denying Americans the chance for profitable business and turning the wheat market over to the Canadians and the computer business to the Europeans. Attempts to control foreign subsidiaries of American companies would cause frictions and, if ineffective, further flights of jobs.

And, as we have noted, the history of attempts to control "strategic" commodities on an international level is not inspiring; how much less likely is agreement to coordinate the economies of the industrialized countries for the attainment of vague, idealistic, controversial political ends—especially as scepticism as to the likelihood of success will probably be even wider and deeper abroad than in the United States?

The practical prospects for the adoption of a technique for using our economic strength to make coexistence with the Soviet Union more endurable, then, would seem exceedingly slim, the more so, perhaps, as successes could scarcely be guaranteed before or trumpeted after the fact. Mistakes would certainly be made, and results would be at best slow in coming. Then why set down such a proposal at all?

One reason is that this book points to the existence of a problem and an opportunity. The problem is that the Soviet Union's foreign trading apparatus is beautifully designed to reap the benefits of the existence of a free-trading, market international economy while paying nothing for the privilege of entering the game. The opportunity is that of exacting a price for participating in it. It seemed obligatory, then, to make some suggestion, however dreamy-eyed, for righting this imbalance.

Another is to draw attention to the inadequacy of the philosophy we are following with respect to trade with the Soviet Union and to suggest the futility of much of our present apparatus for coping with it. At the least, a realistic look at the real situation may save us a lot of effort and bother.

But, finally, the basic reason for advancing this outline of one conceivable way of gaining advantage from our economic strength in the interest of our political well-being is that if we recognize the problem and see the opportunity, a more practical plan of dealing with them may occur to more ingenious minds. It is possible that we have overstated the difficulties; most of them are psychological, not technical, and could, one is inclined to suggest, be coped with if the will were there. In any case, it might be feasible to *begin working* consciously toward an American and an all-Western technique and determination to use our economic strength to gain our political ends. New ideas, whether they suggest techniques for dealing with the problem or improvements in the present suggestions, may be forthcoming. If so, the prospects for a more tolerable world order would be vastly improved.

Note

1. Samuel Pisar, *Coexistence and Commerce* (New York: McGraw-Hill, 1970), p. 5.

Appendix
Foreign Service Despatch No. 574

Date: April 24, 1958
From: American Embassy, Moscow.
To: The Department of State, Washington, D.C.
Subject: The Imperial Tailors on the Imperial Pants: Soviet Economists
Demonstrate Poverty of Soviet Price Theory.

After considerable delay and confusion, a meeting between two Embassy officers
and several prominent Soviet economists arranged by the Institute of Economics
of the Academy of Sciences took place on March 29. During the course of two
and a half hours of friendly, and not uninformative discussion, the Soviet conception of the law of value, including its influence on consumption, pricing, and
investment, was clarified—though, as will appear, the clarity attained can best
be described as an admission of the transparency, if not the nonexistence, of the
theory.

The economists who took part in the discussion were YA. A. KRONROD,
L. GATOVSKI, A. A. KURSKI, T. S. KHACHATUROV, G. SOROKIN, and
Professor KLIMENKO. The first five are, of course, well known through their
writings, and of them, only Kurski and Khachaturov were new acquaintances for
the Embassy officers.

By way of background, initiative for the discussion came from YU. V.
BELOV, the junior employee of the Institute who has been frequently mentioned
in recent Embassy despatches. He urged a series of bi-weekly or monthly meet-
ings between one of the Embassy officers, who has a particular interest in planning,
and economists from the Institute. Independently of this proposal, which was
eagerly accepted by the Embassy officer, a request was submitted to the Ministry
of Foreign Affairs, asking that interviews be arranged for two Embassy officers
with Khachaturov, Mme. SPIRIDONOVA of Moscow University, and Professor
TURETSKI. The Ministry replied that a request for these three interviews
should be sent through it to the Ministry of Higher Education, and after a further
delay of several weeks, a list of questions for each interview was sent to the Ministry, at its request. Meanwhile, Belov informed an Embassy officer that the
Presidium of the Academy of Sciences had telephoned him to ask whether the
names TURPIN and HARMSTONE meant anything. The Presidium had been
sent a letter from the Ministry of Foreign Affairs asking about setting up interviews for these two. Belov replied that he knew the Americans, that they were
frequent visitors at the Institute of Economics, and that the Academy should
cooperate in the arrangements. The Presidium worker then said, somewhat
doubtfully, that perhaps he should speak to the director of the Institute, but
Belov told him not to be silly and to get on with the arrangements. In the same

conversation, Belov said that he had arranged for the group meeting which took place on March 29; two days later, the Foreign Ministry telephoned the same information to the Embassy. Arrangements were further complicated by the necessity of postponing the meeting for one day, as one of the Embassy officers was on a trip, and by a minor misunderstanding about the final confirmation with Belov, but, although the latter was doubtful up to the last minute about who would appear, the meeting finally came off on schedule, with attendance as indicated above.

This narrative is included here as an illustration of the complications which can arise in Moscow over a relatively simple form of Embassy contacts with Soviet institutions, even when both sides are cooperating to their utmost.

No reference was made at any time during the discussion to the questions presented through the Foreign Ministry for the conversation with Professor Khachaturov. Moreover, the Embassy officers were not given a lecture, as is so often done in interviews of this sort. Instead, they were allowed to guide the discussion as they chose, within the limitations imposed by the eagerness of the six economists to talk.

The first question concerned the Soviet conception of a social, specifically an economic, law. Kronrod replied that a law meant an expression of a set of regularities in natural or social phenomena, including an explanation of the cause-and-effect relationships involved where possible. Referring to his own definitions in his article on the Law of Value (*Voprosy Ekonomiki*, no. 2, 1957), he formulated the law of value as follows: The value of a commodity is determined by the amount of socially necessary labor expended on its production. The law has three aspects: *In production*, it requires that labor be expended in accordance with the demands of society and this means, concretely, a constant effort to *reduce costs* (*sebestoimost*); *in exchange*, it determines that commodities shall exchange in proportion to the amount of labor they embody; and *in accounting*, the law expresses the necessity of social accounting (*ucheta*) both qualitatively and quantitatively. "Qualitatively," he explained, means here "from the point of view of society," and "quantitatively" means that the calculations shall be based on the average expenditure of labor, not on *optima or pessima.* "Social labor" he defined as a qualitative indicator, which is defined as that labor which meets, in the proper proportions, the demands of society. "Socially necessary labor" is a quantitative indicator, differing in every branch of production, and defined as the weighted average of the hours of labor actually worked per unit of product in that branch. (The weights are the proportions of each item of production to the total production of the branch.)

The Soviet economists were careful to emphasize that the role of prices in the Soviet economy is primarily that of a stimulus to economies in production. They explained at length that in principle all industries should work at a profit, but that this profit should be low enough to keep them on their toes. They said that, as a result of the price policy followed during the early years of industrialization (for a more complete description of this, see D. D. KONDRASHEV, *Price Formation in the Industry of the USSR,* Moscow, 1956), too many enterprises ran at deficits for too long, but that on the whole this situation had been liquidated after the wholesale price reform of 1949. They explained that after this general raising of wholesale prices, there had been an equal and equally general reduction, but said, on questioning, that the changes on individual commodities had not cancelled each other out, even though the net effect had allegedly been to leave the level of wholesale prices the same as it had been in 1949.

However, Gatovski argued, and Kronrod agreed, that the "deviation of prices from value" in the means of production is still large and should be reduced. Gatovski holds, though Kronrod disagrees, that there should be some upward revision of the prices of some producers' goods, at least temporarily; then the "price lever" should be used to exert a steady pressure for economies and price reductions.

Kurski remarked in this connection that most of Soviet industry, including heavy industry, is operating at a profit; he and Kronrod put the average profitability of all industry at about 10 percent. Gatovski thought the figure too low, but Kronrod insisted that it is correct. As a normal rate of profit of 4-5 percent has been mentioned for heavy industry, this figure is either surprisingly high or light industry must be even more profitable than 10 percent. (It was stressed that the profitability figures do not include turnover tax, and they are calculated as "percentage of the sale price of a unit of production.)

At this point, one of the Embassy officers asked how the relationships between living and embodied labor were expressed in these calculations, intending then to raise the question of the calculus by which all "living labor" is theoretically reducible to "simple labor." Kronrod and Gatovski, who were carrying the ball at this point, explained with patience the system of cost calculations based on "*sebestoimost,*" cited the example of coal mining, where, they said, the proportion of "living" to "embodied" labor, at about 60 to 40, is at a maximum. Capital goods, they said, are valued in monetary terms. Kronrod was careful to point out that in this case price was the monetary expression of value, and that, roughly speaking, this indirect measure was satisfactory. In any case, he said, direct calculation of the amount of labor "embodied" in the means of production is impossible and impractical, and indeed it is perfectly true that only Strumilin, to the best of the Embassy's knowledge, has ever though otherwise. (See on this point Ostrovityanov's remarks as reported in Embassy Despatch No. 451, March 4, 1958.)

(It seemed clearly implied, and was taken for granted at least by the Americans, that the same reasoning applies to the reduction of skilled to unskilled labor. As is well known, Soviet wage accounting practice in fact is based on adding rubles, not hours, and this practice can only be squared with the labor theory of value by arguing that the greater average value of skilled labor is proportionate to the additional pay it receives and that this extra value has been added through training and education, to the "simple" worker.)

At this point the objection was put that surely here Soviet economic theory is involved in an infinite regress, since it was obviously impossible to eliminate, by any process of abstraction, all the arbitrary elements introduced into this process by prices arbitrarily fixed by the state.

Kronrod immediately agreed, and other heads down the table nodded. "You see," he said, "it is not the case that we started price formation in a vacuum. We had a working set of prices when the process of industrialization began, and the deviations of prices from value was a deliberate policy, proper for that time, though out of date now."

This concession seems quite significant, despite the fact that it is obviously true, and has been apparent to students of Soviet economics for some time. The reasons for its significance are two. First, it is a candid admission that Soviet economists cannot explain prices by means of the labor theory of value, and it seemed quite evident that this was perfectly clear to all concerned. Thus when Ostrovityanov argues, as he did in his *Kommunist* article, for an historical and against an overly theoretical approach to questions of value and prices, he is instructing Soviet economists to abandon the attempt to construct an economic system on a Marxist "labor value" basis, and, the Embassy would submit, putting his readers on notice that talk about "social labor" and "socially necessary labor" is purely liturgical.

Why is it an admission that Marxist economics cannot explain prices? For the reason, it seems clear, that Kronrod, with the agreement of his colleagues, was consciously passing from a theoretical explanation to an announcement that prices are something which have appeared, historically, from the interplay of market forces in NEP days, and which have been altered in accordance with state policy, but which have no theoretical basis.

Secondly, though perhaps more doubtfully, there seemed to be running through the whole argument a systematically ambiguous use of the word "value." Although it cannot be proved, it has been the impression of the reporting officers before, in reading Soviet treatments of value and prices, that when Soviet economists talk about the deviation of prices from value they have in mind, not at all anything to do with socially necessary labor, but "real" values in the precise sense of those values which supply and demand would have established under Soviet conditions. (These are "rational prices" in the sense in which the term was defined by Peter Wiles in his article, "Are Adjusted Rubles Rational," in *Soviet Studies*, vol. VII, no. 2, 1955.) In short, the Marxist definition goes completely by the board when Soviet economists are talking seriously about real-life problems, just as does the rest of their "theory" of value.

Since this interpretation of the Soviet economists' argument clearly seemed to be correct, there appeared to be no use in bringing up those objections to the labor theory which seem insuperable, and as Gatovski immediately set off on another tack, the discussion of the "law of value" ended there, not without some palpable relief to the Soviet economists.

Gatovski seized on the words "supply and demand," and set out, with Kurski and Klimenko, to make three major points. First, the Soviet government (specifically Gosplan, the Ministry of Trade, and the Ministry of Finances) devotes great attention to determining which goods the consumers want. Secondly, far more retail prices are set in decentralized fashion than are determined in Moscow. And third, he rejected, lightly but firmly, any implication that there could possibly be any divergence between the state's preferences and those of the mass of consumers. Each point needs some amplification.

The question of "polling" consumers on their preferences was discussed in detail by D. D. Kondrashev in his interview with Professor Loucks, reported in the Embassy's Despatch No. 206, October 2, 1975, and Gatovski gave it only the new twist of emphasizing the degree to which direct interenterprise contracting makes this process more effective and more realistic. In consequence, he and his colleagues heartily favor expanding the practice—but he emphatically rejected any suggestion that the enterprises might be given more control over prices. Sorokin amended Gatovski's statement that the State does vary prices to adjust to supply and demand by saying that "of course," the government could not allow the prices of goods of primary necessity to rise enough to balance supply and demand. (The Soviet state prefers empty shelves and physical controls to that.) It was emphasized that *"ostatki"* (leftovers) are the best possible indicators that the wrong sorts of goods have been produced; this is itself a relatively new phenomenon for this tightly belted scarcity economy. Gatovski smilingly refused to take up the suggestion that possibly the labor embodied in commodities which nobody wants is not exactly socially necessary, passing it off with the remark that "of course we make mistakes"—but not seeing, any more than Kronrod would admit to seeing in the case mentioned above, that he was thereby dealing another fatal blow to the applicability of Marxist economic theory to Soviet practice.

Professor Klimenko asserted that the degree to which price formation is centralized in Moscow is often exaggerated by Westerners. Only about a quarter of the total volume of retail trade, he said, is now carried on at prices set uniformly for the whole country in Moscow: 55-60 percent of it is at prices set locally, and the remainder are set centrally, but are differentiated by locality (*poyasnye tseny*). There was some discussion of this point with the Embassy officers remarking that consumers' durables, at least, seemed to be uniformly priced throughout the country (with the exception, of course, of the rural markup), and with the group agreeing that prices set locally are, for the most part, on food products and some basic textiles. The percentage breakdown given above, it was said specifically, does not include cooperative trade or handicrafts (i.e., tailor shop products, etc.). It was also noted that state procurement (*zagatovka*) prices on fruits and on some vegetables are set on the basis of *kolkhoz* market prices.

The clear implication of the discussion on these two points seemed to be that Soviet price policy is being adjusted to the relatively greater abundance of consumers' goods which is visible in the country (especially, of course, in Moscow) and that these economists, at least, expected the trend to continue. They seemed to be unanimously in favor of modifications of the rigidities of central planning of consumers' goods in the direction of what Westerners would regard as more reasonable and normal practices, and seemed equally clearly to expect such a development. As indicated above, theory seems unlikely to be much of an obstacle.

It is hardly necessary to add the warning that this somewhat rosy picture would hardly be recognized by a Soviet worker as having much relation to the reality he knows. However, whatever allowances one makes for the camouflage function of the discipline of economics in the Soviet Union, it seems likely that something of this sort represents the hopes, if not the intentions, of the Soviet regime.

On the third point, there is little that needs to be said. The idea that the Party knows best what the people "really" demand (*trebovat*) is hardly one that this group of economists, whose professional existence depends on their maintaining it, would question. The extent to which they are willing to go, as was shown by Professor Khachaturov's remarks on investment policy, is indicated by their limitation of the influence of consumer demand to decisions on matters of taste, within general limits set, as always, from above.

On the subject of "supply and demand," Gatovski pointed out that the Soviet system of planning permits more than a mere investigation of consumer preferences: by its control over the incomes of the population, as set forth in the balance of the Money Incomes and Expenditures of the Population, which is part of the Plan, it controls the effective demand which is generated. This mention of this balance was rather striking to the Embassy officer who has spent some time on a study of Soviet planning methods, because it seems to be rarely mentioned in the literature. (There is a prewar book on the subject, but it reads more like a proposal than like a description of a planning technique in ordinary use. Still, it is so obvious and necessary a part of the planning process that it must certainly have long been in use. Perhaps the notorious inability of the Soviet planners to keep the growth of wage income within bounds laid down by the plan explains the unpopularity of this balance.) As this point is one of the key links between the physical and financial aspects of the planning process, it is hoped that a further interview on this precise question can be arranged. Gatovski also said the Soviet government carries out careful investigations of the budgets of workers and of kolkhozniks. (See, on this point, V. Starovski in *Vestnik Statistiki* no. 1, 1958, p. 12.)

The discussion then turned to questions of investment and obsolescence policy, this being Khachaturov's specialty, but the Embassy officers deliberately avoided discussing this question in much detail, having won Khachaturov's agreement to consider it at greater length at a subsequent meeting, when, it is hoped, he may be less inhibited by the presence of colleagues from another institution than his own institute.

Khachaturov did, however, outline the basic scheme of investment planning, beginning from the amount of money which the state has available for the replacement of the means and objects of production (i.e., capital goods and raw materials). The remaining "national income" is then, as a rule, divided in the proportions of 75 percent for consumption (including "social and cultural" expenditures) and 25 percent for investment.*

One of the Embassy officers expressed surprise that the starting point for investment decisions should be financial; it had been his impression that investment planning was done, primarily at least, in physical terms, with the financial planning being adjusted to these goals. He pointed out that Khrushchev, in giving the fifteen-year goals, had set targets in physical terms. Kurski and Gatovski replied that Khrushchev had not grabbed these figures out of the air, but that they were the end result of a lot of calculation. They did say, however, that in the prewar years, certainly, most investment planning had been done with physical goals as the basis, but that the economy has now become too complicated for that to be a practical procedure. They specifically mentioned, however, that the level of investment was a political decision as much as an economic one, and referred more than once to the Party as the agency responsible for making the basic decisions, including the distribution of investment funds among industries as well as between the consumer and investment goods groups.

This reference to the early days of industrialization led Professor Klimenko to embark on a rather elaborate description of an early planning error. Some

---

*This 25 percent rate of net investment is higher than is usually estimated, e.g., by Norman Kaplan in *Soviet Economic Growth*, and while the 25 percent figure has been used before by Soviet economists, it has not, as a rule, been used to mean that 25 percent of the net national product is used for net new investment. It had been the Embassy's impression that gross investment out of gross national product was what the Soviets were talking about. What the true figure would be, if investment goods were priced at their "real" value instead of at arbitrarily low prices is a difficult question. It is interesting to note that when one of the Embassy officers put forward this question as one in which he was interested, but on which he despaired of getting results, there was a slight difference of opinion among the Soviet economists. Kronrod argued that since a retail price index was given in *The Achievements of the Soviet Power in 40 Years*, it should be easy to calculate the proportion of national income going to investment, but Khachaturov agreed with the Embassy officer that far more data would be needed for this purpose, and that these data have not been published. Kronrod then agreed, and rejoined that he was having some trouble with certain American census figures in which the coverage of some industries was no greater than 60 percent.

comrades, he said, thought in 1929-30 that metallurgy was the branch which should get the heaviest emphasis, but the Party had correctly decided that machine-building was the branch which should have priority. One of the reasons which had justified this policy was the systematic economizing on the metal content (*metaloemkost*) of Soviet machinery. Between 1928 and 1956, the metal consumption in the turbine industry per kilowatt of capacity produced had been reduced seven to eight times by building lighter machinery of higher capacity. It seemed unkind to ruffle Klimenko's goatee by reminding him of such fresh complaints about the excessive weight of Soviet machinery as those in, for example, G.I. Baklanov's *The Analysis of the Economic Activity of the Industrial Enterprise*, Moscow, 1956, p. 36, where a ZIS-150 truck chassis is said to be half again as heavy as that of a 1954 Studebaker of comparable size.

The group laid considerable emphasis in this part of the discussion on the gains to be made by improving the use of existing capacity during the coming years.

It was also suggested that a proposal to expand considerably the role of loans from the State Bank in investment operations is being favorably considered, although it was carefully pointed out that no decision had been reached. If the scheme is adopted, investment funds will be allocated through the banks, instead of directly from the budget, and the bank will be given the responsibility of turning over to the enterprises completed projects with the payment by the bank for each new installation taking place only when it is ready to go into operation. This will eliminate the present system by which construction enterprises are paid as work progresses, and will, the economists think, greatly speed up the completion of investments. (For some horrible examples of the operation of the present system, see I. A. Kulev, *On the Further Perfecting of the Planning and Administration of the Economy*, Moscow, 1957, p. 10.)

The system would be similar to the present arrangements under which a director may borrow relatively small sums directly from the bank to carry out improvements which will pay for themselves in two or three years. Gatovski could not be drawn out on the question of whether the director has the right to demand such a credit on his own responsibility, as the Embassy understands to be the case, but he did correct the Embassy officer's view that such a credit could not exceed one million rubles. He said firmly that there is no limit.

At the close of the meeting, some effort was made to sound the group on the problem of obsolescence, but the answer, from Khachaturov, on when obsolescence occurs was oriented primarily toward technical matters, and it seemed clear that Soviet theory on this score achieved its major victory a few years ago when it was allowed to admit that obsolescence can occur.

Comment: Gatovski said that he would review with interest any discussion which the Embassy submits on this subject, and it is planned to prepare a theoretical piece on the law of value and prices in Soviet planning and to allow the

Institute's economists to comment on it. If the Department has any questions which could logically spring from the conversation reported in this despatch, the Embassy would appreciate their submission for use when another round is possible.

Selected Bibliography

Selected Bibliography

Books

Aleksandrov, A. *Finansovaya Sistema SSSR* (The Financial System of the USSR). Moscow: Gosfinizdat, 1956.

Baibakov, N., ed. *Gosudarstvenyi Plan Razvitiya Narodnogo Khozyaistva SSSR na 1971-1975 gg.* (State Plan of the Development of the Economy of the USSR for 1971-1975). Moscow: Izdatelstvo Politicheskoi Literatury, 1972.

Batyrev, Valdimir M. *Denezhnoye Obrashcheniye v SSSR: Voprosy Teorii, Organizatsii, i Planirovaniya* (Monetary Circulation in the USSR: Questions of Theory, Organization, and Planning). Moscow: Gosfinizdat, 1959.

Baykov, Alexander. *Soviet Foreign Trade.* Princeton University Press, 1946.

Becker, Abraham S. *Comparisons of United States and USSR National Output. Some Rules of the Game.* Santa Monica, Calif.: The Rand Corporation, 1960.

_____. *Prices of Producers Durables in the United States and the USSR in 1955.* RM 2432. Santa Monica, Calif.: The Rand Corporation, 1959.

_____. *Ruble Price Levels and Dollar-Ruble Ratios of Soviet Machinery in the 1960's.* Santa Monica, Calif.: The Rand Corporation, 1973.

Belkin, V. D. *Tseny Yedinogo Urovnya i Ekonomicheskie Izmereniya na ikh Osnov* (Prices of a Uniform Level and Economic Measurements on the Basis of Them). Moscow: Izdatelstvo Ekonomicheskoi Literatury, 1963.

Belousov, P. A. *Obshchestvenno Neobokhodimye Zatraty Truda i Uroven Optovykh Tsen* (Socially Necessary Outlays of Labor and the Level of Wholesale Prices). Moscow: Izdatelstvo "Mysl," 1969.

Bergson, Abram. *The Economics of Soviet Planning.* New Haven and London: Yale University Press, 1964.

_____, and Kuznets, Simon, eds. *Economic Trends on the Soviet Union.* Cambridge, Mass.: Harvard University Press, 1963.

_____. *Social National Income and Product in 1937.* New York: Columbia University Press, 1953.

Bernard, Philippe J. *Planning in the Soviet Union.* Oxford: The Pergamon Press, 1966.

Blair, John M. *Economic Concentration: Structure, Behavior, and Public Policy.* New York: Harcourt, Brace, Jovanovich, 1972.

Blaug, M. *Economic Theory in Retrospect.* Homewood, Ill.: Richard D. Irwin, 1962.

Boltho, Andrea. *Foreign Trade Criteria in Socialist Economies.* Cambridge: The University Press, 1971.

Bor, M. Z. *Planovyi Balans Narodnogo Khozyaistva SSSR* (The Planned Balance of the Economy of the USSR). Moscow: Gosplanizdat, 1959.

Bornstein, Morris, ed. *Plan and Market: Economic Reform in Eastern Europe.* New Haven and London: Yale University Press, 1973.

Brown, Alan A., and Neuberger, Egon, eds. *International Trade and Central Planning.* Berkeley and Los Angeles: University of California Press, 1968.

Breev, M. V. *Planirovaniye Narodnogo Khozyaistva SSSR (Planning the Economy of the USSR).* Moscow: Izdatelstvo Politicheskoi Literatury, 1963.

Brus, Wlodzimierz. *The Economics and Politics of Socialism.* London: Routledge and Kegan Paul, 1973.

Byakovskaya, V. S. *Perspektivnoye Planirovaniye Napravlyenii Tekhnicheskogo Progresa* (The Long-Term Planning of the Directions of Technical Progress). Moscow: Ekonomika, 1973.

Bykov, Alexander. *Untapped Reserves of World Trade.* N.p. (New Delhi?): Novosti Press Publishing House, n.d.

Campbell, Robert W. *The Soviet Type Economies,* 3rd ed., Boston: The Houghton Mifflin Company, 1974.

_____, and Marer, Paul, eds. *East-West Trade and Technology Transfer.* Bloomington: Indiana University, 1974.

Caves, Richard E. *Trade and Economic Structure: Models and Methods.* Cambridge, Mass.: Harvard University Press, 1963.

_____, and Jones, Ronald W. *World Trade and Payments: An Introduction.* Boston: Little, Brown, 1973.

Cherviakov, P. *Organizatsiya i Tekhnika Vneshnei Torgovlyi SSSR* (The Organization and Techniques of the Foreign Trade of the USSR), 1st ed. Moscow: Vneshtorgizdat, 1958 (2nd ed., 1962).

Cohen, Peter. *The Gospel According to the Harvard Business School.* New York: Penguin Books, 1973.

Collective of Authors. *Politicheskoya Ekonomika: Uchebnik* (Political Economy: A Textbook). Moscow: Gosudarstvenoye Izdatelstvo Politicheskoi Literatury, 1954.

Committee on Foreign Relations, U.S. Senate. *East-West Trade, A Compilation of Views of Businessmen, Bankers, and Academic Experts.* Washington, D.C.: U.S. Government Printing Office, 1964.

Connolly, Michael B., and Swoboda, Alexander, eds. *International Trade and Money.* London: George Allen Unwin, Ltd., 1973.

Degras, Jane, and Nove, Alex, eds. *Soviet Planning: Essays in Honour of Naum Jasny.* Oxford: Basil Blackwell, 1964.

Dellin, L. A. D., and Gross, Hermann, eds. *Reforms in the Soviet and Eastern European Economies.* Lexington, Mass.: D. C. Heath, 1972.

Devons, Ely. *Planning in Practice: Essays in Aircraft Planning in Wartime.* Cambridge University Press, 1950.

Djilas, Milovan. *The New Class.* New York: Frederick A. Praeger, 1957.

Dorfman, Robert, Samuelson, Paul A., and Solow, Robert M. *Linear Programming and Economic Analysis.* New York: McGraw Hill, 1958.

Doroshin, I. A., ed. *Direktivy i Stimuly v Mekhanizme Upravleniya Ekonomiki* (Directives and Incentives in the Mechanism of Running the Economy). Moscow: Mysl, 1969.

Dragilev, M. S., Faminsky, I. P., and Osmova, M. N. *Problemy Razvitiya Ekonomicheskikh Otnoshenii Mezhdu Sotsialisticheskimi i Kapitalisticheskimi Stranami* (Problems of the Development of Economic Relations between Socialist and Capitalist Countries). Moscow: Moscow University Press, 1974.

Dyachenko, V. P., ed. *Uchet Sootnosheniya Sprosa i Predlozheniya v Tsenoobrazovanii* (Calculating the Relationship of Supply and Demand in Price Formation). Moscow: Izdatelstvo Nauka, 1964.

Efimov, A. N. *Mezhotraslivoi Balans i Proportsii Nardnogo Khozyaistva* (The Interbranch Balance and the Proportions of the Economy). Moscow: Izdatelstvo Ekonomika, 1969.

Ellman, Michael. *Soviet Planning Today: Proposals for an Optimally Functioning Economic System.* Cambridge: The University Press, 1972.

Erlich, Alexander. *The Soviet Industrialization Debate, 1924-1928.* Cambridge, Mass.: Harvard University Press, 1960.

Fokin, D. F. *Vneshnaya Torgovlya SSSR (1946-1963 gg.)* (The Foreign Trade of the USSR (1946-1963). Moscow: Mezhdunarodnye Otnosheniya, 1964.

Frei, L. I. *Mezhdunarodnye Raschety i Finansirovaniye Vneshnei Torgovlyi Sotsialisticheskikh Stran* (International Accounts and the Financing of the Foreign Trade of Socialist Countries). Moscow: Vneshtorgizdat, 1960.

von Gajzago, Oliver. *Der Sowjetische Aussenhandel mit den Industrielaendern.* Berlin: Duncker & Hunboldt, 1960.

Gerschenkron, Alexander. *Economic Relations with the USSR.* New York: The Committee on International Economic Policy, 1945.

Gerashchenko, V. S. *Denezhnoye Obrashcheniye i Kredit SSSR* (Monetary Circulation and Credit of the USSR). Moscow: Finansy, 1960.

Giffen, James Henry. *The Legal and Practical Aspects of Trade with the Soviet Union.* New York: Frederick A. Praeger, 1969.

Gilbert, Milton, and Kravis, Irving B. *An International Comparison of National Products and the Purchasing Power of Currencies.* Paris: Organization for European Economic Cooperation, n.d. (1954?).

Godelier, Maurice. *Rationalité el Irrationalité en Économie.* Paris: Francois Maspero, 1966.

Gosplan USSR: *Ukazaniya k Razrabotke Gosudarstvenykh Planov Razvitiya Narodnogo Khozyaistva SSSR* (Directives for the Elaboration of State Plans for the Development of the Economy of the USSR). Moscow: Eknomika, 1974.

Gosplan USSR: *Vremennaya Metodika Opredeleniya Ekonomicheskoi Effecktivnosti Vneshnei Torgovlyi* (Temporary Methodology for Determining the Economic Effectiveness of Foreign Trade). Mimeographed, n.p., n.d. ("Confirmed by Gosplan USSR in March, 1968.")

Grossman, Gregory, ed. *Essays in Socialism and Planning in Honor of Carl Landauer.* Englewood Cliffs, N.J.: Prentice-Hall, 1970.

_____, ed. *Money and Plan–Financial Aspects of East European Economic Reforms.* Berkeley and Los Angeles: University of California Press, 1968.

_____, ed. *Value and Plan: Economic Calculation and Organization in Eastern Europe.* Berkeley and Los Angeles: University of California Press, 1960.

Gruzinov, Vladimir Petrovich. *Upravlenie Vneshnei Torgovlyi. Tseli, Funktsii, Metody* (The Administration of Foreign Trade, Goals, Functions, Methods). Moscow: Mezhdunarodonye Otnosheniya, 1975.

Haberler, Gottfried. *A Survey of International Trade Theory,* rev. and enlarged ed., Princeton, N.J.: International Finance Section, Department of Economics, Princeton University, 1961.

_____. *The Theory of International Trade, with its Applications to Commercial Policy,* translated by Alfred Stonier and Frederic Benham. New York: MacMillan, 1936.

Hague, D. C. *Price Formation in Various Economies.* London: MacMillan; New York: St. Martin's Press, 1967.

Hardt, John P. *Economic Insights on Current Soviet Policy and Strategy.* McLean, Va.: Research Analysis Corporation, 1969.

_____, and Treml, Valdimir, eds. *Soviet Economic Statistics.* Durham, N.C.: Duke University Press, 1972.

Hawkins, C. J. *Theory of the Firm.* London and Basingstoke: The MacMillan Press, Ltd., 1973.

von Hayek, F. A., ed. *Collectivist Economic Planning.* London: George Routledge & Sons, Ltd., 1935.

Hewett, Edward A. *Foreign Trade Pricing in the Council for Mutual Economic Assistance.* New York: Cambridge University Press, 1974.

Holzman, Franklyn D. *Foreign Trade Under Central Planning.* Cambridge, Mass.: Harvard University Press, 1974.

Jasny, Naum. *Essays on the Soviet Economy*. Munich: Institute for the Study of the USSR, 1962.

Joint Economic Committee, U.S. Congress. *Comparisons of United States and Soviet Economies*. Washington, D.C.: U.S. Government Printing Office, 1959 (Papers); 1960, (Hearings).

_____. *Economic Performance and the Military Burden in the USSR*. Washington, D.C.: U.S. Government Printing Office, 1970.

_____. *Hearings on East-West Trade*. Washington, D.C.: U.S. Government Printing Office, 1964.

_____. *New Directions in the Soviet Economy*. Washington, D.C.: U.S. Government Printing Office, 1966.

_____. *The Soviet Economic Outlook*. Washington, D.C.: U.S. Government Printing Office, 1973.

_____. *Soviet Economic Performance, 1966-1967*. Washington, D.C.: U.S. Government Printing Office, 1968.

_____. *Soviet Economic Prospects for the Seventies*. Washington, D.C.: U.S. Government Printing Office, 1973.

_____. *Soviet Economy in a New Perspective*. Washington, D.C.: U.S. Government Printing Office, 1976.

Kantorovich, L.V. *Ekonomicheskiy Raschet Nailushego Ispolzovaniya Resursov* (The Economic Calculation of the Best Use of Resources). Moscow: Izdatelstvo Akademii Nauk SSSR, 1960.

Kaplan, A. D. H., Dirlam, Joel B., and Lanzilotti, Robert F. *Pricing in Big Business: A Case Approach*. Washington, D.C.: The Brookings Institution, 1958.

Kaser, Michael. *Comecon: Integration Problems of the Planned Economies*, 2nd ed. London: Oxford University Press, 1967.

_____. *Soviet Economics*. New York: World University Library, McGraw-Hill Book Company, 1970.

_____, and Portes, R., eds. *Planning and Market Relations*. London and Basingstoke: International Economic Association, 1971.

Kawan, Louis. *La Nouvelle Orientation du Commerce Extérieur Soviètique*. Brussels: Centre National pour l'Étude des Pays à Régime Communiste, 1958.

Kindleberger, Charles P. *Foreign Trade and the National Economy*. New Haven and London: Yale University Press, 1962.

Klinsky, A. I. *Planirovaniye Ekonomicheskogo i Sotsialnogo Razvitiya* (Planning Economic and Social Development). Moscow: Mysl, 1974.

Kolodny, M. G. and Stephanov, A. P. *Planirovaniye Narodnogo Knozyaistva SSSR* (Planning the Economy of the USSR). Kiev: Vishcha Shkola, 1975.

Kondrashev, D. D. *Tsenoobrazovaniye v Promyshlennosti SSSR* (Price Formation in the Industry of the USSR). Moscow: Gosfinizdat, 1956.

Kostinsky, Barry F. *Description and Analysis of Soviet Foreign Trade Statistics.* Washington, D.C.: U.S. Department of Commerce, 1974.

Kozlov, G. A., and Pervushin, S. P., eds., *Kratkiy Ekonomicheskiy Slovar* (Short Economic Dictionary) Moscow: Gosudarstvennoye Izdatelstvo Politicheskoi Literatury, 1958.

Kronrod, Ya. A. *Sotsialisticheskoye Vosproizvodstvo* (Socialist Reproduction). Moscow: Gospolitizdat, 1955.

Kurskiy, A. A. *Planirovaniye Narodnogo Khozyaistva SSSR* (Planning the Economy of the USSR). Moscow: Gospolitizdat, 1955.

Lane, Frederic C. *Venice and History.* Baltimore, Md.: The Johns Hopkins Press, 1966.

Larionov, K. A. *Dva Mira–Dve Valyutnye Sistemye* (Two Worlds–Two Foreign Exchange Systems). Moscow: Finansye, 1973.

Legislative Reference Service, U.S. Congress. *A Background Study of East-West Trade.* Washington, D.C.: U.S. Government Printing Office, 1965.

Levin, I. M. *Planirovaniye Truda i Zarabotnoi Platy Na Promyshlennykh Predpriyatiakh* (Planning Labor and Wages in Industrial Enterprises). Moscow: Gospolitizdat, 1958.

Lewin, Moshe. *Russian Peasants and Soviet Power.* Evanston, Ill.: Northwestern University Press, 1968.

Lokshin, E. Yu., ed. *Ekonomika Materialnogo-tekhnicheskogo Snabzheniya* (The Economics of Material-technical Supply). Moscow: Gosudarstvennoye Izdatlstvo Politicheskoi Literatury, 1960.

Lyashchenko, P. I. *Istoriya Narodnogo Khozyaistva SSSR, Tom III, Sotsializm* (History of the Economy of the USSR, Volume III, Socialism). Moscow: Gosudavstvennoye Izdatlstvo Politicheskoi Literatury, 1956.

Marer, Paul. *Postwar Price and Price Patterns in Soviet Foreign Trade.* Bloomington: International Development Research Center, Indiana University, 1972.

_____. *Soviet and East European Foreign Trade, 1946-1969.* Bloomington and London: Indiana University Press, 1972.

Meade, J. E. *The Stationary Economy.* Chicago: The Aldine Publishing Company, 1965.

Mendelson, A. *Stoimost i Tsena* (Value and Price). Moscow: Izdatelstvo Ekonomicheskoi Literatury, 1963.

Mendershausen, Horst. *The Terms of Soviet-Satellite Trade, 1955-1959.* Santa Monica, Calif.: The Rand Corporation, 1962.

_____. *Terms of Trade between the Soviet Union and Smaller Communist Countries, 1956-1957.* Santa Monica, Calif.: The Rand Corporation, 1959.

Mikesell, Raymond F., and Behrman, Jack N. *Financing Free-World Trade with the Sino-Soviet Bloc.* Princeton, N.J.: Princeton University Press, 1958.

Ministerstvo Vneshnei Torgovlyi SSSR (Ministry of Foreign Trade of the USSR). *Vneshnaya Torgovlya SSSR za 19___ g. 19___.* (*Foreign Trade of the USSR for 19___.*) (Moscow: Izdatelstvo Mezhdunarodnye Otnosheniya), various years.

Mishustin, D. D. *Vheshnaya Torgovlya SSSR* (Foreign Trade of the USSR). Moscow: V/O Mezhdunarodnaya Kniga, 1941.

Montias, John Michael. *Economic Development in Communist Rumania.* Cambridge, Mass. and London: The MIT Press, 1967.

Moorsteen, Richard. *Prices and Production of Machinery in the Soviet Union, 1928-1958.* Cambridge, Mass.: The Colonial Press for Harvard University Press, 1962.

Morgenstern, Oskar. *On the Accuracy of Economic Observations.* Princeton, N.J.: Princeton University Press, 1963.

Moskovskii Institut Narodnogo Khozyaistva imeni G. V. Plekhanova (Moscow Economic Institute G. V. Plekhanov). *Planirovaniye Narodnogo Khozyaistva SSSR* (Planning the Economy of the USSR). Moscow: Izdatelstvo Ekonomicheskoi Literatury, 1963.

Nauchno-Issledovatelskii Konyunkturny Institut Ministerstva Vneshnei Torgovlyi SSSR (Scientific-Research Business Institute of the Ministry of Foreign Trade of the USSR). *Vneshnaya Torgovlya SSSR s Kapitalisticheskimi Stranami* (Foreign Trade of the USSR with Capitalist Countries). Moscow: Vneshtorgizdat, 1957.

Nove, A. *Economic Rationality and Soviet Politics.* New York: Praeger, 1964.

_____. *The Soviet Economy.* New York: Frederick A. Praeger, 1961.

_____, and Donnelly, Desmond. *Trade with Communist Countries.* London: Hutchinson for the Institute of Economic Affairs, 1960.

Oertal, R. Roland. *Das System der Sowjetwirtschaft.* Berlin: Duncker & Humboldt, 1957.

Patolichev, Nikolai. *Foreign Trade.* N.p. (New Delhi?): Novosti Press Publishing House, n.d.

Peterson, Peter G. *U.S.-Soviet Commercial Relationships in a New Era.* Washington, D.C.: U.S. Department of Commerce, 1972.

Pisar, Samuel. *Coexistence and Commerce. Guidelines for Transactions between East and West.* New York: McGraw-Hill, 1970.

Potapov, I. S., Roginski, G. S., and Kapelinski, Yu. N. *Mezhdunarodnaya Torgovlya* (International Trade). Moscow: Vneshtorgizdat, 1954.

Pozdnyakov, V. S. *Gosudarstvennaya Monopoliya Vneshnei Torgovlyi v SSSR* (The State Monopoly of Foreign Trade in the USSR). Moscow: Mezhdunarodnye Otnosheniya, 1969.

Prokhorov, G. M. *Vneshne-ekonomicheskie Svyazi i Ekonomicheski Rost Sotsialisticheskikh Stran* (Foreign Economic Ties and the Economic Growth of Socialist Countries). Moscow: Mezhdunarodnye Otnosheniya, 1972.

Pryor, Frederic L. *Barriers to Market Socialism in Eastern Europe in the Mid 1960s.* Reprinted from *Studies in Comparative Communism,* vol. 3, no. 2, April 1970.

_____. *The Communist Foreign Trade System.* Cambridge, Mass.: MIT Press, 1963.

Quigley, John. *The Soviet Foreign Trade Monopoly. Institutions and Laws.* Columbus: The Ohio State University Press, 1974.

Robertson, H. M. *Aspects of the Rise of Economic Individualism.* Cambridge: At the University Press, 1933.

Roll, Erich. *A History of Economic Thought.* London: Faber & Faber, Ltd., 1938.

Rosenfielde, Steven. *Soviet International Trade in Heckscher-Ohlin Perspective.* Lexington, Mass.: D. C. Heath, Lexington Books, 1973.

Rosovsky, Henry, ed. *Industrialization in Two Systems: Essays in Honor of Alexander Gerschenkron.* New York: John Wiley & Sons, 1966.

Rotleider, A. Ya. *Mezhdunarodnye Kreditnye Organizatsii Stran-chlenov SEV* (International Credit Organizations of the Member Countries of CEMA). Moscow: Finansy, 1973.

Rozen, Marvin E. *Comparative Economic Planning.* Boston: D. C. Heath, 1967.

Samuelson, Paul., ed. *International Economic Relations: Proceedings of the Third Congress of the International Economic Association.* New York: St. Martin's Press, 1969.

Schaeffer, Henry Wilcox. *Comecon and the Politics of Integration.* New York: Praeger, 1972.

Schenk, Fritz. *Magie der Planwirtschaft.* Berlin/Koeln: Kiefenheur & Witsch, 1960.

Schwartz, Harry. *Russia's Soviet Economy,* 2nd ed. Englewood Cliffs, N.J.: Prentice-Hall, 1954.

Selucky, Radoslav. *Economic Reforms in Eastern Europe: Political Background and Economic Significance.* New York: Praeger Publishers, 1972.

Shaffer, Harry G., ed. *The Soviet Economy, a Collection of Western and Soviet Views,* 2nd ed. New York: Appleton-Century Crofts, 1969.

Shein, P. A. *Materialno-tekhnicheskoye Snabzheniye Sotsialnogo Promyshlennogo Predpriyatiya* (The Material-technical Supply of the Socialist Industrial Enterprise). Moscow: Gospolitizdat, 1959.

Shekhet, N. I. *Planovaya Tsena v Sistemye Ekonomicheskikh Kategorii Sotsialisma.* (The Planned Price in the System of Economic Categories of Socialism). Moscow: Izdatelstvo Moskovskogo Universiteta, 1972.

Shereshevsky, M. G. *Organizovaniye Formy i Tekhnika Vneshnetorgovykh Operatsii na Kapitalisticheskikh Rynkakh* (The Organization of the Form and the Technique of Foreign Trade Operations on Capitalist Markets). Moscow: Vneshtorgizdat, 1957.

Shone, R. *The Pure Theory of International Trade.* MacMillan Studies in Economics. London and Basingstoke: The MacMillan Press, 1972.

Sitnin, V. *Dengi i Denezhnoye Obrashchenye v SSSR* (Money and Monetary Circulation in the USSR). Moscow: Gosfinizdat, 1957.

Skilling, H. Gordon, and Griffiths, Franklyn. *Interest Groups in Soviet Politics.* Princeton, N.J.: Princeton University Press, 1971.

Smirnov, A. M. *Mezhdunarodnye Valyutnye i Kreditnye Otnosheniya SSSR* (The International Foreign Exchange and Credit Relations of the USSR). Moscow: Vneshtorgizdat, 1960.

Smith, Glen Alden. *Soviet Foreign Trade: Organization, Operations, and Policy, 1918-1971.* New York: Praeger Publishers, 1973.

Spulber, Nicholas. *Soviet Strategy for Economic Growth.* Bloomington and London: Indiana University Press, 1967.

Stolyarov, S. G. *O Tsenakh i Tsenoobrazovanii v SSSR* (On Prices and Price Formation in the USSR, 3rd ed., expanded and revised). Moscow: Statistika, 1969.

Sutton, Anthony C. *Western Technology and Soviet Economic Development,* Vol. I, 1917 to 1930; Vol. II, 1930-1945; Vol. III, 1945-1965. Stanford, Calif.: Hoover Institution on War, Revolution, and Peace, Stanford University Press, 1968-1973.

Trager, James, *Amber Waves of Grain.* New York: Arthur Fields Books, 1973.

Treml, Vladimir G., ed. *The Development of the Soviet Economy: Plan and Performance.* New York, Washington, and London: Frederick A. Praeger, 1968.

Tsentralnoye Statisticheskoye Upravlyeniye (Central Statistical Administration). *Strana Sovietov za 50 Let* (The Land of the Soviets for 50 Years). Moscow: Statistika, 1967.

Tuchkin, G. M. *Ekonomicheskaya Effecktivnost Vneshnei Torgovlyi* (The Economic Effectiveness of Foreign Trade). Moscow: Mezhdunarodnye Otnosheniya, 1969.

Twenty-fifth Congress of the CPSU. *Osnovnye Napravlyeniya Rasvitiya Narodnogo Khozyaistva SSSR na 1976-1980 gody* (Basic Directions of the Development of the Economy of the USSR for 1976-1980). Moscow: Politizdat, 1976.

United Nations Economic Survey of Europe in 1962, Part 2. Economic Planning in Europe. Geneva: Secretariat of the Economic Commission for Europe, 1965.

U.S. Department of Commerce. *U.S. Soviet Commercial Agreements 1972.*

Texts, Summaries, and Supporting Papers. Washington, D.C.: U.S. Government Printing Office, 1973.

U.S. Department of Commerce, Joint Publications Research Service. *State Five Year Plan for the Development of the USSR National Economy for the Period of 1971-1975.* Washington, D.C.: U.S. Government Printing Office, 1972.

U.S. Department of State. *The Battle Act Report.* Washington, D.C.: U.S. Government Printing Office, various years.

Vaganov, B. S., ed. *Vneshnaya Torgovlya Sotsialisticheskikh Stran (Voprosy Teorii)* (The Foreign Trade of the Socialist Countries [Questions of Theory]). Moscow: Mezhdunarodnye Otnosheniya, 1966.

Vernadsky, George. *A History of Russia.* New York: New Home Library, 1944.

Voinov, A. M., Lokshin, V. A., and Rodina, L. A. *Ekonomichiskie Otnosheniya Mezhdu Sotsialisticheskimi i Razvitimi Kapitalisticheskimi Stranami* (Economic Relations Between Socialist and Developed Capitalist Countries). Moscow: Nauka, 1975.

Voronov, K. G., and Pavlov, K. A. *Organizatsiya i Tekhnika Vneshnei Torgovlyi SSSR* (The Organization and Technique of the Foreign Trade of the USSR). Moscow: Mezhdunarodnye Otnosheniya, 1966.

Wilczynski, Jozef. *The Economics and Politics of East-West Trade.* New York and Washington: Frederick A. Praeger, 1969.

_____. *Socialist Economic Development and Reform.* New York and Washington: Praeger, 1972.

Wiles, P. J. D. *Communist International Economics.* Oxford: Basil Blackwell, 1968.

_____. *Price, Cost, and Output.* Oxford: Basil Blackwell, 1956.

Wolf, Charles, Jr. *Technology Exchange between the United States and the Soviet Union.* Santa Monica, Calif.: The Rand Corporation, 1973.

Wyndham White, E. *Looking Outwards.* Geneva: General Agreement on Tariffs and Trade, 1960.

Yanson, J. D. *Foreign Trade in the USSR.* London: Victor Gollancz, Ltd., 1934.

Zaleski, Eugène. *Planning for Economic Growth in the Soviet Union, 1918-1932.* Chapel Hill: The University of North Carolina Press, 1971.

_____. *Planning Reform in the Soviet Union, 1962-1966.* Chapel Hill: The University of North Carolina Press, 1967.

Zavyalkov, A. G. *Tseny i Tsenoobrazovaniye v SSSR.* Minsk: Izdatelstvo Vyushaya Shkola, 1971.

Zovilovich, M. A. *Osnovy Metodologii Planirovaniya Narodnogo Khozyaistva* (The Bases of the Methodology of Planning the Economy). Moscow: Gosudarstvennoye Izdatelstvo Torgovoi Literatury, 1958.

Zotschew, Theodor D. *Die Aussenwirtschaftlichen Verbindungen der Sowjetunion.* Kieler Studien, No. 97. Tuebingen: J. C. B. Mohr (Paul Siebeck), 1969.

Zwass, Adam. *Die Waehrung im Aussenhandel der RGW-Laender.* Vienna: Wiener Institut fuer Internationale Wirtschaftsvergleich beim Oester-reichischen Institut fuer Wirtschaftsforschung, 1973.

Annual Statement of the Overseas Trade of the United Kingdom, 1972, Vol. II. *Imports of Commodities Analyzed by Country.* London: Her Majesty's Stationery Office, 1973.

Statistiques du Commerce Extérieur de la France: Importations, Exportations, en n.g.p., Année 1973. Paris: Ministère de l'économie et des Finances, Direction Générale des Douanes et Droits Indirects, 1974.

Statistisches Bundessamt. Der Aussenhandel der Bundesrepublik Deutschland. Stuttgart and Mainz: Verlag W. Kohlhammer, 1974.

Journals and Articles

Principal Soviet Journals Cited

Planovoye Khozyaistvo (Planned Economy), cited as *PK.*
Vneshnaya Torgovlya (Foreign Trade), cited as *VT.*
Voprosy Ekonomiki (Questions of Economics), cited as *VE.*

Articles

Altman, Oscar A. "Russian Gold and the Ruble." *IMF Staff Papers,* vol. 7, no. 3, April 1960, pp. 416-38.

Anisimov-Spiridonov, A. D. "Nekotorye Voprosy Effektivnosti Vneshnei Torgovlyi" (Some Questions of the Effectiveness of Foreign Trade). *VT,* no. 2, 1967, p. 22.

Baghwati, Jagdash. "The Pure Theory of International Trade." American Economic Association, *Surveys of Economic Theory,* Vol. 2, *Growth and Development.* London: MacMillan; New York: St. Martin's Press, 1965.

Bakhtov, K. "Monopoliya Vneshnei Torgovlyi SSSR i Ravitiye ee Organizatsionnykh Form" (The Monopoly of Foreign Trade of the USSR and the Development of Its Organizational Forms). *VT,* no. 10, 1964, p. 44.

Bash, Yu. "Finding the Most Effective Ratio Between Exports and Imports." *Foreign Trade,* no. 5, May 1975, p. 49.

Berliner, Joseph. " 'Blat' Is Higher than Stalin." *Problems of Communism,* vol. III, no. 1, January-February, 1954, p. 22.

_____. "The Informal Organization of the Soviet Firm." *Quarterly Journal of Economics,* August 1952, p. 52.

Boehme, Hans. "Price Formation under the New Economic System." *Soviet Studies,* vol. XIX, no. 3, 1967-68, p. 340.

Bor, M. "Zakon Stoimosti i Tsenoobrazovaniye na Produktsiyu Promyshlennosti SSSR" (The Law of Value and Price Formation in the Output of Industry of the USSR) *VE,* no. 3, 1957, p. 106.

Borisenko, A. "Formirovaniye Struktury Eksporta i Importa" (Forming the Structure of Exports and Imports). *VT,* no. 2, 1967, p. 17.

_____. "K Voprosu ob Effektivnosti Sotsialisticheskoi Vneshnei Torgovlyi" (On the Question of the Effectiveness of Socialist Foreign Trade). *VT,* no. 10, 1964, p. 8.

_____. "Povysheniye Effektivnosti Vneshnei Torgovlyi—Vazhnaya Narodno-khozyaistvennaya Zadacha" (Increasing the Effectiveness of Foreign Trade—An Important Economic Task). *VT,* no. 7, 1966, p. 9.

Bornstein, Morris, "Ideology and the Soviet Economy." *Soviet Studies,* vol. XVII, no. 1, July 1966, p. 75.

Brunner, K., and A. H. Maltzer. "The Uses of Money in the Theory of an Exchange Economy." *American Economic Review,* vol. LXI, no. 5, December 1971, p. 784.

Cairncross, Alec. "The Moscow Economic Conference." *Soviet Studies,* vol. IV, no. 2, October 1952, p. 113.

Dobb, Maurice. "Soviet Price Policy." *Soviet Studies XII,* 1, July 1960, p. 87.

Doroshin, I. "Trudovaya Otsenka Narodnokhozyaistvennykh Velichin v Planirovaniye" (Estimates by Labor of Economic Magnitudes in Planning). *PK,* no. 2, 1963, p. 8.

Familton, R. J. "East-West Trade and Payments Relations." *IMF Staff Papers,* March 1970, p. 170.

Gourvitch, Alexander. "The Problem of Prices and Valuation in the Soviet System." *American Economic Review,* vol. XXVI, no. 1, Supplement, March 1936, p. 267.

Holesovsky, Vaclav, "Financial Aspects of the Czechoslovak Reform. "In Gregory Grossman, ed., *Money and Plan—Financial Aspects of East European Economic Reforms* (Berkeley and Los Angeles: University of California Press, 1968), p. 94.

Holzman, Franklyn D. "The Operation of Some Traditional Adjustment Mechanisms in the Foreign Trade of Centrally Planned Economies." In Jean Bancal, ed., *Economies et Societes,* tome II, no. 2, February 1968, p. 407.

_____. *More on Soviet Bloc Trade Discrimination. Soviet Studies,* vol. XVII, no. 1, July 1965.

_____. "The Ruble Exchange Rate and Soviet Foreign Trade Pricing Policies, 1929-1961." *American Economic Review,* September 1968, p. 803.

Ishchenko, A., Rozenberg, M., and Zatsepnin, B. "O Vzaimootnosheniyakh

Vneshnetorgovykh Obyedinyenii s Sovetskimi Postavshchikov Tovarov
Dyla Eksporta" (On Mutual Relations of Foreign Trade Corporations
with Soviet Suppliers of Goods for Export). *VT*, no. 6, 1960, p. 37.

Ivanov, Yu. "Matrichnoye Opisaniye Sistemy Natsionalnykh Shchetov i Balansa
Narodnogo Khozyaistva" (A Matrix Description of the System of National
Accounts and the Balance of the Economy). *Vestnik Statistiki*, no. 5, 1968,
p. 51.

Kaplan, N. "Investment Alternatives in Soviet Economic Theory." *Journal of
Political Economy*, April 1952, p. 133.

Knight, Frank H. "The Place of Marginal Economics in a Collectivist System."
American Economic Review, vol. XXVI, no. 1, Supplement, March 1936,
p. 225.

Ladygin, G., and Motorin, I. "Raschet Effektivnosti Eksporta Toplivo-syrivykh
Tovarov" (The Effectiveness of the Export of Fuel and Raw Materials). *VT*,
no. 9, 1967, p. 19.

Lettiche, J.M. "Soviet Views on Keynes. A Review Article Surveying the Literature." *Journal of Economic Literature*, vol. IX, no. 2, p. 449.

Lewin, Moshe. "The Disappearance of Planning in the Plan." *Slavic Review*,
June 1973, p. 287.

Lowenthal, Richard. "The Conservative Utopia." *Encounter*, June 1974, p. 1.

Manove, Michael. "A Model of Soviet Type Economic Planning." *American
Economic Review*, vol. LXI, June 1971, p. 390.

McAuley, Alastair N.D. "Rationality and Central Planning." *Soviet Studies*,
January 1967, p. 340.

Medvedyev, E. "Polyeznoye Izdaniye" (A Useful Edition). Review of M.G. Rozen-
berg, *Pravovoye Regulirovaniye Otnoshenii Mezhdu Vsesoyuznyimi
Vneshnetorgovymi Obyedinyenyami i Sovetskimi Organizatsiyami-zakazchi-
kami Importnykh Tovarov* (The Legal Regulation of Relations between All-
Union Foreign Trade Corporations and Soviet Organizations Purchasing
Imported Goods). *VT*, no. 1, 1967, p. 57.

Montias, J.M. "Rational Prices and Marginal Costs in Soviet-Type Economies."
Soviet Studies, April 1959, p. 369.

_____. "Background and Origins of the Rumanian Dispute with Comecon."
Soviet Studies, vol. XVI, no. 2, October 1964, p. 125.

O'Brien, Patrick. "On the Adequacy of the Concept of Totalitarianism." *Studies
in Comparative Communism*, January 1970.

Odom, William E. "Who Controls Whom in Moscow?" *Foreign Policy*, no. 19,
Summer 1975, p. 109.

Olgen, C. "The Ninth FYP and the 'Reform'." *Bulletin for the Study of the
USSR*, March 1971, p. 3.

Patolichev, N. "Stroitelstvo Materialno-tekhnicheskogo Bazy Kommunizma v
SSSR" (Building the Material-technical Basis of Communism in the USSR).
VT, no. 11, 1967, p. 3.

Probst, A. "Ob Opredelenyi Ekonomicheskogo Effekta Vneshei Torgovlyi" (On Determining the Economic Effect of Foreign Trade). *PK*, no. 11, 1965, p. 40.

Pryor, F. "Foreign Trade Theory in the Communist Bloc." *Soviet Studies*, vol. XIV, no. 1, July 1962, p. 41.

Robinson, Joan. "Mr. Wiles' Rationality: A Comment." *Soviet Studies*, January 1956, p. 209.

Samuelson, P.A. "International Trade and the Equilization of Factor Prices." *The Economic Journal*, June 1948, p. 163.

_____. "Understanding the Marxian Notion of Exploitation: A Summary of the So-called Transformation Problem between Marxian Values and Competitive Prices." *Journal of Economic Literature*, June 1971, p. 399.

Schlichter, Sumner H. "Free Private Enterprise." In P.A. Samuelson, Robert L. Bishop, and John R. Coleman, eds., *Reading in Economics.* New York: McGraw-Hill, 1952, p. 24.

Schroeder, Gertrude E. "Soviet Economic Reform at an Impasse." *Problems of Communism*, July-August 1971, p. 36.

_____. "Soviet Economic Reforms—A Study in Contradictions." *Soviet Studies*, July 1968.

Shagalov, G. "Ekonomicheskaya Effektivnost Vneshnei Torgovlyi Sotsialisticheskikh Stran" (The Economic Effectiveness of the Foreign Trade of Socialist Countries). *VE*, no. 6, 1965, p. 89.

_____. "Optimalnoye Planirovaniye Vneshneekonomicheskikh Svyazei" (The Optimal Planning of External Economic Ties). *VE*, no. 11, 1972, p. 63.

Shishkov, Yu. *Mezhdunarodnoye Khozyaistvennye Otnosheniya i Ekonomicheskaya Integratsiya Dvukh Tipov* (International Economic Relations and Economic Integration of Two Types). *VE*, no. 1 January 1975, p. 91.

Smelyakov, N. "Delovye Vstrechi" (Business Encounters). *Novyi Mir*, no. 12, 1973, p. 203.

Smirnov, G. "K Voprosu ob Otsenki Ekonomicheskoi Effektivnosti Vneshnei Torgovlyi SSSR" (On the Question of Evaluating the Effectiveness of the Foreign Trade of the USSR). *VE*, no. 12, 1965, p. 94.

_____ , Zotov, B., and Shagalov, G. "Otsenka Ekonomicheskoi Effektivnosti Vneshnei Torgovlyi" (Evaluating the Effectiveness of Foreign Trade). *PK*, no. 8, 1964, p. 25.

Solzhenitsyn, Aleksandr. "Letter to the Soviet Leaders." *The Times* (London), March 3, 1974.

Sorokin, G.M. "Perspektivnoye Planirovaniye Narodnogo Khozyaistva SSSR" (The Long-Term Planning of the Economy of the USSR). *Planovoye Khozyaistvo*, no. 1, 1956, p. 34.

Spulber, Nicholas. "The Soviet Bloc Foreign Trade System." In Morris
Bornstein, ed., *Comparative Economic Systems.* Homewood, Ill.: Richard
D. Irwin, 1965, p. 344.

Strumilin, S.G. "Materialnoye Stimulirovaniye i Planirovaniye v SSSR" (Material
Incentives and Planning in the USSR). *PK*, no. 3, 1963, p. 22.

Thornton, Judith. "Differential Capital Charges and Resource Allocation in
Soviet Industry." *Journal of Political Economy,* May-June 1971, p. 545.

Turetsky, Sh. Ya. "O Voprosye Otpusknykh Tsen Na Sredstvakh Proizvodstva"
(On the Question of the Sale Prices of Means of Production). *Promyshlenno-
Ekonomicheskaya Gazeta,* February 10, 1957.

Turpin, William N. "The Outlook for the Soviet Consumer." *Problems of
Communism,* vol. IX, no. 6, November-December 1960.

Usenko, E. "Sushchnost i Formy Sotsialisticheskoi Monopolii Vneshnei
Torgovlyi" (The Essence and Forms of the Socialist Monopoly Foreign
Trade). *VT*, no. 6, 1967, p. 34.

Wiles, P.J.D. "The Political and Social Prerequisites for a Soviet-type Economy."
Economica, February 1967, p. 1.

_____. "On Purely Financial Convertibility." In *Banking, Money, and Credit in
Eastern Europe. Main Findings.* Brussels: NATO Directorate of Economic
Affairs, 1973, p. 119.

_____. "Soviet Economics." *Soviet Studies,* October 1952, p. 133.

Wyczalkowski, Martin R. "Communist Economics and Currency Convertibility."
IMF Staff Papers, July 1966, p. 155.

Zakharov, C., and Sulyagin, V. *Raschety Effektivnosti Vneshne-ekonomicheskikh
Svyazei* (The Accounts of the Effectiveness of Foreign Economic Connections).
PK, no. 6, June 1973, p. 78.

Zauberman, Alfred. "On the Objective Function for the Soviet Economy."
Economica, August 1965, p. 323.

_____. "The Criterion of Efficiency of Foreign Trade in Soviet-type Economies."
Economica, February 1964, p. 5.

Index

Index

About the Author

William Nelson Turpin is an assistant professor of economics at Appalachian State University, Boone, North Carolina. As a member of the U.S. Foreign Service, he served as an economic officer in the Hague, Mexico City, Belgrade, Moscow, and Saigon. Professor Turpin was detailed to the Treasury in 1961 as Special Assistant to the Secretary, and in 1972 was detailed to the U.S. Information Agency as Economic Advisor. Professor Turpin received the B.A. from Dartmouth, the B.A. and M.A. degrees from Oxford University, where he was a Rhodes Scholar, and the Ph.D. degree in economics from The George Washington University.